DOUG & MARY

DOUG & MARY

A Biography of
Douglas Fairbanks
⋯◦◦⃟ & ⃟◦◦⋯
Mary Pickford
by
GARY CAREY

E. P. DUTTON | NEW YORK

For
My Mother and Father

Photographs courtesy of The Museum of Modern Art Film Stills Archive.

Library of Congress Cataloging in Publication Data

Carey, Gary.
  Doug and Mary.
  1. Fairbanks, Douglas, 1883-1939. 2. Pickford,
Mary, 1893-   3. Moving-picture actors and
actresses—United States—Biography. I. Title.
PN2287.F3C3   791.43′028′0922   [B]   77-8886

ISBN: 0–525–09512–8

Published simultaneously in Canada by Clarke, Irwin & Company Limited, Toronto and Vancouver.

10 9 8 7 6 5 4 3 2 1
First Edition

Preface

On the telecast of the 1976 Oscar ceremony, there was a film clip of a fragile, old lady accepting an honorary award from The Academy of Motion Picture Arts and Sciences. Her eyes were overbright, her wig as patently artificial as that worn by the boudoir doll sitting beside her, and as she struggled to find appropriate words of gratitude, her voice wavered and thinned out almost to the point of inaudibility. The Oscar ceremony has always been notorious for exposing the time-ravaged monuments of Hollywood history, but this travesty surpassed all others in unconscious cruelty.

Watching this sad spectacle with a group of friends, I averted my eyes from the screen, but the majority of my guests watched and moaned in disbelief. "Why did she do it?" some one asked. A number of explanations were offered, none very complimentary. Then one small voice piped up, "Who is she?"

"Mary Pickford, America's Sweetheart," was one answer.
"She was married to Douglas Fairbanks."
"She played little girls for most of her career."
"Yes, but who was she?" the small voice asked again. "What did she do to deserve this award?"

No one took time to answer because by then two TV nonentities were presenting another award, and the conversation shifted to an analysis of their trash getups. Meanwhile my mind had wandered from the set as I tried to come up with an adequate response to the question, "Who is Mary Pickford?" Not that the earlier answers had been wrong. At one time she had been America's golden-curled Sweetheart; she did play little girl roles until she was past thirty; she was the first of the great movie superstars and was married to the third of the great superstars, Douglas Fairbanks. (Charles Chaplin came in-between.) Their honeymoon was, in the words of Alexander Woollcott, "the most conspicuous in the history of the marriage institution," and afterward, at "Pickfair," their world-renowned home, they reigned unchallenged as the king and queen of Hollywood for more than a decade.

But, as this book intends to show, there is more to Mary and Doug's story than these few well-known highlights. The writer who wants to set down an account of their lives will soon find himself embroiled in film history and the shifting social attitudes of the 1910s and 1920s. Any biography of Pickford and Fairbanks must also be a biography of the American movie as it grew from infancy to young adulthood; and it must be a study of a certain kind of celebrity, one that the Fairbankses fostered and one that is held in contempt by many current stars.

Doug and Mary is not meant as a formal, comprehensive biography. It concentrates on the years of the Fairbankses' romance and marriage (1916–1933), and examines this period from a very specific point of view. Mainly it is the story of how they shaped the film industry; how the industry affected their private lives and of how Mary, Doug and the movies influenced (and were influenced by) the mores of the American public.

In researching the book, I started with the clipping files in the collections of the New York Public Library and the Film Department of The Museum of Modern Art. The material was voluminous, so much so that I began to wonder whether any show-business personalities had ever received more coverage than Mary and Doug. Plowing through the crumbling scrapbooks and sepia-tinged newsprint was great fun, partly because many of the articles were unconsciously funny to the point of absurdity, mainly because they were so enlightening about how Mary and Doug presented themselves to their fans. I wish to thank the staff at both institutions, the anonymous faces at the Library as well as my friends at the Museum, Eileen Bowser, Mary Corliss, Charles Silver and Emily Sieger.

I am also indebted to several books for information and incidental anecdotes. The most important are Mary Pickford's autobiography, *Sunshine and Shadow,* Robert Windeler's *Sweetheart* and two biographies of Fairbanks, Ralph Hancock and Letitia Fairbanks's *The Fourth Musketeer* and Richard Schickel's *His Picture in the Papers.* Probably I should also mention two other books which provided insights and factual data: Alistair Cooke's *Douglas Fairbanks: The Making of a Screen Character* and *Film Notes* (edited by Eileen Bowser), both published by The Museum of Modern Art.

Over the past six years I have talked about Mary and Doug with many people, both in connection with this biography and an earlier project which was abandoned. They include Anita Loos, Blanche Sweet, Ben Lyon, Marian Nixon, Leatrice Joy, Allan Dwan, Clarence Brown, Peggy Fears, David Gray, Mildred Zukor Loew, James Kirkwood, Jr., Allene Talmey, Lois Wilson, John Cromwell, and the late Adolph Zukor, Lila Lee, Louise Huff and Betty Bronson. I am grateful to all of them for caring enough about American film history to share their memories with me.

For encouragement, hospitality or helpful suggestions, I am also indebted to John Greenleaf, Selma Herbert, Patricia Stander, Mary Loos, Patrick Finnegan, John Alfred Avant and Beverly Walker. Finally a deep bow of thanks to five special people: my agent and good friend, Ray Pierre Corsini; my editor, William Whitehead; my mother-in-law, Regina Koshinskie; and most of all, my wife, Carol, and son, Sean.

Gary Carey

1

There had been heavy rain the night before, and on this Sunday morning in November 1915, the skies were still ominously gray. Looking out the window of her Hotel Knickerbocker apartment, Mary Pickford sipped her cup of room-service tea and wondered whether this was the ideal day for an outing in the country. Besides the threat of rain, there was an early winter chill in the air—just the sound of the wind was enough to freeze the blood. Mary was nearly ready to cancel the trip when she remembered the black velvet dress and expensive Russian boots she had bought especially for this occasion. And it really was something of an occasion. Her old friend, Elsie Janis, was back on Broadway after a triumphant tour of Europe, and to celebrate her return, "The International Star and Darling of Queens" (as Elsie was now billed) was holding a Sunday "at home" at Phillips Manor, her country estate near Tarrytown, New York.

All things considered, Mary and Owen Moore, her husband, decided to go ahead with their plans for the day. Shortly before noon, they walked through the Knickerbocker lobby and climbed into the back seat of the taffy-colored, chauffeur-driven Cadillac Mary had bought on the day her salary was raised to $1,000 a week. Moore was taciturn and scowling, and Mary gave him a wide berth—by trial and error she had learned that her husband couldn't be jollied out of his black Irish moods. She pressed herself against her side of the car and stared out the window at the passing Manhattan landscape.

A few blocks away at the Algonquin Hotel, Doug Fairbanks, another of Elsie Janis's Sunday guests, was finishing up his daily dozen in the improvised gymnasium he had created from the bedroom furniture of his hotel suite. Doug never needed the equipment of an athletic club to keep up his muscle tone—two sturdy chairs were a good substitute for the parallel bars, a coat rack served as a high bar and a desk or a lowboy was every bit as challenging as a horse-vault.

His exercises behind him, Doug bathed, shaved and hopped into a tweed sack suit which, in keeping with the male fashions of the day, turned his body into a box. (Only 5' 8" in height, with a full-moon, slightly doughy face, Fairbanks always looked a little squat and square in clothes.) Centering his jauntily knotted foulard bow tie, he then checked up on his wife, who was dawdling before her closet, and he began pacing the hotel suite, throwing himself in and out of chairs, leapfrogging over end tables and magazine stands, not exactly like the typical impatient husband, but like, well, Doug—the hyperactive kid who had never grown up.

Plump, blond and pretty Beth Fairbanks paid him no mind. She was caught up in the problem of what to wear. A tailored outfit, simply but elegantly cut, was then the appropriate costume for the country, with a plumed hat adding a festive note. But whatever Beth Fairbanks may have chosen to wear, it was undoubtedly "correct." According to one catty friend, Beth was Emily Post's ideal society matron—"she had only two interests in life: doing the right thing and seeing that others did the same"—and even those people who remember her kindly, speak of her with respect, not the warmth of true affection.

On this particular November morning of 1915, once she had chosen the right hat and secured it with the right hat pin, once she was sure that six-year-old Doug, Jr. (or "Young Doug" as he is still called by old family friends) was safe with his paternal grandmother who lived only a few blocks away, Beth told Doug she was ready to leave. Reaching the Algonquin lobby, Beth kept her eyes straight ahead while Doug flashed his sunburst smile at the passers-by who looked over their shoulders in belated recognition. Outside, Doug helped Beth into a flashy, low-slung roadster, piled the leopard throw around her and ripped off at a speed that Beth found decidedly vulgar.

Somewhere along the road to Tarrytown, Mary's chauffeur lost the way, and with no map to guide him, he pulled to the side of the road and waited for help. Pretty soon a car sped by, then doubled back and pulled alongside the limousine. Doug Fairbanks had spotted Owen Moore, a nodding acquaintance, and had turned around to see what the trouble was. When they discovered they were all heading for Phillips Manor, Fairbanks offered to lead the way, and a few minutes later they were back on the road, the Cadillac staying a discreet distance behind Doug's tar-hugging sportsmobile.

Before driving off, Moore had introduced Fairbanks to Mary. Both had seen the other in the movies, but this was the first time they had met face to face. And Mary's initial impression was not precisely favorable. The sports car, the leopard throw, his jumping-jack vitality all seemed a bit too flashy, too smart-alecky, for her taste.

Her opinion didn't change as she watched him bounding about among Elsie Janis's distinguished Broadway friends. On arrival at Phillips Manor, she had retreated to a secluded corner where she riffled through the pages of an out-of-date *Vanity Fair*. Always timid and reserved among strangers, on this occasion Mary was perhaps more self-conscious than usual. Though she was the highest paid actress in America, she was a *film* actress, and for theatre people, acting in "the galloping tintypes" was only one step above working in a carnival. The acclaim awarded *The Birth of a Nation*, first released in early 1915, had spilled over and showered the entire film industry with new prestige, but Mary, who had been working in the movies since the nickelodeon days, was not yet able to forget that at one time picture people were the third-class citizens of the acting profession.

Compared to Mary, Doug was a Johnny-come-lately to film. So far he had made only two pictures, and his reputation came from his solid, if lightweight, career as a roisterous Broadway juvenile. He was on an equal footing with Elsie Janis's other visitors. Destiny seemed to have intended him to be the life of the party; he was outgoing, hearty, exuberant, sometimes disturbingly so. Meeting Doug for the first time, said one acquaintance, was like stepping into the path of a hurricane—"there was no room, no space big enough to contain him."

Doug had a social temperament; Mary didn't. She had neither the time nor the desire to be a party girl. She had been working nearly nonstop since she was five years old, and even now she was making eight or nine feature-length pictures a year. When she did have a night off, she preferred spending it quietly at home with her family—sister Lottie, brother Jack and her beloved mother, Charlotte. "Ma" Pickford, as she was known to all her friends, played a double role in her daughter's life—she was both business manager and trusted confidante. For Mary, a girl's best friend would always be her mother.

By 1915, Owen Moore had become only a shadowy figure in Mary's private life. From the outset, their marriage had been a long series of fights, separations and reconciliations, culminating in an ugly incident in the lobby of the Hotel Knickerbocker only a few weeks before this trip to Phillips Manor. Moore had openly abused Ma Pickford, Mary had demanded an apology, he had refused and for a while it looked as though this would be the end of the marriage. But Mary, a devout Catholic, took her wedding vows seriously, and within a few days some kind of a reconciliation had been worked out. So it was Moore who escorted Mary to Tarry-town, not Charlotte Pickford, who usually acted as her daughter's escort on such occasions.

When he wasn't around Ma Pickford and wasn't boozing, Owen Moore could be very charming, and on this particular day, he was on his very best behavior—he had sworn off the hard stuff and was drinking only beer or wine. He left Mary to her pile of magazines and wandered off to chat with his hostess and Doug Fairbanks. Just then the sun came out, and Elsie slipped her arm through Doug's, took Owen by the hand, and pulled them outdoors for a promenade around the grounds of her estate. Beth Fairbanks looked on disapprovingly. Tomboyish, with a bold, lantern-jawed face, Elsie Janis was no beauty, and it was well-known that she usually formed romantic attachments only with her leading men. But she was ready to flirt with nearly anyone, and Mrs. Fairbanks was not blind to Doug's susceptibility to feminine wiles. She dragged Mary away from the pages of a *Pictorial Review* and pushed her along as they tried to catch up with Elsie's walking tour.

It was tough going. The sun had taken the chill out of the air, but the ground was wet and muddy, and with sinking heart Mary realized that her precious Russian boots would have to be discarded after this misadventure. The hem of her velvet skirt was splattered and sodden, but she trudged along gamely until she came to a brook that had overflowed its banks. Beth Fairbanks, wearing a sensible pair of brogans, jumped across without difficulty, but Mary knew she could never manage it.

Doug came to her rescue. Leaping over the brook, he swept Mary into his arms, winked, leaped again and set her safely down on the other side. Mary was totally captivated by Doug's gallantry, so unlike anything Owen Moore had ever done for her, but she put no romantic interpretation on it. She told herself Fairbanks would have done the same for any lady in distress.

If Mary thought about this incident in the weeks ahead, it figured as no more than a pleasant memory in a time filled with trouble and unpleasantness. Owen Moore was back on the bottle, and the picture she was working on, a rag-barrel

5

melodrama called *The Foundling,* showed every sign of being an out-and-out clinker. No one liked it much except Lillian Gish who was enchanted by a flashback sequence in which Mary appeared in a pinafore and pigtails. She suggested that someday an entire story be built around "that adorable little girl or someone like her," and Mary said she'd think about it, but she had doubts whether people wanted to see a picture with no love interest.

While shooting *The Foundling,* Mary was invited to a dinner-dance given by Frank Case at his Algonquin Hotel. Case was Broadway's leading innkeeper—at one time or another, he had fed, housed, encouraged or extended credit to the Barrymores, Tallulah Bankhead, Constance Collier, Mrs. Pat Campbell, Frank Crowninshield and Doug Fairbanks, his close friend and favorite patron. His parties were the smartest of the day, and being invited to them meant you were somebody; you didn't have to be rich or socially prominent or even famous to be asked to Case's soirées, but you did have to be talented or fun or attractive or a curiosity—everyone was expected to contribute something. Ordinarily Mary didn't go out when she was working, but Case's dinner-dance was on a Saturday night and since Sunday was her day off, she accepted the invitation.

There was no mention of it on the invitation, but Case's party was held in celebration of the opening of Doug's second film, *Double Trouble,* which was then running at the Knickerbocker Theatre on Broadway. So Fairbanks and Case were standing by the door when Mary walked in, and Case, unaware that his guests had met before, made a brief introduction. Since no one corrected him, he later assumed (and often claimed) that he was the cupid who brought Mary and Doug together for the first time.

After some polite chatter, Doug took Mary's arm, waltzed her around the dance floor and out into the lobby where they threw themselves into the depths of an overstuffed couch and started talking about the future of the movies. Mary said that in her opinion Doug and Charlie Chaplin were the bright lights among the newest crop of film stars, and Doug repaid the compliment by insisting that Mary outshone them all with "the naturalness of her acting." This pretty parlor speech brought a blush to Mary's cheeks, and she was startled to find her heart skipping a beat. She thrived on compliments, particularly from men, but there had been so few of them during her years with Moore that Doug's words went straight to her head with unexpected force.

Mary was in fact something of a coquette. "She was the most feminine female I've ever met in my life," said novelist and screenwriter Anita Loos. "She'd flirt with any man, a bellhop or a busboy would do as well as a high-powered producer or the handsomest leading man. I don't like coyness, but with Mary, it wasn't a come-on. It was innocent and absolutely genuine, and it was probably the secret of her success, the one way in which she couldn't be imitated."

Doug had a similar set of masculine traits. Shortly before her death in 1973, actress Lila Lee recalled Fairbanks as "a real smoothie, a complete charmer who knew just what to say and do to bend a girl's heart in his direction. And he did it as a matter of course, even when there was no ulterior motive involved. He was just about the best morale booster I ever ran into."

Obviously then, Mary and Doug were ideally matched for an innocent game of lighthearted flirtation. And at the start, it was no more than that. They spent most of the evening together, two-stepping and talking, but when they left the Algonquin that night, they had set no date for a future rendezvous.

Their next encounter, however, was by appointment. Doug had a mother, Ella, whom he adored every bit as much as Mary adored Charlotte, and though the two matrons were from opposite sides of the moon, they both took an uncommon pride in the careers of their celebrated children. Doug thought they should get acquainted—or so he told Mary; what he meant was that he wanted Ella and Charlotte to chaperon their next meeting.

Mary accepted Doug's pretense without question, and on a January afternoon in 1916, she and Charlotte came to Ella's apartment for tea. Charlotte might have preferred something more potent than orange pekoe, but she had been forewarned that Mrs. Fairbanks was an evangelical teetotaler. When Doug was still a wisp of a boy, Ella made him swear he would never touch liquor, and except for a glass of dinner wine or an occasional watery cocktail, he kept his promise until the last years of his life.

In the next few weeks, Mary and Charlotte were frequent guests at Ella's home. And it was only a short time before the two mothers realized that Doug and Mary were hovering on the brink of a full-fledged affair. Charlotte didn't mind—she had never liked Owen Moore and her Irish peasant blood didn't boil over at the thought of extramarital shenanigans. Ella, however, was disturbed by what was happening. She was tolerably fond of her daughter-in-law, Beth, and she firmly believed that a man's first duty was to his wife and children. Still, she liked Mary, and above all else, she wanted Doug to be happy.

The tea parties came to an end in February 1916 when Doug went West to resume his film career. Mary's schedule also included a spring visit to California, and she realized, as did Doug, that when they met again in Hollywood they would have to resolve their feelings for each other.

At this time it seems unlikely that either of them thought as far ahead as marriage. Doug had been tutored in the horrors of divorce by his mother (who knew what she was speaking of), and like his hero, Teddy Roosevelt, he considered himself married for all time. And Mary, who had every good reason to divorce Moore, had never done so because of religious scruples. The Catholic Church regarded divorce as a permissible, if regrettable, step, but remarriage meant instant excommunication.

It could also mean the end of her career. Divorce was then a very ugly word, though it was not an uncommon practice. As early as 1904, Edith Wharton had written (in *The House of Mirth*), "There is a divorce and a case of appendicitis in every family one knows." But Edith Wharton's families were not the kind of people who went to the movies—they were rich and aristocratic, with enough social crust to flout convention and live as they pleased.

Many of the people who went to Mary Pickford pictures were working-class, a social stratum where man-made conventions were still honored as the laws of God. And for her fans, Mary was the personification of the American girl. What would happen if they learned that beneath the golden curls there lurked a tarnished soul, a divorcée, one of those wicked screen vamps who lured men away from hearth and home? No one knew for sure how the picture public regarded its idols. For centuries show people had been notorious for their vagabond morals, and stage stars shed their spouses as easily as they changed roles. But there were indications that film blurred the boundary between illusion and reality in ways the stage didn't, and that the movie public totally identified an actor with his or her screen personality.

If so, Mary Pickford could be in deep trouble if she stepped out of character and betrayed the curly-headed scamp the American public had taken to its heart. Mary recognized the danger and proceeded with caution. She had worked long and hard to get to the top, and she was not ready to risk everything on what might be no more than a passing infatuation.

2

Mary Pickford was born Gladys Marie Smith in a six-room, two-story brick house in Toronto sometime in the early 1890s. Her arrival was overlooked by the city registrar, an omission that makes it impossible to pinpoint an exact date of birth. Mary has always given her birthday as April 8, 1893, but several film histories claim it occurred a day or two earlier or later, and a recent biographer says there is "strong evidence" that she was born in 1892.

If 1893 is the correct date, then Mary and the movies are the same age, for it was in that year that Thomas Edison patented the first projectable film strip. It's a pleasing parallel—Mary and the movies born at the same time, both in humble surroundings, both to rise to the very summit of the entertainment world. Rags to riches is more than a movie cliché—it's also the story of the movies, and it's Mary Pickford's story, too.

Her parents were first-generation Canadians, Irish Catholic on her mother's side, English Methodist on her father's. Both families, the Hennesseys and the Smiths, had been prosperous in the old world, or so Mary claimed in her autobiography, *Sunshine and Shadow*. The Smiths had sailed across the Atlantic and up the St. Lawrence River in their own ship, an imperial entrance into a brave new world where they quickly frittered away their fortune through unsound investments. By the time Mary's father, the youngest of twelve children, had grown to manhood, the Smiths were established members of that hapless caste, the genteel poor.

John Charles Smith was a delicate, good-looking man with golden brown hair and a huge, curly mustache that was too big for his face. Everybody liked Jack Smith—he was funny and good-natured, and people wanted to help him, but something always went wrong. Before he was 21, Jack had earned a reputation as an ineffectual dreamer who couldn't hold down a job. Salesman, stagehand, Canadian cowboy, farmhand—he drifted from one job to the next, and it wasn't until he married plump and jolly Charlotte Hennessey that he settled down and resigned himself to clerking behind a candy and fruit counter in a fish market.

Jack Smith was no great catch, but in taking an Irish Catholic as his bride, he was probably marrying beneath his station. Or so it must have seemed to his relatives. (To keep harmony between the families, Mary was baptized twice, first as a Methodist and later as a Catholic.) But for the short time it lasted, the marriage was happy and fruitful. Besides three children, Charlotte also gave her husband enough push for him to better himself, and within two years he was running the refreshment concession on a Lake Ontario excursion boat.

This was sunshine employment—the profits dropped off in the winter months—and there was never a lot of money, just enough to maintain a modest household and still keep some for the proverbial rainy day. The bad weather came all too suddenly. One day as Smith was leaving the ship, he hit his head on a pulley dangling from the paddle wheel. It caused a blood clot on his brain, and a year later he died at age twenty-seven.

Whatever savings he had accumulated were spent on medical and funeral expenses. Friends took up a collection, but it went like the wind, a month's groceries and it was gone. There was nothing left over to help Mrs. Smith raise her three young children—Mary was then four, Lottie three and baby Jack only six months old. Charlotte found a job in a grocery store and took in sewing at night, but ends wouldn't meet, and soon she was letting out rooms to lodgers. Roomers were a last resort for the penniless widow, an open admission of poverty. The Smiths were horrified, but instead of material support, they offered to adopt and raise one of the children. Charlotte refused. At whatever cost, she was determined to keep the family together.

John Smith's death was a sharp blow to his eldest child. Lottie had been his favorite (something Mary never forgot) and Jack was the baby, but everyone agreed that "little Gladys" was the spitting image of her father, both in appearance and personality. She was a dreamy, sickly child, and had she grown up under ordinary circumstances, she might have turned out as a dreamy, spoiled, silly young woman. But once Mrs. Smith went to work, Mary was forced to act as "little mother" to her small brother and sister. This responsibility brought out the practical, Hennessey side of her nature, but it did not endear her to Jack and Lottie, who came to regard their sister as a spoilsport who disapproved of anything that was fun.

One of the rooms in the Smith household was rented to a pair of actors working at a local stock company. They were rehearsing a play with a small part for a little girl who looked like Mary. At first Charlotte Smith was horrified at the thought of putting her daughter on the stage, but after visiting the shabby little theatre, she decided that no harm would come of it, particularly after she learned Mary would be paid fifty cents a week for her part in *The Silver King,* a popular melodrama by Henry Arthur Jones.

Mary's part consisted of only one line: "Don't speak to her, girls, her father killed a man." She spat it out on cue and then walked off into the wings and waited for her next scene. This time she had nothing to say, but was to sit and listen while her stage parents carried on a long expository conversation. Surreptitiously Mary had worked out a clever piece of stage business for this scene. While the other actors droned on and on, she built a towering pyramid out of blocks and then plowed it down with a four-wheeled hobby-horse.

So, significantly, Mary began her stage career as a scene-stealer. The other actors were ready to spank her, but the audience was delighted with her improvisation and a few weeks later she was hired for a local vaudeville revue.

The star of the show was "Little Elsie" Bierbower, a nine-year-old song-and-dance girl who brought down the house with her imitations of Anna Held and other "popular artistes" of the day. (Three years later little Miss Bierbower changed her name to Elsie Janis.) Backstage, Mrs. Bierbower told Mrs. Smith that Elsie had been in show business for less than a year and already she was earning fifty-five dollars a week. Charlotte was speechless. Fifty-five dollars was more money than she earned in two months.

Today the stage mother is a figure of scorn, particularly when she is suspected of living out her own ambitions through her children. Charlotte Smith wasn't that sort. She wasn't stagestruck; she had never wanted to be an actress. Her only ambition was to provide security and a good home for her family. The stage seemed the only answer. Certainly it was better than sending one of the children to live with her uppity in-laws, far preferable to putting them to work in an industrial sweatshop.

Of course the theatre had its own sweatshops. Actors rehearsed twelve hours a day, played eight to ten performances a week, and when touring, they rarely spent two nights in the same town. Pay was low, and there were no expense accounts, no per diems, no vacation days. Child actors—or "showbrats," as they were frequently called—were treated as equals. They got no time off for tutoring or for holidays, and there was no organization that looked after their welfare. (The Society for the Prevention of Cruelty to Children—informally known as the Gerry Society—was an ineffectual force in the theatre until the 1920s.)

Mary's childhood ended when she went on the stage. While other little girls were playing with dolls, she was learning lines, mastering the tricks of pleasing an audience, fighting for bigger and better roles. She had no playmates of her

13

own age except Jack and Lottie, who excluded her from most of their games. Her formal education was limited to a few months in a Toronto schoolroom, and she learned to read by picking out words on billboards and posters. Arithmetic was a matter of money, how much she earned, how much she could spend, how much could be salted away. She became a thrifty child, often depriving herself of small luxuries if it meant breaking a dollar bill.

In 1898 and 1899, Mary played a series of roles with Toronto's Valentine Stock Company, and with the Jessie Bonstelle Company in Rochester. She was Little Eva in *Uncle Tom's Cabin,* Little Willy in *East Lynne,* and Dick the Waif in a forgotten melodrama called *Soudan.* She threw herself into all her parts, particularly those with death scenes; then she kept one eye open to count the handkerchiefs in the front rows.

As part of the Toronto season, Mary appeared in a new play that was scheduled to open on Broadway the following fall. The playwright promised to keep Mary in the cast if she was willing to move to New York. Charlotte immediately sold all her furniture, packed up the other family belongings and got the children aboard a train headed for Manhattan.

Meanwhile the playwright had forgotten all about Mary and gave her part to another child actress, Lillian Gish. The Smiths were crushed, but they decided to stay on in New York and look for work in another production. There were no openings on Broadway, and eventually they were forced to join a third-rate touring company. Mary played an important role, Jack and Lottie had walk-ons, Charlotte doubled as general understudy and wardrobe mistress. Their combined salary was twenty dollars a week.

For the next six years, Mary never had a permanent home, just a dreary succession of tenement flats, theatrical boardinghouses and seedy hotels. She was nearly always on the road, traveling from one backwater to the next, often spending sleepless nights stretched out on springless train seats. Whenever possible, the Smiths tried to stay together, but not every play had parts for three kids and a buxom matron, and not every producer wanted Mary badly enough to hire the less talented members of her family. Occasionally Lottie was hired as Mary's understudy, but often Mary toured alone, with one of the older actresses in the company acting as her guardian.

Once, for a first-class production, she earned forty dollars a week, but usually her salary was about twenty-five dollars. After six years in show business, Mary was still at the bottom rung of the theatrical ladder. Mostly she appeared in hokey melodramas on the "ten-twenty-thirty" circuit, so-called because ten to thirty cents was the price range of the theatres on the route. (Broadway theatres then charged about $2.50 for the best seats.) In the spring of 1907, after a grueling and unrewarding engagement in a ramshackle melodrama, Mary made up her mind that she was going to find a part in a Broadway show. And not just any Broadway show, but something with class, something that would link her with the great names of the American theatre.

She started at the top with playwright, director and producer David Belasco, the self-appointed high priest of American drama. In spite of his Jewish heritage, Belasco wore a clergyman's vest and collar, and once claimed he had been born in a San Francisco cellar "because there was no room in any hotel." It wasn't true, but he couldn't resist a biblical parallel anymore than he could resist a crucifix—dozens of medieval and Renaissance crosses lined the walls of his private office.

David Belasco was a charlatan, a great showman, the middle link in a tradition that starts with P. T. Barnum and ends with Cecil B. De Mille. He loved spectacle and glamor and beautiful women, and mixed them together in a series of skillfully-crafted, lurid melodramas that often centered on the sacredness of profane love. Scarlet ladies with golden hearts were his specialty, and though most of his Mary Magdalenes were redeemed by the final curtain, a few remained floozies to the core. At the end of *The Easiest Way*, Belasco's biggest *succès de scandale*, the tainted heroine turns to her colored

15

maid and says, "Annie, dress up my body and paint my face. I'm going to Rector's to make a hit and to hell with the rest!"

This curtain line had ladies reaching for their smelling salts, and during the run of the play the supper trade at Rector's (the Sardi's of the 1900s) dropped off by half. *The Easiest Way* also made a star of a young actress named, appropriately enough, Frances Starr. Belasco had the Svengali touch, and his first Trilby was Mrs. Leslie Carter, the bored and restless wife of the inventer of Carter's Little Liver Pills. Mrs. Carter decided she wanted to be an actress and though she had little to recommend her except a pretty face, a shapely figure and a thatch of carrot-red hair, Belasco took her on. He piled her hair into a flaming pompadour, undraped her bodice as far as decency would allow and pushed her half-nude on stage in a then-risqué French melodrama called *Zaza*. The rest is legend, or at the very least, a footnote in the textbook histories of the American theatre.

Belasco knew how to dress and light his ladies to best advantage. He was able to spot their weaknesses and reshape a script to disguise them; he made them look better than they were. And sometimes he molded them into accomplished actresses; with his help Mrs. Leslie Carter soon became a skillful comedienne. Belasco could be merciless during rehearsals —once, when Frances Starr couldn't scream on cue, he plunged a hat pin into her behind—but the red carpet was rolled out after the first night. Later on little girls dreamed of being movie stars; before that they wanted to be Ziegfeld show girls; but earliest of all, they wanted to be Belasco actresses, rich, pampered, respected and courted by the best stage-door Johnnies of the era. This was Mary's dream, too. There were more prestigious producers, more adventuresome producers, more intelligent producers, but Mary chose Belasco and glamor.

At the end of his life, Belasco frequently reminisced about his first meeting with Mary, and each time his story took on new drama. Mary has been equally inconsistent and today it is all but impossible to sort fact from fiction. But what seems to have happened was that Mary applied for an audition, failed, and in desperation, started prowling the stage alley of the Belasco Theatre on the chance of meeting either the producer or Blanche Bates, who was then appearing in his production of *The Girl of the Golden West*.

Instead, she caught the attention and sympathy of the stage doorman who introduced her to Belasco's assistant, William Dean. (In one version of the story, the doorman looked straight through Mary until she threw herself to the ground, pounded the pavement and kicked her feet in outraged frustration.) Dean told Belasco about Mary and Belasco, who was looking for a young girl with blond curls and a winsome smile for his next play, agreed to see her.

Belasco met Mary backstage at the old Republic Theatre on 42nd Street. He asked her to recite a short poem; she complied, and then, after asking her a few questions about her background, he told her to report back a week later for rehearsals. She had her first part in a Broadway show.

Belasco did one other thing for Gladys Smith—he changed her name to Mary Pickford. She had aways preferred Marie or Mary, her middle name, to Gladys, which was only one step better than Ruby or Pearl or Violet, and Smith was just as drab and working-class. Pickford, her paternal grandmother's maiden name, had a touch of distinction. Mary and Mama Charlotte both liked it, and soon the whole family had adopted it as their last name.

Mary made her New York stage debut on December 3, 1907, in *The Warrens of Virginia,* a Civil War drama by William De Mille. (The playwright's younger brother, Cecil Blount, was also in the cast.) The play, one of the big hits of the season, ran through May 1908, and toured the country for another year. When it closed, Mary joined her family in New York. She was shocked to learn that, despite all the money she had sent home, there was barely enough to see them through the next three months. Since it was off-season on Broadway, Charlotte suggested she look for work in the movies.

If her mother had mentioned white slavery, Mary couldn't have been more appalled. Earlier, when she had been down and out, she had thought about the movies, had even gone so far as to apply for work at the Essanay Company in Chicago and at Kalem in New York. But that was long before *The Warrens of Virginia*. Now she was a Belasco actress, and it was beneath her dignity to "pose" before a motion picture camera.

There was good reason why the movies were held in contempt by polite society. The nickelodeons weren't quaint prototypes of the present-day neighborhood theatre, as they are often nostalgically remembered. They were smelly, urine-stinking, unsanitary firetraps, tucked away in tenement districts, patronized only by immigrants and the poor, sometimes by prostitutes and pickpockets and other denizens of the dark. Nice people didn't go to the nickelodeons, or if they did, they wore big hats and looked over their shoulders before entering.

It is also understandable that the stage community looked down on the movies. Picture salaries were low, and actors received no billing, or opportunity to show their talent. The average movie ran ten minutes or less, enough time to sketch in a brief dramatic anecdote, but not long enough for any detailed plot or character development. Film acting wasn't real acting—it was making faces and funny gestures in front of a black box that added ten pounds to your waist and ten years to your face.

Stage actors went into film only as a last resort, and even then they usually took the precaution of putting on a wig or a false beard before facing the camera. Mary wasn't so hypocritical. Swallowing her pride, she dressed up in her navy blue suit and new Tuscan straw hat, stuffed her stage reviews into her handbag and boarded a streetcar to the Biograph studio on West 14th Street. After a hectic audition, Mary was offered a job at the standard fee of five dollars a day, payable when and as she earned it. "I'm a Belasco actress," Mary said with a smile. "Don't you think I deserve a little more?"

D. W. Griffith, chief director at Biograph, was amused by

this snippet of a girl, this wide-eyed, golden-haired innocent who seemed convinced she was destined to become the next Sarah Bernhardt. Normally Griffith didn't like working with stage actors, and though Mary's audition had been no more than average, he agreed to pay her ten dollars, provided she didn't tell his other actors.

By 1909 Biograph and Griffith were turning out better films than any other production company in America. Nearly everyone sensed the superiority of the Biograph pictures, even the uncritical who couldn't define the quality that made them so vastly superior. It wasn't anything as simple as good acting or careful design or clever material, though generally the Biograph one-reelers were funnier and more dramatic than those produced by other companies. Still, the real difference wasn't the subject matter; it was the way the story was told. Contrary to legend, Griffith discovered none of the devices or techniques that make up the grammar of film. Close-ups, pans, flashbacks, dissolves, crosscutting, disjunctive editing—these had all been "discovered" and used haphazardly by the earliest filmmakers, Edison, Lumière, Méliès, Edwin S. Porter. None of these men, however, fully understood the importance of their innovations. For example, the famous close-up in *The Great Train Robbery* (1903) was not organically related to the story, but could, according to the whim of the projectionist, be placed either at the beginning or end of the film. Only Griffith recognized that these techniques could be used as more than tricks or attention-getters; that they were, in fact, the basic components of narrative film structure. And gradually, through constant experimentation, he started to evolve the basic laws of narrative film structure.

D. W. Griffith came to film in 1907 as a failed stage actor and playwright. Like Mary, he originally thought of his Biograph employment as a stopgap between theatre engagements, but soon he was intrigued by the artistic challenges of the new medium. While other producers and directors *talked* about film equaling the stage and the novel, Griffith set out to accomplish this. It couldn't be done, he realized, by aping the conventions of the novel or the play; instead the director had to find ways of translating these effects into cinematic language. Slowly he began adding dabs of complexity to his stories and characters, always seeking more supple and expressive methods of filmic storytelling. He had embarked on a great creative adventure and nearly all his actors came to share his vision of what movies could become, Mary included. She stayed at Biograph until early 1911, a stretch of a year and a half during which she made seventy-nine films, all but two directed or supervised by Griffith.

In a couple of her early films, Mary was cast as a child, but usually she played girls close to her own age, sixteen to twenty-year-olds. There was no typecasting at Biograph. Mary portrayed schoolgirls, sweethearts, brides, mothers; she was alternately naughty and nice; she disguised herself as Indians and Italians and Mexican senoritas; she went from slapstick to sentimental comedy to blood-chilling melodrama. In the truest sense of the word, Griffith ran a stock company, and so Mary found herself cast in a lead one day, playing a bit part the next.

Although Mary never balked at a small role, she did have her differences with Griffith, who was not accustomed to arguing with his actors. A flint-eyed, hawk-nosed Southerner of aloof and dignified bearing, Griffith was an awe-inspiring figure. Everyone at Biograph was on a first-name basis, but no one called him David; he was always Mr. Griffith. He intimidated Mary, but she wouldn't bow before his every wish; not when she knew he was wrong.

And about acting he was dead wrong. Griffith had liberated film from many of its stage-inspired conventions, but he made no objection to the broad Delsartian gestures used by his actors. Quite early on, Mary realized that in pictures an actor was in intimate contact with his audience, and should scale down his performance accordingly. This she began to do, always checking the results on the screen to see how much more she could or should eliminate.

Griffith disapproved. Often while the cameras were turning, he'd yell at her, telling her to do "more," a demand she always refused to meet. "I will not exaggerate, Mr. Griffith," she'd say firmly at the end of the scene. "I think it's an insult to the audience."

Once Griffith took her by the shoulders and tried to shake some feeling into her. Mary broke loose and said, "Sir, if I am not an actress, you cannot beat it into me. I'm finished with you and motion pictures and the whole thing." Mary would often quit and Griffith let her, only to rehire her a few hours later when they both had calmed down.

Film critics singled out Griffith's new ingenue, and praised the simplicity and charm of her performances. Fans were also captivated by her bounce and perkiness. They asked theatre managers to show more pictures featuring the actress they called "Goldilocks," or "The Biograph Girl." The general public didn't know her name or the name of any picture player. Film producers refused to bill their actors for fear that there might someday be a movie equivalent of the all-powerful Broadway star system.

Anonymity didn't appeal to Mary, who argued and fought for billing, but always lost. Nearly everything else she wanted, she got. Griffith agreed to use Jack and Lottie for extra and bit parts; he promised to cast Mary only in leading roles; he raised her salary to a guaranteed $40, then $100 a week. For the first time Mary and her family were secure; money was coming in every week, enough for a comfortable apartment (first in Brooklyn, later in upper Manhattan), with some left over for a savings account and summer vacations.

A few years later, Mary praised the movies for "putting an end to the vagabond life of the actor. . . . Nothing in the whole history of the world has done so much for the actor as the motion picture. It has given him more sense of security. It has given him a chance to save money. It has given him a voice in his own career. It has given him a chance to have a home."

But the early film actor had to work very hard for the right to live like a middle-class citizen. At Biograph, the hours were nine to eight, six days a week. On Mondays, Griffith would assign parts and conduct rehearsals, really improvisations, during which he and the actors would build up stories from sketchy scenarios provided by some member of the company. (Often they were cribbed from newspapers or popular fiction.) Tuesdays, interiors were filmed in the Biograph studio (formerly a ballroom). Wednesdays, exteriors were shot in New Jersey, Connecticut or upstate New York. On Thursday, rehearsals started for a new film.

Retakes were considered an extravagance, and not much time was wasted on shifting camera angles or retouching makeup. There was a forty-five-minute lunch break, usually sandwiches eaten on the set and provided by the studio. (These catered meals were the forerunner of the Hollywood studio commissary. Producers were quick to learn that actors had to be watched or they would drink, not eat, their lunch.) Biograph was committed to turning out at least two movies a week, and that meant no nonsense on the part of the employees. The company tried to keep up with the schedule, but sometimes there were delays and accidents that couldn't be prevented, and often the actors were still at work long after the 8 P.M. quitting time.

Because of the uncertain hours, film actors had little time for outside social activities and had to depend on each other for companionship. Consequently Biograph was a spawning ground for quick friendships and easy flirtations. Mary was initially put off by the informality of the studio. In the theatre, actors called each other Mr. and Miss, and socialized only with their peers: stars never mingled with supporting players, supporting players didn't mix with extras. At Biograph there was only one status symbol. One side of the communal ladies' dressing room was reserved for "stars," the other for newcomers and bit players.

Mary didn't relax until she had reached the star side of the room. But she was not by nature a lordly person, and whatever affectations she had learned in the theatre were quickly dropped after a few weeks at Biograph. For the first time she had friends that weren't Mama Charlotte's friends; not old ladies, but people her own age. And for the first time she started to express an interest in the opposite sex.

Her first Biograph friend was also her first beau, actor James Kirkwood, a burly, handsome man with a salty sense of humor and huge appetite for booze, women and practical jokes. Prior to joining Biograph, Kirkwood had played romantic leads opposite several top Broadway actresses, and like Mary, he wasn't entirely happy about working in the movies. They had long conversations about their lowly occupation and whether it would ruin them permanently in the legitimate theatre. Mary said no, but Kirkwood wasn't sure. He always put on a false beard or mustache before facing the camera.

Out of these conversations grew a close friendship that lasted until Kirkwood's death in 1963. (One of Mary's last public appearances was at his funeral.) But whether this friendship ever blossomed into a romance, as Kirkwood frequently claimed, is open to question. If so, it must have been of very short duration or occurred at a later time. By early 1910, Mary was already infatuated with the man she would marry a year later.

They met during her first week at Biograph. As she was leaving the studio one afternoon, Griffith asked Mary if she could play a love scene. Though embarrassed and unsure, she answered that she could. He then asked her to demonstrate on a papier-mâché pillar. Even Duse might have blanched at such a request, and Mary, hoping to escape without making a fool of herself, said indignantly, "Mr. Griffith, how can I make love to a cold pillar?"

At that moment Owen Moore walked out of the men's dressing room. "Stand right there," Griffith shouted. "Miss Pickford doesn't like to make love to a lifeless pillar. See if she can do any better with you."

Just as Mary was about to turn on her heel and walk out of the studio forever, she remembered how much money she was making. So she walked up to Moore, nuzzled her nose against his chest, and said, "I love you." There was no kiss—she considered kissing in public "vulgar in the extreme and completely unnecessary in the theatre, where one could pretend."

Griffith wasn't very impressed. "After ten years more of life and rehearsal you should be able to do a love scene very well," he told her. But he gave her the part, and in the film, *The Violin Maker of Cremona*, Mary played her second love scene with Owen Moore.

Ten years older than Mary, Moore had been born in Ireland, the eldest of three brothers, all actors, all handsome, all but one (Matt) moody and introspective. Owen had dark hair, deep blue eyes and a rosy, Irish complexion. He was also, according to Mary, "the Beau Brummell of Biograph, always dressed with immaculate elegance." From the start, she was very much taken with him, and he was equally captivated by her.

At first Mama Charlotte paid no attention, thinking he was too old for Mary and that they both would soon lose interest. But as time went on, and Owen was still hanging around the Pickford apartment, Charlotte began to worry. Somebody warned her that things were serious and that Owen shouldn't be trusted—he was a heavy drinker. Mrs. Pickford told Mary that Moore was no longer welcome in their home and that she was not to see him outside the studio.

For the first time in her life, Mary disobeyed her mother. She went on seeing Moore on the sly, and the clandestine nature of their meetings added a touch of drama to their romance. Owen played the role of the star-crossed lover to the hilt—once, when Mary refused to see him, he got drunk and swam across the East River from Whitestone to Claussen's Point and back, a distance of over three miles. And when she turned down his fourth marriage proposal, he threatened to leave Biograph and never see her again. This was too much for Mary. A week later, on the evening of January 7, 1911, she and Owen took the ferry to Jersey City, where they were married in a drafty and dimly-lit courtroom by a half-crocked justice of the peace.

There is a Hollywood legend that, when asked the question, "Do you take this man . . .", Mary and her mother answered in unison, "We do." It is, of course, only a legend. Mrs. Pickford didn't learn about the wedding until several weeks later, and when Mary told her what she had done, Charlotte burst into a fit of tears that lasted for three days.

But the "we do" story is worth mentioning because it sums up Moore's version of what went wrong with his marriage. Life with Mary, he often implied, was not unlike a split-reel Biograph comedy about the young bride, the gorgon mother-in-law and the frustrated husband. He once told an interviewer about an incident that had occurred when they checked in at a New York hotel. A bellboy took them to a two-bedroom suite which Charlotte inspected carefully before taking the key. "It's fine," she said. "You take that room, Owen. Mary and I will share the other."

That story, too, may be an exaggeration, but there is no question that Mary, only seventeen at the time of her marriage, was still her mother's little girl. She was, as she later admitted, too young and inexperienced to handle a man as difficult as Moore. "Owen was morose and uncommunicative," says actress Leatrice Joy. "He wasn't difficult to work with, there was no trouble on the set, but it wasn't easy to know him." Anita Loos, on the other hand, remembers Moore as "amusing, really quite witty, as long as he wasn't around Mary. Owen's problem was that he had married a girl on the way up while he was standing still. Some men don't mind living in their wives' shadows, but Owen couldn't stand it."

After their marriage, Owen and Mary lived at the Hotel Flanders and later in an apartment on 157th Street. Moore was drunk and abusive most of the time, and according to Mary's divorce testimony, he told her "a wife was a luxury" and that he had no intention of buying her clothes. Later, after one of their early separations, he asked her not to come back. "He said I was the cause of his failure in life," Mary recalled. "He said I made him morbid and caused him to drink. . . ."

But Mary kept coming back and she went on supporting Moore—most of his jobs between 1912 and 1916 were won through her intervention, often as her leading man or director. Within a year people were saying Mary stayed married to Moore only because she was a Catholic. But Leatrice Joy (who made one of her first screen appearances in an early Pickford film) isn't so sure. "It was my impression," Miss Joy said recently, "that Mary was very much in love with Owen. She turned moony whenever he was around."

Shortly after her marriage, Mary left Biograph and went to work for the Independent Motion Picture Company, usually called IMP. Owen Moore was partly responsible for this change. For some time he had been urging Mary to develop a distinctive screen personality, something that couldn't be done at Biograph where there was room for only one star, David Wark Griffith. This was one of the few occasions when Mrs. Pickford agreed with her son-in-law. She opened negotiations with IMP president Carl Laemmle who offered Mary $175 a week and featured billing as "Little Mary." As part of the deal, Charlotte, Jack and Lottie were hired as "atmospheric players" and Moore was promised a position as Mary's leading man. The IMP pictures (several shot in Havana) were directed by Thomas Ince, second only to Griffith in prestige, but as Mary later admitted, they weren't very good. She left IMP after six months, and after an equally brief and unprofitable stay at the Majestic Company, she went back to Biograph.

There was no red carpet rolled out for her return. Her salary dropped to $150 a week, and while her name was used on posters and handbills, she received no screen credit. Worst of all, she discovered she no longer had first claim on the better ingenue roles. Lillian and Dorothy Gish, Blanche Sweet, Mabel Normand, Mae and Marguerite Marsh were now working at Biograph, and they were all suited to Mary's roles. Griffith took sadistic pleasure in playing one off the other—it was an effective way of keeping them all in line.

There would be no stars at Biograph as long as he was in charge of production.

Mary found his attitude petty and backward. She told Griffith that she "didn't like his bringing people in from the outside" and she was going to return to the theatre "where years of study were a safeguard against the encroachment of amateurs." Griffith laughed and said, "You have disgraced yourself. No decent theatre producer would hire a girl who had spent three years in the movies."

Griffith was bluffing, but Mary knew there was some truth in what he said. A few days earlier, while walking along 14th Street, she had run into William De Mille, author of *The Warrens of Virginia,* who was horrified to learn she was working in the movies. Later, he wrote to David Belasco, "Remember Mary Pickford who played Betty in *The Warrens?* Well, the poor kid is actually thinking of. taking motion pictures seriously. . . . I pleaded with her not to waste her professional life and the opportunity to be known to thousands of people, but she's rather stubborn for such a youngster. So I suppose we'll have to say good-bye to Little Mary Pickford. She'll never be heard of again."

To find out whether she would be welcomed back to the theatre, Mary called David Belasco's office and invited the producer and his manager, William Dean, to a screening of her newest comedy, *Lena and The Geese.* Belasco came, much to Griffith's surprise, and at the end of the picture, he had high praise for Mary's performance. As he was leaving, she reminded him of something she had said at the close of *The Warrens of Virginia:* "No matter where I am or what I'm doing, when you want me just let me know and I'll come." Belasco said he would not forget. And less than two months later he called and asked her to play the twelve-year-old blind heroine of *A Good Little Devil,* an adaptation of a French "fairy drama" he was producing later that season.

The play opened on January 8, 1913, with Mary, Ernest Truex and Lillian Gish heading the cast. "Miss Pickford's success in a very difficult role was phenomenal," Belasco wrote. "Nothing like her remarkable performance of a child's part had been seen in New York or elsewhere." But Lillian Gish called the play "a good little failure," and others have expressed reservations about Mary's performance. "She was sweet and ingratiating," remembers actor and director John Cromwell. "But no, I don't think she had any great future in the theatre, not as a serious actress, anyway. She didn't have the kind of background that would have led her to develop and train her talent."

A Good Little Devil ran for several months, supported mainly by movie fans who tended to overlook Mary's breathy vocal delivery and her harsh Canadian "r's." At first Mary was thrilled to be back on the stage, but she really didn't like her stilted and sentimental part, and after a few weeks, she was ready to return to the movies. But only on her own terms. Ever since childhood she had dreamed of earning $500 a week before she was twenty, or so she told Griffith, who said she wasn't worth more than $300 to him.

Fortunately she found a new friend in a diminutive, Hungarian-born producer named Adolph Zukor. A former furrier and nickelodeon-owner, Zukor had entered film production in 1911 with a novel concept called "Famous Players in Famous Plays." His films were "feature-length" (four- or five-reel) visual transcripts of well-known plays starring well-known stage actors. The first Famous Players release was *Queen Elizabeth,* a French import which exploited the reputation and faded charms of the once divine Sarah Bernhardt. This was followed by American-made productions with James Hackett, James O'Neill, Minnie Maddern Fiske and other Broadway actors recreating their most celebrated roles for the camera.

Critics praised the Famous Players films for bringing art and respectability to the movies, but audiences found them dull and lifeless. Poorly photographed and grotesquely made-up, the actors mouthed entire speeches to the silent camera; there were no close-ups, no camera movement, just an endless succession of static scenes. Once the novelty wore off, the public lost interest in the Famous Players films, and by 1913 Zukor realized he needed a smash hit to establish the company as a permanent force within the industry. With this in mind, he bought the screen rights to *A Good Little Devil,* including the right to use Mary and other members of the New York cast. In a separate negotiation, he signed Mary (who was still four months away from her twentieth birthday) to a one-year contract at the salary she requested—$500 a week.

This, at least, is Pickford and Zukor's version of how Mary became a Famous Players star. Blanche Sweet, however, tells a different story. "I'm not all sure it's true, but around Broadway it was said that Zukor was Belasco's silent partner for the stage production of *A Good Little Devil.* He knew he needed a 'famous player' with some screen experience, so he thought of Mary. The only problem was that she wasn't a Broadway star—she had only done that one play by William De Mille. So Zukor went to Belasco and said he'd back any play for him as long as it starred Mary Pickford."

Pickford's career at Famous Players got off to a weak start. The screen version of *A Good Little Devil* was a disaster, and Zukor shelved it till after the release of Mary's next three pictures, none very good. But when she asked to have her salary increased to $1,000 a week, he consented without protest, and for the opening of her third release, *Hearts Adrift,* he prepared a very special surprise. Late one afternoon, he invited her to tea at a New York restaurant directly opposite the theatre where the film was playing. Zukor dawdled over his tea, talking about nothing, reluctant to leave. Then, when it got dark, he took her up to a mezzanine overlooking Broadway, and suddenly she saw (in her own words) "one of the most thrilling sights of my whole career, my name blazing on the marquee in electric lights."

Zukor's showmanship made a hit of *Hearts Adrift,* but it was a mediocre film, and while it did good business, its profits were not large enough to wipe out the losses incurred by the other Famous Players pictures. By the summer of 1914, Zukor was so deep in debt that he had to borrow on his life in-surance to meet the weekly payroll. Everything depended on the next Pickford picture, *Tess of the Storm Country,* the story of a young girl who leads a squatters' revolt against a group of corrupt landowners.

Tess was as crudely made as the other Famous Players films, but the plot was strong and the title role was ideal for Mary. In Tess, she found the screen character she had been looking for. Contrary to current belief, the early Pickford heroine wasn't all sweetness and light and shimmering, sugar-spun curls; she was not one of those Victorian damsels who does nothing but bat her eyes and swoons at the first mention of anything nasty or unpleasant. Like Mary herself, the Pickford heroine was usually a working-class or slum girl, often a plucky tomboy with boundless energy and spirit, capable of handling any adversity that came her way.

Mary's tattered and dirty-faced child-woman today seems a bit quaint, but for the audiences of 1914 she was a recogniz-able and touching figure. *Tess* was an enormous success of far-reaching consequence. Besides establishing Zukor as a major producer and Mary as the first lady of the movies, it also established the star system as a permanent part of the Ameri-can film industry.

Tess did one other thing—it gave Mary the nickname that people still use whenever they speak of her. When the film opened in San Francisco, theatre-owner David Graumann placed this sign on the marquee:

TESS OF THE STORM COUNTY
MARY PICKFORD
AMERICA'S SWEETHEART

3

In 1916, when Mary and Doug met again in California, Hollywood had not yet become the movie capital of America. A few film companies had settled there permanently, but most still kept studios in New York and used them as frequently as they did their West Coast facilities. Broadway was the hub of the American entertainment world, and show people didn't like to stray too far from the action. But the inclement Northeastern winters made location shooting all but impossible, and the producers started moving westward in search of sunshine. The choice of Southern California was no accident. Around 1909 the Los Angeles Chamber of Commerce sent literature East, extolling the climate, the varied scenery, the sun that shone 350 days a year. One by one the film companies bit the bait, and pretty soon the ramshackle Hollywood Hotel was filled to overflowing with New York movie people.

Mary first went to California in 1910 with Griffith and other members of the Biograph stock company. Hollywood was then a sleepy village, populated mainly by elderly couples who had come there, like movie people, for the sun and the dry climate. The area had barely been touched by civilization: a poppy field covered the corner of what is now Hollywood and Vine; pepper trees lined Melrose and La Brea; the Sunset Strip was a cow pasture valued at $500; Beverly Hills was a wilderness of briars and bridle paths, home for no one except deer, coyotes and an occasional wildcat. And above everything towered the royal and date palms, beautiful to those who like them, barbaric to those who don't.

Mary disliked them on sight. Nothing about California appealed to her during her first visit, and it was several years before she really felt at home in Los Angeles. Fairbanks, on the other hand, liked it from the start. In fact, the chance of working and living in California played an important part in his decision to enter the movies. Born in Denver in 1883, a time when Colorado was still the promised land for gold and silver prospectors, Fairbanks grew up on the legends of the Old West, and even as an adult he hankered after those romantic days when a man could be happy with a pistol, a horse and a can of beans. Going to California was for Doug a way of stepping back into his childhood.

He was the first child of Ella and Charles Ulman, an odd couple if there ever was one. By the time she reached Colorado, Ella had led a checkered, much-married existence. Catholic by birth, she came from a well-to-do New Orleans family, and while still a petite, teen-aged Southern belle, she married a wealthy industrialist and plantation owner named John Fairbanks. They were happy for a time, but after the birth of their first son (also named John), Fairbanks contracted tuberculosis and died a few months later. Swindled out of his inheritance by her late husband's relatives, Ella hastily married a handsome, smooth-talking Georgian named Edward Wilcox. He turned out to be an abusive and violent drunk, and Ella divorced him soon after the birth of her second son, Norris.

Ella then fell in love with her divorce attorney, New York lawyer Charles Ulman. The romance did not go smoothly—Ella was Catholic; Ulman, Jewish—but eventually they were wed. Shortly afterward Ulman gave up his law practice and invested all his money in a Colorado mining venture. He then moved Ella and her elder son to Denver. Norris was left in the care of relatives, and though Ella had good intentions, she somehow never got around to sending for him, possibly because she had two new sons—Doug and his younger brother, Robert—to care for.

Ella loathed Denver on sight, but she tried to adapt herself to the dirty frontier town, tried to give her home a touch of elegance with the few things she had salvaged from her New Orleans days. Still, the Ulmans seemed a happy and close-knit family until Charles's mining investments collapsed, and he returned East as a paid speaker for Benjamin Harrison's presidential campaign. Ella never heard from him again.

She turned to her children, especially 5-year-old Doug, for consolation. He was far more troublesome than his brothers—perhaps that was the reason he was her favorite. Doug was always getting into some kind of mischief—climbing trees or walking along the edge of the roof or playing swords with the kitchen carving knives—he wouldn't sit still in school, couldn't concentrate, wouldn't listen. A born show-off, he corralled the other neighborhood kids into playing cowboys-and-Indians and other games based on stories of the Old West.

After Charles had been missing for a year, Ella went back to calling herself Mrs. Fairbanks—Fairbanks had a genteel and Gentile sound that Ulman lacked—and she asked her sons to use the same name. She also wanted to move to New York, but that required a lot of penny-pinching, and first she had to educate her children. And that took time as well as money. Finally John was in college, Robert had decided to become an engineer and Doug had halfheartedly assented to Ella's suggestion that he, too, try for an engineering degree. Then in his senior year in high school, he told his mother he wanted to be an actor.

The Fairbanks family claim Doug's interest in the theatre was spawned by his father, who prided himself on his resemblance to Edwin Booth and who was fond of spouting lengthy passages from Shakespeare. Realizing that his son had inherited some of his theatrical temperament, Ulman enrolled him at a local drama school where Doug made his stage debut in a matinee of "Living Pictures."

A flair for the dramatic was not the only trait Douglas inherited from Charles. They also shared a tendency toward moodiness and what one member of the family called "gypsy-foot." Both were afflicted with wanderlust. This, in fact, may have been at the bottom of Doug's theatrical ambitions, not the desire to become the next Edwin Booth. Probably he dreamed of going on the stage for the same reason other boys ran away from home and joined the circus—it meant romance and excitement, an escape from the encroaching monotony of adult responsibility.

Whatever the reason, Ella was appalled. Unable to dissuade her son from joining a vagabond profession, she consulted a priest who advised her to let the boy have his way. Ella was forced to agree—Doug had deliberately flunked out of school so he could go on the stage. By hanging around the Denver theatres, the seventeen-year-old got a job with a touring company that presented tatty makeshift productions of everything from Shakespeare to Sardou. The overall quality of the troupe was suggested by the critic who gave Doug his first professional notice: "The [entire] supporting company was bad, but worst of all was Douglas Fairbanks as Laertes."

At the end of the tour, Doug had second thoughts about being an actor. He spent a semester at Harvard as a "special student," toured Europe for a summer, then returned to New York where he took a job in a Wall Street brokerage house. Three months later, half-dead from boredom, he went back to Broadway and was lucky enough to find a job almost immediately. Fairbanks had his ups and downs, but compared to most young actors (Mary Pickford, for instance), he established himself as a New York actor without much hardship. He was never out of work for very long.

Shortly after his return to the stage Doug was spotted by actress Grace George who persuaded her husband, producer William Brady, to sign him to a long-term contract. (Miss George had a good eye for young talent; years later she brought Humphrey Bogart to her husband's attention.) Brady began to feature, then star, Fairbanks in a string of light-

weight comedies whose titles—*Two Little Sailor Boys,*
Frenzied Finance, Fantana—fully convey their content and
quality.

In 1906 Fairbanks had his first really substantial success in
The Man of the Hour, an insubstantial comedy by the popular playwright, George Broadhurst. Ella took pride in his
burgeoning career, though, as she often told him, all she really
wanted was to see him settled down with a wife and a couple
of bouncing babies. Doug said he was working on it, and true
to his word, in the fall of 1907, he announced his engagement
to Anna Elizabeth Sully.

Beth was quite a catch for a young and not-so-famous actor.
She was the debutante daughter of Daniel Sully, a cotton
tycoon who maintained lavish homes in New York and
Watch Hill, a Rhode Island resort that ranked just below
Newport in the East Coast social gazetteer. Sully liked Fairbanks, but before consenting to the marriage, he made Doug
swear he would give up the stage and look for a reputable way
to support his daughter. So, after a brief honeymoon, Doug
went to work as a salesman for Buchan's Soap, a company in
which his father-in-law held a small business interest.

Doug genuinely enjoyed his new line of employment. It
kept him out in the fresh air, and on his rounds he met lots of
interesting people, including Frank Case (who agreed to use
Buchan's Soap in all the Algonquin washrooms). And his
theatrical experience came in handy in developing a nearly
foolproof sales pitch. "Listen," he'd say to a prospective client,
"if you don't believe this soap is pure, I'll eat it!"

But for all his skill and zeal, Fairbanks's career as a soap
peddler lasted only a short time. In 1908 Mr. Sully lost most
of his money in a stock market panic and to the chagrin of his
mother and in-laws, Doug had to go back to the stage to help
the Sullys live in the style to which they were accustomed.
The soap business may have been more respectable than show
business, but it didn't pay nearly as well.

Fairbanks came back to Broadway in *All for a Girl,* a flop,
but quickly recovered lost ground with *A Gentleman from*

Mississippi, a personal triumph. Then came a steady stream of hits—*A Gentleman of Leisure, The Cub, Officer 666, Hawthorne of the U.S.A.*—which established him as one of Broadway's most popular matinée idols. But, as he was the first to admit, he was never much of an actor. First of all, he had vocal problems. Offstage, he spoke so fast that his words came out in a jumbled, irregular pattern, and some of this carried over into his theatre work, often making him unintelligible. Also he couldn't play the simplest dramatic situation, not even a love scene, without becoming stiff and self-conscious. "Aw shucks, do I have to kiss [the heroine]?" he asked one producer. "It's silly, and anyway, the audience knows I've got a yen for her."

Doug got by on the strength of his smile—he had the biggest, most infectious grin of any actor in American stage history—and his hijinks. He never walked on stage when he could run, never crossed behind a table when he could leap over it, never registered a thought that wasn't a doubletake. Some serious critics found his bouncing breeziness, his exuberance, close to unbearable, but audiences enjoyed his antics and playwrights started tailoring roles to his personality. These star vehicle roles made Doug's acrobatics a part of his character, but the stage was too small an arena for his skills. He needed a hippodrome or the three rings of a circus or, best of all, a movie screen where space is an illusion and any physical feat looks lighter and easier than it really is.

Early in 1913 Adolph Zukor asked Doug to be one of the original Famous Players, but Fairbanks turned down the offer because, like other stage actors, he held a low opinion of the picture business. Two years later, his attitude hadn't really changed; still, he listened intently when a movie producer came forward with a proposition that was too tempting to be rejected without careful consideration.

The offer came from the California-based Triangle Company, a new organization formed by the then Big Three of motion pictures, Thomas Ince, Mack Sennett and D. W. Griffith (who had left Biograph only a few months after

Mary). To compete with Famous Players, Triangle hired over sixty stage actors (including Mary Boland, Billie Burke, Dustin Farnum, William S. Hart and Herbert Beerbohm Tree) at salaries as high as $4,000 a week. Fairbanks, not quite as illustrious as some of the other Triangle names, was offered a middling salary of $2,000 a week.

At first Doug was reluctant to sign. He discussed the contract with his friend, Frank Case, who told him a man with a wife and young son to support couldn't turn down all that money, far more than Fairbanks could ever hope to earn in the theatre. "I know," Doug sighed, "but the movies!"

He continued to waver, but eventually security and the lure of the wide-open spaces won out over Doug's self-esteem. In the spring of 1915, he went off to California, and enjoyed himself so much that when he returned the following year, he insisted Frank Case come along on a "bachelor's holiday." (Beth and Doug, Jr. stayed behind in New York.) The five-day train trip to the Coast allowed ample opportunity for practical jokes, Fairbanks's and Case's favorite way of killing time. One morning Case awoke to find an Indian, done up in war paint, blanket and feathers, bending over his berth and making menacing noises. Case gave such a start that he bumped noses with his assailant. Catching a whiff of his breath, the Algonquin innkeeper realized the chief was "no true Algonquin."

In Los Angeles, Fairbanks rented a big house on Holly-wood Boulevard near La Brea, and later moved to an even larger home in the desolate, upper terrain of Beverly Hills. There (according to a fan magazine article of the time) "he rose at dawn to trot through dewy grass and jump over fences on his way home." Since the only country club in the area refused his application for membership (actors weren't welcome in Los Angeles society), he played tennis on his own court, worked out in a makeshift cellar gymnasium and rode his own horse through the Beverly Hills brambles.

On one of these expeditions, Doug discovered a mountain-side of shale, sloping from a roadway down a thousand feet to a valley below. At first glance the incline looked still and motionless, but as soon as a foot was placed on it, the entire hill began to move and slide. Doug made a game of it. He pushed people onto the cliff and laughed uproariously as the rocks began to tremble under their feet. Mary was one of his victims. In his memoir, *Tales of a Wayward Inn,* Frank Case remembers her "flying down the mountain like Peter Pan through the window, only faster and much prettier."

Sometimes Mary joined Doug and a bunch of friends for riding parties or for beach picnics at Malibu. And later that spring when Beth arrived from New York, the Pickford family were occasional dinner guests at the Fairbanks home. Whenever they met, Mary and Doug made sure they were part of a crowd. Separately they had decided to fight their feelings for one another and to shield themselves from temptation. Both resumed their former ways of life. Early in 1916 Mary went through another brief reconciliation with Owen Moore and Doug was once again playing the field.

For years Fairbanks had been an ardent ladies' man. "He didn't drink or smoke much, so he thought he had the right to some kind of vice," said Anita Loos. "So he chose women. He went after every girl who crossed the Triangle lot. I don't remember all their names, but Irene Castle was one of them." Doug's philandering was done in a discreet fashion, and he assumed that Beth knew nothing of his transient affairs. Perhaps not, but it's also possible that Mrs. Fairbanks chose to act as practically any woman of her position and background would—she pretended ignorance of her husband's infidelities.

Between women and moviemaking, Fairbanks led a busy life in 1916. He made eleven films that year, all but one feature-length. Two were Western romances; the others were "modern comedies" which followed the pattern of *His Picture in the Papers,* Doug's third film and first big success in pictures. It was directed by John Emerson and written by Anita Loos, a team that created the best of the early Fairbanks films.

When Fairbanks had come to Triangle the year before, he

had been assigned to the Griffith unit. This was fine for Doug, whose disdain for the movies had dwindled after he saw *The Birth of a Nation,* but not such happy news for Griffith. Most of the director's creative energies were being poured into the preproduction planning of his second screen epic, *Intolerance,* and he had little interest in the stage actors who were passed along to him for grooming. Fairbanks he found particularly exasperating.

After watching Doug cavort on one of the sets, Griffith suggested the new actor be put to work in one of Mack Sennett's slapstick comedies. Doug was deeply offended by this remark as were the Triangle production chiefs who saw Fairbanks as a second Francis X. Bushman, then the reigning matinée idol of the screen. So Griffith was stuck with Doug, whom he passed along to the second-string directors of his unit, telling them not to waste much time on the newcomer. "He's got a face like a canteloupe and he can't act," Griffith commented.

On his third time out, Fairbanks drew John Emerson, a Broadway actor turned film director, who was familiar with Doug's stage work. Unlike most theatre people, Emerson was fascinated with the movies, and he looked on his Fairbanks assignment as a challenge. Rummaging through the Triangle scenario files, he came across an unfilmed story which was full of action and sassy, wisecracking titles. Emerson got in touch with its author, Anita Loos, and asked her to write something along the same lines for Doug.

She turned in *His Picture in the Papers,* the story of Pete Prindle, the son of a manufacturer of vegetarian products. He falls in love with a girl who hankers for a man who gets his picture in the papers. To prove he's a man and not a vegetable, Pete goes out and gets involved in a series of outlandish escapades and winds up with his picture on the front page of all the New York dailies.

Griffith took one look at the finished film, and ordered it shelved. All the humor was in the captions, he said, and people wanted to see, not read, movies. The film remained unreleased until a booking crisis forced Triangle to substitute it for another feature scheduled for a New York theatre. A huge success, it guaranteed the future of both Douglas Fairbanks and the printed title as a legitimate form of movie storytelling.

Fairbanks was to work with other directors and writers, but Loos and Emerson were his favorite collaborators for the next two years. All their films were made from the same formula: an Eastern effete or a European playboy or a poor little rich boy proves his manhood through some kind of crazy, romantic adventure. Or, as a variation, the Fairbanks hero was a frustrated dreamer, caught in some humdrum job and longing for romance and excitement.

Years later Doug said that in these early comedies he had tried "to catch the real spirit of youth . . . the spirit that takes short cuts and dashes impetuously at what it wants, that doesn't take time to walk around obstacles, but hurdles them—the fine, restless and impatient, conquering Spirit of youth that scales whatever hazards are in its way."

Though a bit overstated (Doug seems to be parroting his own notices), this description is apt enough. The hundreds of thousands of young American men trapped in monotonous nine-to-five jobs did look on Doug's adventures (in Alistair Cooke's words) "as an antidote, a goal for the fretting city worker to aim at . . . a source of constant inspiration."

Nonetheless, it seems pretty certain that Doug didn't set out to capture the spirit of youth—that was an afterthought. The screen character Anita Loos devised for him was designed to minimize his deficiencies as an actor (all the "acting" came early in the picture) and to give him every opportunity to display his abilities as a gymnast. In *His Picture in the Papers,* he went several rounds with a professional boxer, dove from the deck of an ocean liner and took a breathtaking (and very dangerous) leap from a speeding train. And for the later pictures, Miss Loos recalls that her toughest task was "dreaming up situations that would allow Doug to break loose."

She also acknowledges the important part he played in shaping the scenarios. "Doug contributed a lot. He had a very strong dramatic sense. If you gave him a good idea, he'd take off with it, elaborating it in all sorts of wonderful ideas."

Fairbanks worked out all his stunts in advance, but many of the nonaction scenes were improvised at the last minute— John Emerson always let Doug set the pace of the shooting. Some of these improvisations were never intended for the camera. Doug used the set as a background for elaborate practical jokes, many of them aimed at Emerson, who had a number of personal quirks which alternately amused and enraged his friends. One of the worst was his timidity about driving—he hugged the middle of the road and usually poked along at a snail's pace. Doug, who loved speed and fast cars, decided to give him a good scare.

One day, as Emerson drove away from the studio, he noticed he was being tailed by two mean-looking hoodlums in a fast-moving roadster. The driver honked his horn and made rude gestures indicating that he wanted Emerson to pick up his pace. The director stepped gingerly on the accelerator, but the horn only blew louder and his pursuers kept coming closer and closer. To avoid a collision, Emerson had to go faster and faster until finally the roadster decided to pass him. As they whizzed by, the two hoodlums waved and laughed. Shaking with terror and rage, Emerson recognized his assailants as none other than Doug Fairbanks and one of his Triangle cronies.

One of Fairbanks's better practical jokes occurred during the filming of *The Good Bad Man* in the Mojave Desert. When the picture was finished, Doug gave a party for cast, crew and all rangers and cowboys in the surrounding area. As the evening wore on, people began to dance, and since there were more men than women, some of the cowboys partnered each other. One burly ranchhand asked Frank Case (a visitor on the set) for a waltz. Afraid to refuse, Case sheepishly allowed himself to be pushed around the room till the music stopped. As he was walking back to his seat, the cowboy

41

tugged at his sleeve and pleaded, "Aw, come on, Frank, just one more!"

Case spent the entire night on the dance floor. Finally, as the last song was ending, his cowboy-partner whispered, "God, Frank, I could die waltzing with you!"

This story was one of Case's favorite anecdotes—he told it many times, but he never realized that Doug had stage-managed the whole incident.

By the fall of 1916, Fairbanks was one of the leading stars of America. Among the men, he was second in popularity only to Charles Chaplin. Mary still topped them both. At this time, the fan magazines printed poems written by their readers, the vast majority dedicated to Mary. A sample:

> As Queen or Thrall she holds us all
>   In spell at the photo show
> The evening stars, with golden sheen
>   In tribute rise and fall
> To her who reigns an uncrowned queen—
>   The brightest star of all

The following month the same magazine published a reader's list of "The Six Natural Wonders of America":

1. Yellowstone Park
2. Grand Canyon
3. Mammoth Cave
4. Niagara Falls
5. Yosemite Park
6. Mary Pickford

Undoubtedly some fans would have ranked her even higher, even though many of her recent films had been disappointing.

Famous Players had started to build the Pickford films around the questionable assumption that the public would pay to see Mary in anything, no matter how weak the story or slovenly the direction. She played a wide variety of roles in this period, everything from Cinderella to Nell Gwynne and *Madame Butterfly,* and she made a specialty of ethnic roles. In rapid succession, she was *Hulda from Holland, Poor Little Peppina,* the half-breed Indian heroine of *Little Pal,* a Hindustani slave in *Less than the Dust.*

Critics praised her versatility, but audiences knew it was just little Mary done up in a sari or a kimono or a pair of Dutch braids. And they liked her better without the disguises. When *Less than the Dust,* her last film in 1916, flopped dismally with both critics and the public, Mary realized she must have more control over her career. She also wanted more money. Her salary was now $4,000 a week, a tidy sum, but no more than what some of the Triangle stars were earning, and far less than Charles Chaplin, who had recently signed a $670,000 yearly contract with the Mutual Company. Mary thought she deserved better than Chaplin, a relative new-comer to film, or the Triangle players who, with the exception of Fairbanks and William S. Hart, had all proved to be bad investments. She decided to have a chat with Adolph Zukor.

By this time Famous Players had merged with the Lasky and Paramount companies, but Zukor remained the topmost power of the conglomerate. He negotiated all the Pickford contracts, a chore that kept him up nights, trying to find a way to keep her happy and still stay solvent. "I never had to diet," he once said. "Whenever Mary started to talk money, I auto-matically lost ten pounds."

A soft-spoken, gentle-mannered man, Zukor was nonethe-less a shrewd and ruthless bargainer. ("He'd leave the screen-ing room after weeping buckets over some inane picture and go straight to the conference table where he'd lop off a couple of heads," recalled a former associate.) But he had met his match in Mary. Her demands were presented in a round-about, highly ladylike fashion, often through her mother who was always ready to act as Mary's intermediary. Charlotte would smile sweetly at Zukor and ask, "Don't you think Mary should have a fur coat for winter?" Or "I saw a handsome limousine today. Mary would look darling in it!" Zukor would sigh and start totaling up what the new coat and car would cost in terms of salary.

Just before her 1916 contract expired, Mary was approached by a rival company which offered her $7,000. Out of loyalty to Famous Players, Mary told Zukor about the offer and asked whether he wanted to match it. There followed an intricate series of proposals and counterproposals, stretching over several weeks, but the outcome was that Mary got what she wanted, and more. She signed a two-year contract at $10,000 a week. In addition, she would be head of The Mary Pickford Picture Corporation, which would release its films through Artcraft, a special distribution branch of Famous Players–Lasky–Paramount. Charlotte Pickford was to become treasurer of this corporation, and no money was to be spent without her consent. To insure quality, the number of Pickford films would be reduced from eight to five a year. And, as a token of good will, Zukor threw in a bonus of $300,000 for Mary, $20,000 for Charlotte.

The next day there were banner headlines in *Variety* and the other trade papers: MARY GETS FIRST MILLION DOLLAR CONTRACT. The news spread like wildfire through the industry, pleasing actors, horrifying producers who predicted that star salaries would be the downfall of the picture business. But Mary's demands were not unjustified or irresponsible. She was pretty certain her salary would be comfortably absorbed by the gross profits of her productions. A million dollars was not a figure she had plucked greedily from the sky; it was based on a dispassionate appraisal of her drawing power and an expert knowledge of the ways and means of the film industry.

Nor was the contract quite as extravagant as it sounded. As her own producer Mary was expected to foot the production costs of her films, though she shared the profits equally with Paramount. This part of the arrangement didn't seem quite fair, but there was nothing Mary could do about it, not at this time. . . .

Mary signed her new contract in New York in the fall of 1916. And she was still there when Fairbanks returned to the East Coast to spend the Christmas and New Year holidays with his family. While traveling cross-country, Doug learned that his mother, Ella Fairbanks, had died suddenly of pneumonia. The news came as a terrible shock. Just before Doug left for California, Beth and Ella had gone through one of their periodic squabbles—Beth often accused Ella of being overly possessive. Whenever this happened, Doug had the good sense to side with his wife, even though Ella wouldn't speak to him for weeks afterward. This particular quarrel had never been patched up, and Doug couldn't forget that his mother had died while they were still on bad terms. Arriving in New York, he went straight to the Algonquin and locked himself in his suite, refusing to see anyone except the immediate family.

Finally he turned to Mary Pickford for comfort. After the funeral he called at her hotel and asked her to drive with him through Central Park. She tried to comfort him, recalling all the things she had liked and admired about Ella. After a few minutes, Doug stopped the car and began to cry, unashamedly releasing all the emotion he had pent up over the last week. Turning aside from his private moment of sorrow, Mary gazed silently ahead at the trees, the windshield, the dashboard clock which had stopped, she suddenly noticed, at the precise hour of Ella's death.

Mrs. Fairbanks had always been superstitious about clocks and thought they stopped whenever someone in a family died. Wanting to believe his mother had forgiven him, Doug accepted the broken clock as a sign that Ella's spirit was still with him. From then on, Mary and Doug used the phrase "by the clock" for promises that couldn't be broken.

A few weeks later Doug held a reception in Mary's honor at the Algonquin. It was a bon voyage party for her—she was going back to the Coast for a new film—and also for him; he was soon to join her in Hollywood as a Famous Players–Artcraft star. At the end of 1916 he had left Triangle and signed with Zukor at a salary of $5,000 a week. As part of the deal, he was promised his own production company (Douglas Fairbanks Films) and the right to choose his own writers and directors (Anita Loos, John Emerson, Allan Dwan and others), his own business manager (his half-brother, John) and his own production facilities. He rented a small studio just across the street from the lot where the Pickford unit worked.

In the spring of 1917, after Doug's arrival in California, Mary reciprocated with a picnic on the lawn of her small West Hollywood bungalow. It was nothing fancy, just tea and Mama Charlotte's punch and assorted canapés, but it was Mary's way of introducing Doug to a few of his fellow Famous Players–Lasky–Paramount colleagues—Gloria Swanson, Thomas Meighan, Blanche Sweet, Wally Reid, Mickey Neilan and Fatty Arbuckle were among the guests. The trade press gave routine coverage to the party, never suggesting that Mary and Doug were more than business friends.

4

Looking back, it now seems amazing that Mary and Doug managed to hide their romance for as long as they did. Many of their closest friends were not aware there was an attachment until late 1917, and a full year would pass before any hint of it reached the public. Partly this was because the gossip columnists and show-business reporters of the time laundered their copy; partly because Mary and Doug's popularity made them untouchable; mainly because they conducted the affair with such infinite tact.

Beth Fairbanks was one of the first to suspect something was going on. Around this time, she crossed Mary off her party list, even though she wasn't sure Mary was the reason why Doug was suddenly spending so many nights at the studio. At first Beth was inclined to pin the blame on Anita Loos. Doug often used his business associates as a cover for his amorous activities, usually his publicist, Bennie Zeidman, but recently he had been seeing Miss Loos about a screenplay. Or so he told Beth, who thought there might be more to their collaboration than scriptwriting. She suggested that henceforth Doug and Anita work in the library of the Fairbanks home.

At first, Anita Loos was disconcerted by Beth's glacial welcomes, but after Doug confessed that he had been using her as an alibi, she was greatly amused and willingly became his partner in crime. Like many of Doug's friends, she had grown weary of Beth's haughty airs, and she was happy to see the regal Mrs. Fairbanks brought down a notch or two.

Often, when Beth was otherwise preoccupied, Miss Loos and her future husband, John Emerson, would make up a secret riding party with Mary and Doug. They would sneak off on horseback to the canyons above Los Angeles, Mary and Doug both wearing huge sombreros to hide their faces. If inquisitive riders came too close, Doug would throw them off the scent by saying, "I saw the new Fairbanks picture last night, and is he ever a show-off!" "He couldn't be worse than that Pickford girl," Mary would chime in. "Aren't those curls awful!"

Some Sundays Doug would put on false whiskers and goggles, Mary tied a babushka around her head, and they climbed into a beat-up Ford flivver for a drive through the San Fernando Valley. And every so often they met surreptitiously at night, either at Mary's bungalow or Robert Fairbanks's cottage in Laurel Canyon.

Getting out at night was something of a problem for Doug. He took to making his bed on an upstairs sleeping porch—the night air, he told Beth, was good for the constitution. Then, when everyone else was asleep, he'd climb down a pillar, release the handbrake of his car, coast it down the steep incline of his driveway and start it up on the street where no one would be awakened by the sound of the ignition. Returning home wasn't quite so easy—he had to push the car up the driveway, an Olympian feat that left him exhausted and hungry. He asked his colored valet, Buddy, to leave a piece of cake on his bed table, and he always gulped it down in the dark, afraid he would waken someone if he turned on a light.

One night, the cake had an odd, faintly Oriental taste, but Doug thought nothing of it—he wolfed it down and went right to sleep. The next morning he discovered the reason for the strange taste—on the plate were a few crumbs and a creeping mass of red ants. Doug must have swallowed several hundred of them the night before.

Another obstacle Fairbanks had to overcome was Owen

Moore's wrath. Once Mary and Charlotte had settled in their California home, Moore started besieging his wife with presents and letters, and begged to come back. Mary agreed, and although Charlotte offered to move out, the three of them lived for a time in uneasy coexistence. Mary told him to leave and never come back. His drinking had grown steadily worse, and according to several friends, he had committed some grievous offense that Mary and Charlotte could not forgive. Moore refused to accept the separation as final, and once he got wind of the Fairbanks romance, he was sure this was the reason Mary had kicked him out. In a drunken rage, he swore that the next time he saw Fairbanks, there would be blood.

A few weeks later, they did bump into each other in the lobby of a Hollywood hotel. In one version of the incident, Moore pulled a gun on Fairbanks, but probably the gun was a figment of a fan-magazine writer's overproductive imagination. There was a short scuffle, but no blood was spilled and nobody was hurt. Still, Doug thought it best to stay away from Hollywood until Moore came to his senses.

He started off to make a movie in New York, but halfway across the country he got a better idea. He had never seen the Grand Canyon and his director, Allan Dwan, had always wanted to visit the Canyon de Chelly in the Navajo country near Albuquerque. So, they decided to use these sites as the locales of the movie. Hurriedly, they concocted a scenario, called it *A Modern Musketeer*, and had it before the cameras in less than three weeks.

Meanwhile Mary sat around Hollywood, asking herself (as Anita Loos recalls), "What does Doug Fairbanks want with a shanty Irish girl like me?" It was not entirely a rhetorical question. Doug was a terrible snob, and the Pickfords's raffish reputation disturbed him no end. "Gee, it'd be swell to be married to Mary," he once said to a friend. "But gosh! Her family! How do you handle them?"

Charlotte Pickford was the best of the lot; nearly everybody liked her. She gave herself no airs or pretensions, and even wearing her best Fifth Avenue finery, she looked like an Irish scrubwoman decked out for Sunday Mass. Jolly, down-to-earth, with a lilting, Mother Machree brogue, Ma Pickford's only failing was her thirst for whiskey. Just before Prohibition, she built a vault in the cellar of her home, and crammed it with every bottle it could hold. The keys to the stash were entrusted to no one, certainly not to Lottie or Jack who would have raided the premises faster than Elliott Ness.

Lottie was, in the slang of the time, a madcap. She drank too much, she was rowdy, she flirted with cocaine and other drugs, she wasn't overly fastidious about her love life. Lottie had four husbands, marrying the last of them before she was legally divorced from his predecessor. ("Jeez, will Mary be mad when she hears about this!" she confided to reporters.) Husband number three caused Lottie considerable embarrassment. He was supposed to be a "mortician," but Lottie's maid told the press that it was hooch, not corpses, that he was hauling in the back of his hearse.

Much as she disapproved of Lottie's antics, Mary did everything she could to establish her sister as a front-rank film star. But Lottie wasn't as pretty or talented as Mary, and she wasn't nearly as ambitious. She fluffed her only real chance for stardom, a leading role in a 1914 serial, *The Diamond from the Sky*. Mary got Lottie the job and Charlotte worked out the terms of the contract—$4,000 a week plus a big publicity campaign that would promote Lottie as the new Pearl White.

Lottie was blasé about this unexpected piece of good luck; perhaps because she had more important matters on her mind. A recent bride, she was also an expectant mother, a biological condition she neglected to mention at the time she signed her contract. Her pregnancy might have passed unnoticed in a five-reel film, but it was a real problem in a twenty-four episode serial, shot over a period of four months. For the final installments, Lottie had to be photographed peeking over the tops of screens and picket fences.

Mary barely tolerated her sister's improprieties. Lottie was cast as the black sheep of the family, though brother Jack, equally naughty, really deserved that title. Jack, however, was the baby, and pampered from birth by three doting women, he was wise in the ways of male coquetry. Short, with an equine face, and the body of a Charles Atlas reject, Jack was no Adonis, but he had charm, scads of it, and he knew how to use it at a very young age.

While still in his early teens, Jack met Lillian Lorraine, the queen of the Ziegfeld runway (called "the bridge of thighs" by connoisseurs), and she introduced him to the intoxication of sex and silver fizz cocktails. She must have been a persuasive teacher—Jack never lost his taste for gin and all three of his wives were graduates of the Ziegfeld chorus line.

Jack's friends think he might have become a major star. He had the talent and the personality, but not the drive or discipline. "Working with Jack was no picnic," said Louise Huff, his leading lady between 1915 and 1917. "He was either recovering from a hangover or getting ready for the next one. Often he wouldn't show up in the morning and if he did, he'd have to lie down and take a nap. And you could never be sure he'd return after lunch. But no one could stay mad at Jack. He was a darling—clever, funny and *so* charming. Not many drunks are good company, but Jack was never tedious or obnoxious."

Mary kept tabs on Jack, and often stopped by the set to watch him at work. And though she tried to stay in the background, her presence intimidated Louise Huff. "I came to Famous Players as the next Mary Pickford. Zukor was afraid that one day Mary would fly the coop and I was there to keep her in line. I was supposed to resemble her—I was small and blond and curly, but the similarity ended there. Still, when Mary started hanging around the set, I thought she was jealous. Now, wasn't that silly of me? I was no threat, and she knew it. She couldn't have cared less about me. She was worried about Jack and the way he was destroying his life."

Jack went from one escapade to the next, never worrying about the consequences because he knew that in a pinch Mary or Charlotte would always come to the rescue. But sometimes even they couldn't keep him out of the headlines. In the spring of 1918, less than six months after he had enlisted in the armed forces, he became a key figure in a Navy graft investigation. Allegedly he had been a go-between for a group of "rich slackers" who paid naval officers $10,000 for assignments that kept them off the battlefields of World War I. Jack was threatened with a dishonorable discharge, but Charlotte pulled some strings and in exchange for turning state's evidence, he was let off with an ordinary, honorable discharge. But patriotism was running high in the country, and the incident was never entirely forgotten. It was to haunt Jack for years to come.

Doug wrestled with his snobbism, but for a long time he seemed to be waging a losing battle with his squeamishness about the Pickfords. Mary's real name of Gladys Smith, he reasoned, was a legitimate reason to suppose his sweetheart could lay claim to a proper, if modest, British ancestry. The argument sounded good to him, but just as he was ready to swallow it, Lottie or Jack cut a caper that proved the Pickfords still had their hearts in the bogs of shanty Eire. Beth Fairbanks, now fully aware of what was going on, was not terribly concerned. Either the affair would be killed by Doug's fastidiousness or it would die a natural death.

Beth miscalculated on both counts. The clandestine nature of Mary and Doug's meetings were a cure for boredom—there was something oddly exciting about dodging the public and sneaking up stairs of backstreet hotels. And Mary's status in the film industry was another cure for Doug's snobbism. It was nice being married to a Watch Hill debutante, but it might be even nicer to be married to the First Lady of the Movies, to the woman poet-critic Vachel Lindsay had just crowned "the Queen of the American People."

It seemed impossible, but Mary's popularity continued to grow and now she was virtually in a class by herself. She was the first film actress to be on the covers of national magazines; her curls and her clothes had begun to influence the look of the American woman. People were interested in what she thought and how she lived, and she told them in articles in *Ladies' Home Journal* and *Pictorial Review* (many of them ghost-written by a young reporter named Frances Marion.) And at the end of 1917 the readers of *Woman's Home Companion* voted her "The Ideal American Woman."

Ironically, the ideal American woman was beginning to drift into a second childhood. It was at this time that Mary created the screen character for which she is best remembered. It was a part she didn't want to play in a film she didn't want to make, *A Poor Little Rich Girl*. The title sums up the plot: ten-year-old Gwendolyn, neglected by her wealthy, fun-loving parents, is given an overdose of a sleeping potion by a careless maid. As she hovers near death, her entire life passes before her eyes in a long dream sequence; then she awakens to find her repentant parents sitting by her bed.

Gwendolyn was too helpless and all-suffering for Mary's taste, and she fought against making the picture for several weeks. But Zukor, who had paid a lot of money for the screenrights to the original play, promised her a free hand over the production if she would accept the assignment. Mary brought in Frances Marion as scenarist, and together they conspired to add a few touches of humor and spirit to poor little Gwendolyn. These embellishments did not please director Maurice Tourneur, a Frenchman who prided himself on the "pictorial beauty" of his productions. "I am a dignified director," he said. "My pictures should be dignified." Each time Mary and Frances Marion introduced one of their interpolations, he would stop shooting and ask, "Where, exactly, do you see that in the script, ladies?" Refusing to be intimidated, Mary improvised a temper tantrum in which Gwendolyn throws all her clothes out a window, including the ones she has on her back. It's the best scene in the film, but Tourneur was appalled. *"Mais non, c'est une horreur!"* he screamed.

Adolph Zukor tended to agree. True to his word, he had let Mary have her way during production, but once he saw the results, he told her that, as he had feared, the picture was a fiasco for which she was personally responsible. Mary was so contrite she willingly accepted the penalty of making her next two films with Cecil B. De Mille who was already well on his way to earning the reputation of Hollywood's most tyrannical director.

This is the way Mary tells the story in her autobiography, and Adolph Zukor backed her up in the story of his life, *The Public Are Never Wrong*. But Clarence Brown, assistant director of *Poor Little Rich Girl,* tells a different story. In his version, while Mary and Tourneur had their differences on the set, they were very friendly after hours, too much so for Zukor and Charlotte's liking. To put an end to the friendship, they exiled Mary to California.

The pictures Pickford made with De Mille (*Romance of the Redwoods, The Little American*) were popular, but they were completely overshadowed by the unexpected and spectacular success of *Poor Little Rich Girl.* Contrary to everyone's predictions, this became one of the most beloved and popular of all Pickford films. Today it still stands up well, mainly because of Tourneur's dream sequence, the tough fiber of Mary's performance and some superb close-ups, including several illuminated with a baby spotlight—a Pickford innovation.

Later in 1917, Mary played another child, the title heroine in *Rebecca of Sunnybrook Farm,* which became an even bigger hit than *Poor Little Rich Girl.* It is also a far better film, possibly the best Mary ever made. Sweet, sentimental, but never treacly, it's a classic of its kind. And Mary is a delight; she plays the part without a trace of strain, never winking at the audience to say, "Look, I'm a woman playing a kid, and aren't I cute?"

One thing that helped Pickford create the illusion of youth was her own physical appearance. She was short, just a fraction under five feet tall, and weighed less than a hundred pounds. There was also something childlike about her proportions—her head was too big for her body, her torso a shade too thick for her height. In later films, costumes and sets were carefully designed to enhance this illusion. All furniture and props were scaled one-third larger than life size, doors and windows were bigger than normal, doorknobs higher. And her dresses were padded around the abdomen and hips so that there would be no womanly curves to give her away.

The real secret of her success, however, was the absolute sincerity she brought to her little girl parts. "I didn't act—I *was* the characters I played on the screen," she once said. "During a picture, I didn't leave the character at the studio; I took it home with me. I lived my parts." She had, in fact, found the little girl she had never been. Many of her friends felt that in playing Rebecca and Pollyanna and the other "glad girls," she was actually living out the childhood she had never had.

Most people knew that offscreen Mary was a young woman in her twenties, but some fans, particularly the younger ones, preferred the illusion to the reality. For thousands of young girls, she *was* Rebecca of Sunnybrook Farm, and to live up to their expectations, Mary had to pretend she was nine going on twenty-nine. She never went so far as to wear pinafores and Mary Janes (as did one of her imitators), but her off-screen dresses were junior-miss designs, simple and without a trace of sophistication. Formerly she had often pinned up her curls; now they always hung loose. Charlotte was her chaperon at public affairs and Owen Moore was edited out of all biographies and press releases. Mary's fans were quite happy to forget she had ever been married, and weren't prepared for her to have a boyfriend—or so Adolph Zukor and Mrs. Pickford believed. Mary wasn't pleased about acting half her age—she liked glamorous clothes and male companionship—but her career always came first. She went along with the decision.

To give up a glamorous dress is one thing; to give up a glamorous man is something quite different. Previously Mary had sacrificed her personal life to her career partly because there hadn't been much personal life to sacrifice. Now there was Douglas Fairbanks, whose ardor was becoming an increasingly serious problem. Mary's instinct for professional survival told her to discourage him, but her personal feelings kept her attentive. Every day she was the middleman in a game of tug-of-war, Fairbanks pulling one way, Charlotte and Zukor the other. And, as usual, Mrs. Pickford carried a lot of weight.

Charlotte was fond of Doug, and at first she had no objections to the romance. Then, when things took a serious turn, her attitude changed and she warned Mary of the possible consequences of any impetuous action. Her fears were not only for her daughter's career, but also for her personal happiness. Knowing of Doug's reputation as a ladies' man, she worried that someday he would again begin to wander and treat Mary as he now treated Beth Fairbanks. She also thought Doug was in love with Mary's fame, not Mary herself.

There is strong evidence that Doug was indeed fascinated with the adulation that surrounded Mary. It was both an attraction and a challenge. Once, after a film premiere, he asked Adela Rogers St. John, "Do you think I got as much applause as Mary?"

Doug had no cause for concern. Though he didn't rank quite as high as Mary in the popularity polls, he was always one of the top five. The senior class at Yale voted him their favorite actor and, in March 1917, he had a mountain in Yosemite Park named after him—"Douglas Fairbanks Peak." And like Pickford (who was the subject of a poem in Vachel Lindsay's popular collection, *The Congo and Other Poems*), Fairbanks was beginning to capture the imagination of the country's leading literary and intellectual figures. Around this time, novelist Booth Tarkington wrote this charming tribute for *Photoplay:*

> "Fairbanks is a faun who has been to Sunday school.
> He has a pagan body which yields instantly to any
> heathen or gypsy impulse . . . but he has a mind re-

liably furnished with a full set of morals and proprieties. He would be a sympathetic companion for anyone's aunt. I don't know his age. I think he hasn't any. Certainly he will never get older—unless quicksilver can get older."

As often happens, this attention came to Fairbanks at a time when the quality of his work was beginning to fall off. In the summer of 1917, the Fairbanks-Loos-Emerson team broke up amicably—Loos and Emerson wanted to work in New York, he wanted to stay in California—and without Miss Loos's witty, well-constructed plots as a rein, Doug's exuberance ran roughshod over the pictures. The balance between comedy and action had been upset, intentionally so, since Fairbanks announced that from now on, he would make straightforward adventure films. But the plan hadn't been thought through, and the new films resembled the old, only they weren't so neatly crafted or amusing.

Critics carped about the unmotivated action of the new Fairbanks films, but kids weren't so persnickety. The boys of America worshiped Fairbanks along with such fictional heros as Robin Hood, Tom Swift and Frank Merriwell. And Doug returned their affection—he was a bountiful big brother for his little fans. The Boy Scouts of America elected him as an honorary official, and occasionally he made a guest appearance at one of their summer camps or national conferences. In his role as den father, he put out under his name a series of books designed to guide the young boy through the rites of manhood. Titled *Laugh and Live, Making Life Worthwhile* and *Taking Stock of Ourselves,* these 5-and-10 cent store best sellers were ghost-written by Kenneth Davenport (an actor-writer who was Doug's close friend), but in style and philosophy they were pure Fairbanks.

They're nearly unreadable, but a quick perusal shows that Doug advocated the benefits of self-denial, positive thinking and strenuous exercise. "The boy who wishes to get to the front in athletics must adopt a program of mental and bodily cleanliness," he wrote. He was anti-liquor ("the greatest foe of athletic success among college men") and pro-laughter. "Play, play, play. . . . we are getting too serious, too methodical. Let us start a crusade for the glory of play. Troubles are what you make of them. It's easier to laugh than to cry, but if you must cry, get a joyful kick out of it."

Sex was not mentioned in the books, but Doug did have some thoughts on love and marriage. "Marry early," he advised, "and remain faithful to the bride of your youth." Apparently he had no scruples about preaching what he didn't practice.

Patriotism was another subject not discussed in the self-help books, but had Doug put his mind to it, he would assuredly have come up with some rousing jingoist slogans. He was no warmonger, but like his hero, Teddy Roosevelt, he was always ready to fight for his country's honor. In late 1916, when America was divided into "preparedness" and "pacifist" camps, Anita Loos wrote a comedy, *In Again, Out Again,* which poked fun at the controversy and also mocked Doug's worship of Roosevelt. In the picture, Fairbanks plays Teddy Rutherford, "a pacifist who is always prepared." Doug, who could always laugh at himself, thought it was a capital joke.

When America finally entered the war in 1917, Fairbanks was thirty-four, too old for active service. But he was ready to do his bit on the home front. To aid the Red Cross, he organized a colossal rodeo in San Francisco. A two-hundred-cowboy band playing "When Johnny Comes Marching Home" led the parade of guest celebrities (Dustin Farnum, Hoot and Helen Gibson, Art Acord) into the arena, followed by thirty girls in Red Cross uniforms who held up signs showing dollar signs and American eagles. Next came the world's champion buck-horse rider, Prairie Rue, followed by three Hollywood starlets dressed as chickens for a mock cock-fight. The climax of the spectacle came when Fairbanks, the master of ceremonies, rode into the arena while executing a hand-stand on top of an automobile.

Douglas also donated his services for several short propaganda films produced by the War Relief Organization. One was *Swat the Kaiser!*, a boxing match between Democracy (Fairbanks) and Prussianism, with Uncle Sam acting as referee.

Mary also was active in war work. Besides starting a "tobacco fund" for the boys overseas, she adopted the second battalion of the First California Field Artillery. In her role of "war mother," she made frequent visits to Camp Kearney near San Diego, and presented each of the six hundred recruits with a gold locket containing her picture. She bought thousands of dollars worth of Liberty Bonds, and spent thousands more in subscriptions to the Canadian War Loan.

Mary and Doug's patriotism caught the attention of William McAdoo, Secretary of the Treasury and President Wilson's son-in-law. He asked them to join Charlie Chaplin on a tour to sell and promote Liberty Bonds. This was an historic moment on two counts: it was the first alliance between Hollywood and Washington; it was also the first time Pickford and Fairbanks appeared together in public.

In every city, huge crowds turned out to greet the stars. Sometimes they appeared in theatres, sometimes on makeshift platforms out-of-doors, but always there were more people than could be comfortably fitted into the allotted space. First Mary would come on, toting a megaphone she could barely lift. "I'm only five foot tall and weigh a hundred pounds," she shouted. "But every inch and ounce of me is fighting American!" (She was, however, still a Canadian citizen.)

Next came Chaplin twirling his cane and walking like the little tramp. And then Doug, flashing grins and bounding off every pillar and post in sight. At the Academy of Music in Philadelphia, he shinnied up the proscenium arch and leaped into the stage boxes, then jumped to the stage, vaulted across the orchestra pit and ran up the aisles begging for pledges. A Washington business firm promised a million dollars if he flew to New York in a mail plane and picked up a similar contribution on Wall Street. Doug made the flight—a daredevil feat in those days—and got the money. He also got headlines on the front page of most New York dailies.

The first stage of the tour ended with the three stars making a lunchtime appearance on the steps of the sub-Treasury Building in Wall Street. Over 20,000 people came to shake their hands and listen to them speak. ("We lived on coffee and handshakes," Mary remembered.) "Germany is at your doors!" Mary shouted. "But we can stop them!" Chaplin cried. "And we *will* stop them if *you* buy Liberty Bonds!" Doug yelled. By the end of the day, the crowd had pledged over $3,000,000.

On the tour Mary was accompanied by her mother and Doug traveled with his publicity manager Bennie Zeidman. Though frequently together on train journeys, they always stayed in separate hotels. In New York Mary and Charlotte went to the Ritz-Carlton and Doug moved into the Sherry-Netherland.

This was the indication that something was seriously wrong in the Fairbanks household. Beth and Doug, Jr., had come East a few days earlier and were staying as usual at the Algonquin. For the past few weeks rumors had been circulating that Mary and Doug were deep into an intrigue, and newsmen interpreted Fairbanks's absence from the family apartment as a sign that he had left, or was about to leave, his wife. Reporters started hanging around the Algonquin lobby. Late one afternoon Doug arrived and spent several hours with Beth. When he left he had nothing to say except that he was leaving immediately for a Liberty Bond appearance in Detroit.

Two days later Beth gave the reporters their story. She announced that she was separated from her husband and might, in the near future, file for divorce.

5

For months Doug had wavered on the question of divorce. Teddy Roosevelt and the boy scouts of America would certainly be disappointed if he ever took such an unchivalrous step. He kept turning the problem over in his mind and finally he came up with historical precedents that eased his conscience. "Why not divorce?" he asked Anita Loos. "Julius Caesar did it! Napoleon did it!"

Beth Fairbanks, however, had no intention of playing Caesar's wife. She was hopping mad and had no qualms about naming Mary Pickford as her rival. She blurted everything out to a reporter, but then, after a moment's reflection, she asked to withdraw her comments. A true gentleman, the reporter swore he would never print what he had just heard. Beth then issued a statement of dignified self-abnegation.

"Mr. Fairbanks has admitted his love for someone else and it is only for his sake—to give him time to find out if he really does love her—that I have agreed to remain in the East while he 'baches it' in the West. They both feel that theirs is the one big love and that nothing else matters, and because I adore Mr. Fairbanks and have always put his happiness above everything else, I have decided that I am big enough to stand aside until they find out if it really is that big love."

In the first newspaper accounts of the separation, Beth's rival was described as "an actress with whom Fairbanks has at times been thrown into contact professionally." In case readers failed to identify the mystery woman, the newspapers also carried a statement from Mary: "If Mr. and Mrs. Fairbanks have separated it is no concern of mine or of any other person but themselves as far as I can see. We are simply associated in business."

Still in Detroit when the story broke, Doug was accosted by a mob of reporters in the lobby of his hotel. Caught unawares, Fairbanks babbled an idiotic denial of the whole affair. "It's all German propaganda. I'm campaigning for the Liberty Loan, and these ridiculous stories are being circulated. They've had me shot three times already . . . And now they start this story of a separation. It's false from beginning to end."

This was too much for Beth. The next morning, she again spoke to reporters, and this time she had a warning for Doug and Mary. "We have separated. There is no question about it. I do not understand why Mr. Fairbanks should continue to deny it. . . . An actress has told all my friends, some of my relatives and my representatives that she is in love with Mr. Fairbanks, and I do not understand why she should deny it publicly. . . . If no statement is made within the next few days, either by my husband or by the woman I can name responsible for our separation, I shall verify my statements by proofs."

The threat was clear: Mary and Doug would either refrain from professing their innocence or she would sue for divorce, naming Mary as corespondent. Before they had time to digest this piece of information, Mary and Doug received another low blow, this one from Owen Moore, who threatened to sue Fairbanks for alienation of affections. This action, Moore told the press, was prompted by Beth's request that her rival speak out. "The other woman is now ill and under great nervous strain. So I feel it obligatory upon myself to make a statement to save her from humiliation."

He went on to describe Mary as "little more than a child, with a child's winsomeness, appealingness and trust in others." Their life together had been "one of mutual sympathy and affection" before she met Doug who "combined a strong fascination for women with an instinct for possession." Bringing action against Fairbanks was "repugnant and distasteful" but necessary "for Mary's own protection."

Moore was right about one thing. Mary was sick with worry, and his ill-advised intrusion into the affair only added to her emotional strain. He was, as she was well aware, just irrational enough to go ahead with a suit he had no conceivable chance of winning. The whole situation was becoming progressively more sordid. Only a few days before Moore's threat, Doug had been approached by a stranger who handed him a photocopy of a page from an Atlantic City hotel register: there was an entry for "Mr. and Mrs. Owen Moore"; there was also an eyewitness to testify that the Mrs. Moore of that occasion wasn't Mary Pickford.

Doug wanted no part of this dirty business, so the man approached Owen Moore, who promptly had him arrested and charged with attempted blackmail, thereby calling public attention to the incident. Deeply distressed, Mary talked to Zukor who talked to the other leaders of the industry; they then issued a joint ultimatum to Moore. Either he desist from making any further comment about Mary and Doug or he would never again work for a major American film company.

Possibly similar, if gentler, pressure was used to persuade Beth Fairbanks to exercise restraint when talking to the press. Or perhaps she naturally mellowed as the months passed. Whatever the reason, she declined to name a corespondent when she sued Fairbanks for divorce in October 1918, and there was no mention of Mary in court testimony the following December. Two witnesses testified to Doug's indiscretions. Musical comedy star Clifton Crawford recalled that in January 1916, after dinner at the Lambs Club, he and Fairbanks had gone to "a party in a 33rd Street house where there were beautiful girls." Shortly after their arrival, Doug followed a lightly clad woman into a bedroom where Crawford saw them lounging on a sofa and smoking cigarettes. John Emerson then testified that Fairbanks had later told him this boys'-night-out had been "the best time he had ever had in his life."

It was flimsy evidence, but since Doug did not contest the suit, Beth got her divorce. She also got $500,000 and sole custody of Doug, Jr. And for a while, it looked as though she might also get the last laugh. A week after her decree became final, she married Pittsburgh stockbroker James J. Evans, but the marriage ended in divorce in 1924. Several years later, she married stage actor Jack Whiting, and this marriage, a happy one, lasted until her death in 1963.

Doug had hoped that his divorce would encourage Mary to take the same step, but she continued to bide her time. She was held back by her religious beliefs and pride—she hated to admit publicly that her marriage to Moore was a failure. And she was still not prepared to marry Fairbanks. In her autobiography, Mary remembered asking Doug, "If we both lose our careers, will our love be sufficient for our future happiness?"

"I can't answer for you, Mary," Doug replied, "but I know that my feeling for you is not of the moment . . . I love you for yourself."

A pretty speech, but Mary questioned whether Doug had really examined his own feelings or come to grips with the realities of what they were facing. "Every force, individual and collective, in Hollywood," she later wrote, "warned that our pictures might become total failures . . . that our hard-won prestige would be buried under an avalanche of malignant gossip and denunciation." And, if either she or Doug had any doubts about the validity of these arguments, they had only to consider the unhappy case of Francis X. Bushman.

Between 1911 and 1916, Bushman was "King Romeo," the reigning matinée idol of the day. Young girls swooned at his pictures, and once, during a personal appearance in Chicago, they nearly stripped him of his clothes. (Many young ladies paid high prices for seminude photographs of Bushman, taken when he was an artist's model.) Often he appeared with a phlegmatic blond beauty named Beverly Bayne, but his studio hastened to tell the fans that Bushman was available for any girl who had the wiles to ensnare him.

His studio, however, wasn't speaking the truth. All the time his lady fans were dreaming of having him all to themselves, Bushman was living it up with Beverly Bayne, either at his Manhattan penthouse apartment or at The Gedney Inn in White Hills, New York, where they washed down four-course lobster dinners with hot Scotch toddies and buckets of beer and wine. And that was only the beginning of the deception. Besides a mistress, Bushman also had a wife and five children whom he kept hidden at "Bushmanor," a country estate in Maryland where he raised Great Danes.

The bubble burst in the spring of 1918 when a forlorn and neglected Mrs. Bushman came forward and talked about the Scotch toddies and the Great Danes which, she claimed, were better treated than she and her children. Bushman had beat her, but had never laid a hand on the hounds. Mrs. Bushman got a divorce and King Romeo got his comeuppance. Under a photograph of a frowning Bushman, one newspaper carried a column that opened: "Oh, see the handsome man. He looks worried. Why should the nice man be worried?" The article went on to tell why Bushman's brow was furrowed and then went in for the kill. "Millions of sweet young girls in America with more affection than good sense have stayed awake mooning over this face. Now is the time to tear up the picture and go to sleep. Francis X. Bushman is a fake."

A few weeks after his divorce and marriage to Beverly Bayne, several theatre chains cancelled their bookings for Bushman films, and later his studio told him his contract would not be renewed. By early 1919 Bushman and Bayne were running advertisements in *Vanity Fair* for Bushmanor, "A Great Kennel for Great Danes." Dog-breeding had become their major source of revenue.

Bushman had been ruined by the discrepancy between his screen personality and his private life. The same could happen to Mary and Doug. "Whether we wanted it or not, the roles we portrayed on the screen had built up a special picture of Douglas and me in the world's eyes," Mary said. "Both of us, I perhaps more acutely than Douglas, felt this obligation to the public."

Following the Liberty Bond tour, Mary stopped appearing in public with Fairbanks, though she was a frequent guest at his big Spanish-style Beverly Hills home. (Originally built by Syl Spaulding, the sports-goods manufacturer, the thirty-six-room house was bought in the late 1960s by actor George Hamilton.) But these visits, had they come to the attention of the public, could have been passed off as business meetings of the newly created United Artists, a production and distribution company Mary and Doug formed with Chaplin and D. W. Griffith in January 1919.

United Artists was the outcome of a complicated set of moves and countermoves that started with the expiration of Mary's Famous Players contract the previous summer. At that time, the new First National Company, which had stolen several stars from Zukor's list of players, asked Mary to act in three films at $750,000 against fifty percent of the gross receipts. Zukor refused to match the deal. In common with the other film magnates, he was concerned about the spiraling costs of star salaries and decided the line had to be drawn somewhere, specifically at Mary Pickford, who was the worst offender. Zukor loved Mary as if she were his own daughter, but he had to agree with Cecil B. De Mille, who advised, "Let her go—it'll take some of the swelling out of her head. She can't act as her own producer—she'll ruin First National and First National will ruin her."

De Mille's prediction proved false—Mary's first First National picture, *Daddy Long Legs,* was one of her biggest hits. Having failed to make an example of Pickford, Zukor and his business cohorts set out on a new tack—there were rumors of forthcoming mergers between several of the top companies, including First National and Famous Players–Lasky–Paramount (and possibly Metro). If these mergers went through, it could mean that someday there would be only two or three large studios in America, an arrangement that would severely limit the bargaining power of the star.

All actors recognized the threat, but only Mary did something about it. Inspired by an offhand comment from Secretary of the Treasury William McAdoo—"Why don't you make and distribute your movies; then you'd reap all the profits"—she came up with the idea of a company owned and managed by the leading talents of the picture industry.

Each of the four founding members contributed $125,000 toward the running of the corporation, doling it out over a period of years "as the company needed it." Stock was divided evenly among the four, and if for any reason one of them decided to withdraw, he was honor-bound to sell his shares within the company. McAdoo refused the presidency, but was retained as general counsel at a salary of $100,000. At his suggestion, Oscar Price was installed as president and George Clifton as secretary and treasurer. (Both were former members of McAdoo's staff.) Fairbanks's and Pickford's attorney, Dennis O'Brien, became vice-president.

Fairbanks's announcement of the formation of United Artists was greeted with the now-famous quip, "The lunatics have taken over the asylum." Years later Mary was able to answer, "Yes, but we lunatics had a lot of fun." But at the beginning they also had a lot of headaches.

The biggest problem was getting the company off the drawing board. Three of the four united artists had commitments elsewhere—Pickford and Chaplin owed films to First National and Griffith was working on two pictures for Paramount. Only Doug was free to work; his $10,000 weekly contract with Famous Players had expired at the end of 1918. So the first two United Artists releases were Fairbanks pictures, and like many of his recent films, they were slipshod.

His next-to-last Paramount film, *Arizona,* had been an out-and-out fiasco, one of the few of his career. Critics jumped on it, objecting to the mania for action that marred much of Fairbanks's work. "His recent films have only one speed, and that's third," wrote one reviewer, and another complained, "To the mania of doing something every moment, he has added the mania of doing it so fast that nobody can see it." The time had come for Fairbanks to change the pace and direction of his career, but as yet he didn't know which road he should take.

His first films for United Artists made money, but it took Mary to prove that the lunatics knew how to run the asylum. Considerable thought went into the choice of her first picture for the new company. For years, her fans had been urging her to film *Pollyanna,* Eleanor H. Porter's best-selling novel about a crippled orphan girl who spreads joy and happiness wherever she goes. Pollyanna, "The Glad Girl," was cut from the same cloth as Gwendolyn, the poor little rich girl, and Mary was "appalled at the prospect of eight weeks of un-relieved goodness." But since it was important to get United Artists off to a powerful start, she bowed to the wishes of her fans.

Halfway through production, Mary became exasperated with Pollyanna's unfailing saintliness and decided the little girl should have a few lapses to show she was human. One day while the camera was turning, she caught a fly that had landed on a table, scooped it up and said, "Little fly, do you want to go to heaven?" Then she smacked her hands together. "You have!"

This scene is the best moment in a film that could kill anyone suffering from sugar in the blood. But her fans loved the whole thing. To Mary's chagrin, Pollyanna became the role with which she was most identified. "If reincarnation should prove to be true," she once said, "and I had to come back as one of my roles, I suppose some avenging fate would return me to earth as Pollyanna."

Making the picture was an ordeal for Mary. A few months earlier she had contracted a virulent case of the Spanish flu and for several days her condition was critical. (*The New*

York Tribune noted that her "ardent admirers follow the news of her illness as devotedly and sympathetically as if it were a personal sorrow.") Her recovery had been slow and she was still weak when she started work on *Pollyanna*. Poor health and the strain of the Fairbanks problem brought Mary to the verge of a nervous collapse, but she wouldn't halt production as her doctor ordered. Nor did she take a vacation when the film was finished. Instead she went off on schedule for a personal appearance tour that took her to Chicago and New York.

The major event of the tour was a parade in which Mary was to lead a bunch of parochial schoolgirls and their nun-instructors on a march down Fifth Avenue. Before the parade Mary and Charlotte were entertaining a few friends including Adolph Zukor and Frances Marion when the phone rang in the bedroom of the hotel suite. Doug was calling to give Mary an ultimatum: either they got married or he would never see her again.

According to Frances Marion, Mary was in tears when she hung up the receiver. Charlotte tried to calm her. "Let him go, Mary. There must be no divorce . . ." "Think what you mean to millions of people," piped in Adolph Zukor, "You're their idol . . ." But Mary had made her decision. She was now ready to become the second Mrs. Douglas Fairbanks.

But at the moment she was still Mrs. Owen Moore. And Owen flew into a rage as soon as Mary mentioned divorce. Once again he threatened to shoot Fairbanks, "that climbing monkey," but later he cooled down, and told Mary's lawyers he would cooperate provided he received a settlement. Buying a divorce was distasteful to Mary, but there was no alternative, and so Charlotte and she went to their bank and cashed in some bonds they had put away for their old age. They then handed $150,000 to Owen's lawyer.

The transaction was carried out with the greatest secrecy. Mary did not want to face the accusation of "buying off one husband to acquire another." She also wanted a quiet and private divorce, which precluded filing suit in California or

New York, the two states in which she could claim legal residence. The only other alternative was Nevada.

In 1920 Nevada was already well on its way to becoming the divorce capital of America. Other states were just as liberal about the grounds for divorce, but Nevada's six-month residency requirement was the shortest in the country. And there was a way for the prospective divorcée to shorten these six months to a couple of days. Any visitor could enter a Nevada court and ask for a divorce, provided she could swear that: a) she intended to live permanently in the state; b) she had by sheer coincidence met her estranged spouse within the state's boundaries; c) she had given her spouse enough time to contest the suit.

Nevada was particularly handy for the unhappily married couples of Hollywood. It was nearby, yet far off the beaten track of most reporters, and since the state was frequently used for location shooting, there was nothing unusual about a star staying there for a few weeks. One of the first Hollywood celebrities to take advantage of the liberal Nevada divorce laws was actress Pauline Bush, wife of director Allan Dwan. In 1918 she went to Minden, the seat of Douglas County, a one-street, frontier town twenty miles southeast of Lake Tahoe. A few days after her arrival, Dwan passed through Minden, staying just long enough to be served with divorce papers; a week later, Pauline went to court and came out a free woman only a few hours later.

The Dwans were minor Hollywood figures, so their divorce didn't stir up much interest until March 1920 when Mary traveled the same route. The parallel seemed too close to be entirely coincidental, especially since Dwan was one of Doug's buddies. Mary, however, insisted she went to Nevada for her health. Charlotte had bought a home near Lake Tahoe, she said; this was the main reason she chose Nevada for her vacation.

She never explained why she wasn't living in Lake Tahoe at the time of her divorce. As soon as she arrived in Nevada,

Mary and her traveling companions (Charlotte, New York attorney Dennis O'Brien and a maid named Fernanda) went into hiding at a guest ranch outside of Minden. Mary went everywhere dressed in basic incognito—smoked glasses, slouch hats, shawl-collared coats—and none of the sagebrush yokels saw through this transparent disguise. "Lots of high-priced chippies pass this way," one local told a reporter. "We don't pay 'em no mind."

Four days later, Owen Moore came to Minden and sat around the spittoon-festooned lobby of the Minden Hotel long enough to receive divorce papers. Four days later Mary came to court with her two attorneys, O'Brien and Judge P. A. McCarren, Nevada's leading legal authority. McCarren did most of the talking in court. (O'Brien anticipated—correctly, as it turned out—that if there should ever be a dispute over the legitimacy of Mary's divorce, McCarren could be a very persuasive witness for the defense.) Mary was sworn in as Gladys Smith Moore, and the presiding judge showed little interest in her or her story until she explained why Owen Moore had come to Minden. "Well . . . it's something about business," Mary said, "something about a coal mine."

The judge snapped out of his lethargy, O'Brien coughed discreetly, and Mary hastily corrected herself and said that of course she meant a gold mine—Owen was scouting locations for a gold rush picture. Regaining her composure, she sailed through the rest of her testimony, remaining unflurried even when the discussion touched on the reasons for her presence in Nevada:

Q: Is it your purpose and intention to remain in the state of Nevada and particularly in the county of Douglas?

A: Yes, sir.

Q: Is it your purpose to build here?

A: Well . . . if I can find a place to suit me, I will.

71

Mary went on to describe her life with Moore, and when she had finished, the judge asked her why she had not filed for a divorce before this. Mary said that now she was famous and well-to-do, she wished to leave a will that could never be contested by any undeserving claimant.

At 7 P.M. that evening Mrs. Owen Moore was once again Mary (Gladys Smith) Pickford. But the next morning, she was still traveling incognito when she left Nevada for California. To outfox the reporters (who were hot on her trail) she took a circuitous route back to Los Angeles. Mary, Charlotte and Fernanda drove to Tahoe where they boarded a train to Oakland, California. There they jumped into a waiting limousine which drove them to San Jose where they caught the milk train to Los Angeles. When they arrived at Union Station, they were welcomed by every reporter and photographer within a hundred mile radius. Mary pulled herself up to the full measure of her dignity, raised a hand for silence and swept through the crowd without a word or a backward glance.

A few days later she agreed to meet the press. Gracious, though pale and visibly nervous, she apologized for her behavior at the station, explaining that her mother had been overtired and anxious to return home. Then she tried to answer all questions about her divorce. Concerning Moore and the rumor that he had been paid for his cooperation, she said, "He did not receive any sum of money from me with the request he refuse to contest the suit. Such a thought never entered my mind, for I know that Mr. Moore is a gentleman . . . who would not permit such a thought to enter his mind."

About her religious beliefs, she had this to say: "Statements have been published that I will be excommunicated from the Catholic Church if I marry again. There is no danger. I shall never be excommunicated. In the eyes of the Church my divorce was not illegal. The Church sanctions such an act, but it will not sanction my second marriage. . . ."

The reports that she would marry Fairbanks were "absurd."

Her only desire was "making people happy. My aim is to fill their hearts with gladness through my appearance in picture shows. If I have done anything to offend the public, I am so sorry."

6

Three weeks later, the license clerk for Los Angeles County was guest of honor at a Fairbanks dinner party. R. S. Sparks ("Cupid" to his friends) was not accustomed to hobnobbing with the Hollywood rich, so he suspected there was some devious reason for the invitation. "I had a hunch I might be asked for something in the license line when I was asked to dinner," he said. "So I took along the necessary document."

On the Friday night "Cupid" came to dinner, Doug was already living in the stucco and shingle house (actually a converted hunting lodge) that would soon be named "Pickfair." There were several guests that evening, including Bennie Ziedman, Charlotte Pickford and Mary (looking, Sparks remembered, "real pretty in a sparkly white dress"). Doug asked "Cupid" if he had any idea why he had been invited.

Pulling the license out of his pocket, "Cupid" replied with a wink, "I knew I'd get you two sooner or later." After Mary and Doug had filled out the form, he said, "Jeepers, this is my masterpiece in marriage licenses. I can never stage anything better than this."

Doug wanted to be married the next day, but Mary insisted on a Sunday wedding. So the date was set for two days hence, Sunday, March 28. Reverend J. Whitcombe Brougher, a Baptist minister known across the country as a kind of bush-league Billy Sunday, agreed to perform the ceremony at his home in Glendale. All arrangements were private—Lottie and Jack weren't invited because they couldn't be trusted with a secret. To keep up an appearance of normality, Doug spent Sunday afternoon at one of his favorite haunts, the Los Angeles Speedway, where he signed autographs and joked nonchalantly with his fans.

At ten that evening the guests started to arrive at Reverend Brougher's house. Among them were Doug's brothers, Robert and John, and their wives; actress Marjorie Daw, who served as Mary's maid of honor; Charlotte, dressed in Georgette crepe; and the bride, wearing (in the words of novelist Djuna Barnes, then a syndicated fashion columnist) "a pearl santoir" (whatever that may have been) and "a lovely dress of white satin and overdrape of net, caught up with contrasting knots of green and mustard."

The double-ring ceremony ended with Brougher reading the famous passage about marriage from St. Paul's epistle to the Ephesians. ("Wives, submit yourselves unto your husbands, as unto the Lord . . .") Doug chose the selection and asked Brougher to read it from a Bible that had been a childhood present from his mother. Later he passed out expensive Havana cigars to the men, each encased in a souvenir box. Autographing one, Mary signed "Mrs. Douglas Fairbanks" for the first time, and one of the guests pointed out that she was now entitled to American citizenship. Just as the guests were sitting down to a midnight supper, Lottie called, crying because she hadn't been invited to the wedding. Suddenly Doug remembered that in all the excitement he had forgotten to tell Charlie Chaplin and rushed to the phone to correct this oversight.

Two days passed before the rest of the world learned of the marriage. On March 30 Mary and Doug announced their wedding at a small dinner party and the next day the news was splashed across the front page of every paper in the country. No marriage, not even the wedding of a monarch or president, had ever created such excitement, and sixteen years would pass before Wallis Simpson and Edward VIII finally overshadowed Doug and Mary. The first stories were factual, no-opinion reports, but these were quickly followed by accounts of the controversy the marriage had stirred up.

As often happens in controversies of this kind, the yea-sayers were given short shrift—people who condone are rarely as colorful or vehement as those who chastise. The Hollywood community, which might have been expected to stand staunchly behind Mary and Doug, was fairly guarded in its response. Actress Clara Kimball Young, for example, said, "Really, it's nobody's business but Mary and Doug's." Then, pressed to answer whether the marriage had taken her by surprise, she answered, "Well, no, not exactly . . . there have been rumors for months."

Those rumors damaged Mary's reputation more than anything else. Why, if she loved Doug and planned to marry him, had she refused to admit this at the time of her divorce? Her faithful fans had chosen to believe her when she said she was planning to devote her life to "making people happy"; now they felt they had been betrayed.

Mary hadn't been entirely dishonest when she said she had no plans to marry Fairbanks. Originally, she had intended to wait for at least a year during which she and Charlotte would tour Europe. In this way Mary hoped to avoid the accusation of having divorced Owen only because she wanted to marry Doug. But Fairbanks refused to wait: he had no intention of twiddling his thumbs in Hollywood while Mary and Charlotte barnstormed the capitals of Europe. Mary was stubborn, but Doug could be very persuasive, and this time he won out.

The harshest criticism of the marriage came, as expected, from the Church. Though there was no mention of Mary and Doug, Bishop Cantwell of the Catholic diocese of Monterey and Los Angeles issued a statement on divorce, calling it "the greatest of all modern evils." He feared that "the people of

Los Angeles are not giving to the world at large an example of the Christian life . . . Laws wisely made for the government of civil and social life should not be easily set aside. . . . [they] must be obeyed for conscience' sake."

Reverend Brougher was openly rebuked for taking part in the ceremony. He defended himself by saying that the Baptist church had no rules or laws regulating remarriage and that most ministers would marry divorced persons provided that the cause of divorce had been "a scriptural one." He had known Mary and Doug for five years, and had interviewed them at length before deciding their divorces were "scriptural." Several of Brougher's colleagues disagreed, and he came close to being ousted from the executive committee of the Northern Baptist Alliance.

The final blow was delivered by Leonard J. Fowler, attorney general of Nevada, who announced that he was reviewing the Pickford-Moore divorce, and might start proceedings to annul the decree. A week later, he did bring suit against Mary and Doug on grounds of collusion. (He also considered charging Mary with perjury, but later decided against it.)

Mary's representatives promptly denied the allegation and questioned the legality of Fowler's action: it was doubtful whether the attorney general of Nevada had jurisdiction over California residents and was invested with the power to institute such a suit. Mary's attorney argued that only the judge who had originally heard her case could ask to review it. For a while they hinted that Mary might refuse to take part in the trial, but this stratagem was abandoned when an attorney pointed out that Mary could be tried *in absentia.* And, if found guilty, she would be open to prosecution for bigamy.

Fowler claimed he was acting for the upright citizens of Nevada who were alarmed at the way the state's divorce laws were being abused. In Hollywood there was (and still is) a story that Owen Moore was behind the whole affair—he wanted vengeance as well as his $150,000—but there's no

77

proof for this accusation. Fowler was acting for himself and with the sole purpose of furthering his own political ambitions. (A year later he ran for the United States Senate.)

Fowler's action backfired. Though not every aspect of Mary's divorce could stand up under legal scrutiny, she was no more guilty of playing fast and loose with the law than were hundreds of other women who had come to Nevada for quick divorces. No one had asked to review their decrees—so why pick on Mary? The answer was obvious: as a national celebrity, she would call attention to Fowler's crusade to make Nevada safe for clean-living, law-abiding Christians. The hypocrisy was too blatant to go undetected.

Public opinion began to turn in Mary's favor when the papers, carrying on their own review of her divorce, printed large hunks of her testimony about Moore. People were shocked by what they read. After so much misery, Mary was entitled to her share of happiness, and what form of happiness could be better than Douglas Fairbanks? If marriages were truly made in heaven, then Mary would have drawn Doug straight off—America's Sweetheart deserved no less than America's favorite screen cavalier.

Newspapers all over the country began carrying editorials in Mary's defense, with *Variety* being especially outraged at the way she had been maligned. A writer for this trade publication decried "the woodsmen" who used "the halberd and shield of the Protestant church to attack Miss Pickford . . . the ablest ambassador, the most persuasive maker of friends the United States ever sent out in the world at large." Then he went on to say:

> To destroy this ideal is to hurt her personally, but it is also money and good will out of every pocket of every American business man, out of the inheritance of every American child, and your children's children will remember what you do today, for her pictures have been clean pictures, and she has stood for clean things in terms more beautiful, effective, more sure of appeal

than any within the reach of the most eloquent clergyman in the greatest cathedral. Where they [sic] speak
in one place to thousands, she speaks in many to millions,
and in simpler, more certain terms . . . She remains
and will remain what she has been and is, one of the
glories of American art.

This breathless mixture of money, religion, loose grammar
and inflated rhetoric is only slightly more effusive than the
other tributes paid to Mary. Practically overnight she was
canonized as the patron saint of the film industry, a living
emblem of all that was best about the American way of life.
Probably no actor in history had ever been asked to carry so
heavy a burden; certainly no film star since Mary has been so
conscientious in trying to fulfill her fans' expectations.

Despite the indications that the public was on her side,
Mary remained troubled and apprehensive for several weeks.
The idle speculation about her romance with Fairbanks, the
publication of the intimate details of her life with Moore, the
legal battle with Fowler and the state of Nevada—these were
complications she hadn't bargained for. Nor was she prepared
for the gossipy explanation of why she had married Doug so
soon after her divorce. According to a whispering campaign
that soon reached the ears of the press, she was pregnant,
though no one could agree on whether Fairbanks or Moore
was the prospective father. These rumors circulated for the
better part of a year, and once Mary was said to have booked
a room in the maternity ward of a Los Angeles hospital. But
there was to be no heir; Mary was unable to have children because of an accident or illness that had occurred during her
first marriage.

Mary wisely decided that her best defense was to lay low
and go about her business as though nothing had happened.
The day after the wedding, she pasted an adhesive band over
her new platinum ring and went to the studio to work on
Suds, her second film for United Artists. This was one of her

periodic escapes from childhood into young adulthood; in the film she played Amanda, a Cockney laundress who saves a carthorse, her best friend, from the glue factory. Amanda was an unglamorous role that allowed no opportunity for flowing curls, pretty dresses or flattering close-ups, all of which the fans expected when they paid their money for a Pickford picture. Certainly it was a risky part for Mary to have undertaken at this particular time, but two years earlier she had had a great success as a misshapen slavey in *Stella Maris,* and was probably hoping to repeat that success with *Suds.*

When they weren't working, Mary and Doug stayed close to Pickfair, seeing only a few close friends and talking only vaguely about their plans for the future. Everything was up in the air. They weren't sure whether they would stay in Doug's home or sell it and go ahead with Mary's plans to build a $250,000 home on Fremont Place in Los Angeles. They hoped to get away on a honeymoon, but the date was indefinite, certainly not until they had finished their current films and probably not before they heard the ruling of the Nevada court on the legality of Mary's divorce.

One of their few public appearances during this period was a trip to a Hopi Indian reservation in Arizona where Doug had shot location scenes for his latest film, *The Molly-coddle.* This was supposed to be a "holiday," but like so many of Mary and Doug's later vacations, it was really a cross between a royal tour and a publicity junket. Their entourage included Bennie Zeidman, their publicity manager; a maid and a valet; several friends; and a horde of reporters and photographers. In Arizona Mary was made an honorary member of the Hopi tribe and Doug showed scenes from *The Molly-coddle* to all the people who lived on the reservation. One of the Indians who had played a bit role in the film had subsequently died, and when his friends saw him appear on the screen, they ran away in terror. In 1920 this incident seemed highly amusing and was widely reported in newspapers.

Shortly after their return from Arizona, Mary and Doug decided it was safe to take off on their European honeymoon.

As they were leaving Los Angeles for New York, they learned that a Nevada court had upheld Mary's divorce, and while there was every reason to believe Fowler would appeal the decision, there was also good reason to believe they would win out in the end. (Both predictions were correct: the case dragged on for another year before the Nevada Supreme Court decided in Mary's favor.) Mary was almost speechless when she heard the good news. "I am very, very happy, more happy than I can express." Doug did a backward somersault and quipped, "This business about America's Sweetheart has got to stop. From now on she's *my* sweetheart!"

Mary and Doug arrived in New York with Charlotte, Zeidman, a maid, a valet, a secretary and forty pieces of luggage. An hour after they checked in at the Ritz-Carlton, the bellboys were still lugging the trunks up to their suite which was filled with flowers, candy, telegrams and twenty or thirty members of the New York press. Doug suggested that everyone go up to the roof for some photographs where he performed handstands on the building ledge while Mary wrung her hands in mock horror. The schedule for interviews was so heavy that he and Mary had to spell each other. While she shampooed her hair (castile soap, lemon juice and several rinsings in tepid water), he chatted with the visitors; then she took over while he went to see his buddies at the Lambs Club.

Nearly every evening they went to the theatre and nearly every time they walked down the center aisle, the audience rose to their feet and applauded. Sometimes they waited until the lights had dimmed before taking their seats, but they were always spotted. The 1920 summer edition of the *Ziegfeld Follies* featured a mild little song-and-dance sketch about "Mr. and Mrs. Fairbanks," and one night as it came to a close, the actors walked to the front of the stage and said, "If you don't like us, ask the real ones to come up and do it!" Then a spotlight picked out Mary and Doug in the third row, and the audience stomped and whistled and screamed with joy.

What precisely was all the excitement about? Well, for one

thing, Mary and Doug were the perfect storybook couple, Cinderella and Prince Charming magically transformed into two down-to-earth, all-American sweethearts. And they looked good together—dark, swarthy and muscular, he pointed up her fragility; she wasn't tall enough to overshadow him as a statuesque woman might have done. Their personalities were complementary, too. He was brash and breezy whenever she became too dignified or sugar-sweet; she was a soothing presence when he overplayed the athletics and manic energy.

Movie fans (and, to a lesser degree, theatre fans) had always found vicarious pleasure in sharing the private lives of their favorites, but never so much as with Mary and Doug. Of course, no previous celebrities had been quite so ready to open the doors and invite the public into their living rooms. In the next few years, Doug and Mary were to create a new brand of stardom that would have a later generation of actors yelping about "the invasion of privacy." Without too much exaggeration, one could say that their films soon became side events to the main attraction, the unfolding drama of their marriage.

There was probably another reason for the furor over Mary and Doug. In 1920, they gave Americans something they badly needed at this time—a touch of old-fashioned romance. The country hadn't been devastated by World War I as Europe had, but an economic depression, the flu epidemic of 1918 and a changing moral climate made many people long for the halcyon days of the prewar era. Despite the fact that they had taken the distinctly modern step of divorce and remarriage, Doug and Mary were nostalgically linked to the values of a happier, more innocent age. The world was going jazz-crazy, but they were as simple and wholesome as ever—or so the public wanted to believe.

Eventually this nostalgia was to create problems for Pickford and Fairbanks. They became frozen in time, never allowed to age or take on sophistication, simply because their fans didn't care to be reminded that the world was changing and they, too, were growing older. But in 1920 no one thought about the consequences—all that mattered was that

Mary and Doug were adored as no two actors had ever been. Having taken New York by storm, they decided it was time to conquer Europe, and on June 12, they boarded the S.S. *Lapland* for the second leg of what one reporter later called "the most famous and frenetic honeymoon of modern history."

"Ma" Pickford stayed behind, but Bennie Zeidman, the maid, the valet, the secretary and forty pieces of luggage all went along on the trip. The ship sailed in the afternoon, and just as it was passing Sandy Hook, a low-flying plane showered it with flowers, a tribute to Mary and Doug. The wind blew most of the bouquets out to sea, but Doug leaped on a deck railing and managed to catch one, which he presented to Mary with a cavalier flourish. Needless to say, the bystanders gave him a round of loud applause.

For most of the crossing, Doug and Mary stayed close to their stateroom, taking turns reading aloud Charles Dickens's *Child's History of England* in preparation for their visit to London. The book awakened in Mary a sense of her ancestral past, and she made a long list of all the sights she wanted to see. But as it turned out, England saw more of Mary than Mary saw of England.

Outside the Ritz Hotel in London, they were met by a mob of people that grew ever larger throughout the day. The crowd was orderly and good-natured, but noisy, and whenever the din became too ferocious, Mary and Doug appeared on the balcony of their suite, blowing kisses and waving to quiet their British fans. Everywhere they went they were pursued by throngs of well-wishers, some asking for autographs, others offering small gifts, many handmade.

Such devotion was touching and exciting, but also a little frightening. Doug took it all in stride and was even able to joke about it with the press. "At first, when I saw the entire British nation advancing, I wondered what was up," he said. "But all they wanted was to kiss Mary. I had to tell 'em that was my business."

Mary managed a weak smile, but the furor was too much for her. Unable to sleep because of the excitement, she was on the brink of nervous exhaustion when a member of the British peerage asked her to spend a weekend at his country home on the Isle of Wight. Mary and Doug gratefully accepted the invitation.

On their return to London, they were invited to a charity bazaar in Kensington Gardens, a fashionable affair sponsored by leading members of the English stage. Making an appearance in such a public and open place was courting disaster, but Mary and Doug decided to risk it. He put on his new tweeds and bow tie, she dressed up in an organdy tea gown and matching hat, and they drove off to Kensington Gardens in a long, open-topped limousine.

Inside the grounds of the park, the car inched along and was frequently blocked by people asking for autographs or a handshake. A man held out his hand, Mary took it and before she realized what was happening, she had been pulled out of the car and thrown against a fender. The crowd rushed forward and nearly crushed Mary before Doug and a London bobby were able to pull her to safety. Doug lifted her onto his shoulder, and pushed, shoved and elbowed his way through the mob. He knocked several people to the ground, including one well-dressed gentleman who clutched at Fairbanks's ankles and pleaded, "Aw, come on, Doug, give us an autograph!"

Mary was so badly shaken by this incident that she wanted to leave England immediately. Two days later, with Frances Marion and her husband, Fred Thompson, as traveling companions, they left London for Holland where the crowds were thick and noisy, but not violent. From there they traveled by train through Germany and Switzerland to Italy where Doug hired a car and chauffeur to drive them across the French border at Ventigimilia. As they drove along the curving, coastal roads of the Italian Riviera, people ran out to greet "Maria e Lampo" (or "Lightning," as Doug was called in Italy), and at the border they were whisked through customs when the chauffeur shouted, *"Attention! Attention! Monsieur et Madame Fairbanks!"*

The last stop on their itinerary was the Hotel Crillon in Paris. Mary went on a couturier shopping spree and bought twenty-eight gowns from Patou and Lanvin (who was to become her favorite designer in the 1920s). She and Doug spent a few evenings at the Comédie Française, and later dined with the stars of the company, Cécile Sorel and the rouged and bedizened Edouard de Max. Mme Sorel suggested that Doug make a picture with herself and Sarah Bernhardt and de Max proposed a film version of *The Three Musketeers* in which he would play Richelieu to Fairbanks's D'Artagnan. Apparently no projects were mentioned for Mary, possibly because neither Sorel nor de Max cared much for women.

Sight-seeing in Paris was nearly as dangerous as in London, and once again, Mary was nearly the victim of mass ravishment at Les Halles, the outdoor market on the Left Bank. This time she was saved by two butchers who picked her up and locked her in a meat cage where she stayed until a squadron of gendarmes arrived and escorted her to safety. From then on, all their sight-seeing was done at night. "Fortunately, there was a full moon," Mary commented wryly.

The European press was at a loss to explain the furor over the Fairbanks honeymoon, particularly the ugly incidents at Les Halles and Kensington Gardens. What had happened to French gallantry and English reserve? Journalists at first wrote off the whole affair as a brilliant example of superior American showmanship. They weren't entirely mistaken. Bennie Zeidman came along on the tour in the dual capacity of traveling companion and publicity manager, and according to *The New York Times,* a corps of publicity men preceded the newlyweds on their journey. (In Venice, a separate gondola of photographers went along on the couple's moonlight ride.) Doug and Mary relished the adulation as long as it was free of the violence that had ruined their visits to London and Paris. Doug enjoyed it more than Mary, but neither was happy when they were ignored by the Germans who had seen few American films since the beginning of World War I. They spent their few days in Germany mostly with the American occupation troops who knew and loved them, and gave them a twenty-four gun salute at a Fourth of July celebration in Coblenz.

But no matter how much calculation went into the demonstrations, there was twice as much spontaneity—not even P. T. Barnum could have arranged such freewheeling, enthusiastic displays of affection. Eventually even the staid *London Times* had to admit that Mary and Doug's popularity was a phenomenon that required serious editorial consideration. The *Times* centered its comments on Mary who, by virtue of her Canadian birth, was regarded as belonging as much to England as to the United States:

> "The appeal of Miss Pickford's acting is always to the sense of chivalry which, in however a sentimental form, is characteristic of the English temperament. She is truly an ambassadress of our race. Thus our welcome, while it expresses the new and vast influence of the film, is no mere gratitude for pleasure accorded; it is rather the recognition of a touch that makes the whole English-speaking world kin."

The French couldn't link themselves to Mary through the bond of a common language or heritage, so they decided she belonged to the world. "No one speaks the new international language of film as eloquently as Mary Pickford," wrote the *Lanterne*. The paper went on to compare Mary to Georges Carpentier, then the light-heavyweight boxing champion of the world. "They are true ambassadors; they are real propagandists . . . They cost less in our budget than the other kind and they do far more good. . . . We found Doug and Mary regular folks."

"Ambassador" was a word that turned up frequently in reports of the Fairbanks honeymoon, and Mary liked it so much she began using it herself. She later wrote that the cheering and adulation was a tribute to "the American motion picture and the American people and the world of make-believe." For that reason, she and Doug were "in a large sense, ambassadors, not only of the motion picture industry, but of our country."

Mary and Doug's European triumph virtually eliminated all opposition to their marriage. In fact, their foreign success was seen as something of a challenge to their American fans. Adored abroad but criticized at home, Mary and Doug were reportedly thinking of becoming permanent members of the expatriot set. There is no evidence that they ever seriously considered taking such a step, but the idea may have appealed to them, particularly to Doug, who had enjoyed rubbing shoulders with the British aristocracy. Economically it would have been a very sound move—the currency exchange rate made European film production a very profitable investment for Americans.

True or false, the rumor put America on guard, and when Mary and Doug returned to New York at the end of July, they were met by a brass band and a welcoming committee that included Jack Dempsey, several prominent Broadway actors and hundreds of cheering fans. A motorcycle escort was needed to keep the crowds away from Mary and Doug's limousine, which was decorated with white orchids and American flags. The all-male Friars and Lambs clubs granted Mary an honorary membership; people stood and cheered when she and Doug went to the theatre; there was a riot when they showed up in Hackensack, New Jersey, for the tryout of a Broadway comedy featuring Ernest Truex, who had appeared with Mary in *A Good Little Devil*.

It was a week-long love feast during which all the criticism of the past was temporarily laid to rest. Everybody jumped on Mary and Doug's bandwagon, even *Photoplay,* the leading fan magazine of the period, which had previously hedged about taking sides on the Fairbanks-Pickford controversy. A month after their honeymoon, the magazine printed this "telegram":

A WESTERN UNION

MR. AND MRS. DOUGLAS FAIRBANKS
HONEYMOON LANE
HAPPINESS ALWAYS

      COME HOME   ALL IS FORGIVEN

          PHOTOPLAY

7

By 1922 Pickfair and the White House were the two most famous homes in America. And Pickfair was probably the more celebrated of the two. No one much cared about how Mrs. Harding or Mrs. Coolidge ran 1600 Pennsylvania Avenue, but Mary's boudoir, her servant problems, the table she set, her scheme of interior decoration—these were fascinating topics for the American public, and the papers kept readers informed of each new development at Pickfair. When Doug decided to build a wall outside the house, photographers rushed over to take candid shots of Mary handing him the bricks; when they went for a tramp in the woods, a reporter went along to describe how Mary brewed coffee over a campfire while Doug cooked beans in a tin pan; when she switched from blue to green for her bathroom towels, readers were advised to take note and do the same.

Mary and Doug opened the door of Pickfair to the press, and practically every newspaper in the country carried an account of a typical day in the Fairbankses' life. They got up early, around 5 A.M. when they were filming, with Doug being the first to rise—he didn't have to worry about disturbing Mary because they had separate suites. He went out and jogged around the gravel path that circled the house, jumped over a few bushes and lawn chairs, dashed through his knee-bends, push-ups and waist-bends, and then faced the problem of what to wear. Which of his forty suits should he put on?

Which of the dozens of ties, shirts and socks would match it? Mary was always asked in for a last-minute consultation. Then, after a light breakfast, they drove to the studio where Fairbanks shed his Italian and Saville Row finery and put on an old shirt and a pair of worn flannel slacks.

By 1922 Mary and Douglas were working on the same lot—the old Jesse Durham Hampton studio on Santa Monica Boulevard in West Hollywood, which they had purchased and renamed the Pickford-Fairbanks studio. (Today it is known as the Goldwyn studio.) They went their separate ways until lunch, when they met in the paneled dining room of Mary's fully-staffed, five-room studio bungalow. Then Doug worked out in his private, professionally equipped gymnasium and later spent a half hour in his Turkish bath. (He often held conferences in the steam room, a practice that exasperated those movie executives who didn't have the physique for talking business in the buff.)

For location filming, Doug and Mary both had specially built trailers which provided them with nearly all the amenities of the studio. But they always returned to Pickfair for dinner. They later boasted that for the first eight years of marriage they had never been separated for an entire evening.

Dinner was served at 7 P.M. Since Doug had a habit of extending last-minute invitations, Mary left strict orders that the table was always to be set for fifteen. When working, Mary often suffered from nervous indigestion and ate only spinach and milk; Doug had to watch his weight and dieted during the week. But guests were always served a multicourse meal, a typical menu including "hors d'oeuvres, cream soup, fish, an entrée, salad, parfait and fresh fruits."

After dinner Mary had her daily French lesson, after which she joined Doug and their guests in the living room where they spent the rest of the evening watching movies on a screen that was built into one of the walls. If they were alone, Mary and Doug snuggled on a big chintz couch and munched chocolates or popcorn balls while watching the picture. Then, at around eleven, Albert, "the majordomo," passed around fruit and cups of Ovaltine, the guests went home and Mary and Doug climbed the stairs to bed.

Life at Pickfair as it emerges from these faded and crumbling newspaper accounts was not so very different from the kind of existence led in thousands of suburban bungalows across the country—this, at least, was the impression reporters tried to convey. It was cozy, serene, informal, a harmonious blend of all the simple pleasures of family life. And Mary was presented as the typical housewife. "Offscreen Mary Pickford contents herself with being Mrs. Douglas Fairbanks," said *Ladies' Home Journal.* "She is the 'little woman' whose sole concern is her husband's happiness."

Not many "little women" had such big budgets as Mrs. Douglas Fairbanks, but Mary assured them that money wasn't everything. "Cluttered minds make cluttered homes, and disordered homes constantly threaten happiness and wholesome development," she once said. "It isn't the amount and cost of one's possessions that insure satisfaction. Riches lie in few and simple things required for use and personal culture, instead of show, and it is with this in mind that Mr. Fairbanks and I manage the home which gives us daily refreshment and inspiration. I should feel that unless I could achieve this result in a five-room bungalow or on a moderate income, I should fail even more miserably in a fifty-room palace."

Pickfair wasn't a palace, but it wasn't a bungalow, either. It was a large L-shaped house (far bigger than it looks in photographs), with two stories and a basement. On the first floor there was a spacious center hallway with a blue and white tiled floor, living room, sun parlor, dining room, kitchen, butler's pantry, back porch and breakfast room. The decor was something of a mishmash—tapestries, Doug's collection of Remington and Russell paintings, portraits of Mary, oriental rugs, chintz, mahogany, wicker and a few hand-carved antique Italian chairs.

Upstairs there was another hallway, so big it doubled as a sitting room. Off it were five bedrooms, baths and several sleeping porches, all furnished in painted "modern" furniture.

Mary's apartment was lavender and dull green. Doug's was brown, and a rose room was reserved for Chaplin, who frequently spent the night at Pickfair, though he owned a house only a block away.

In back of the house there were kennels, stables, a tennis court, a miniature golf course, two garages and an oyster-shaped swimming pool with a sliding board and a bathhouse fully equipped with "swim-suits for all sizes, from fatsos to the teeniest of tiny-tots." The fifteen live-in servants who ran the household had their own separate quarters, a gabled cottage for the majordomo, and a dormitory for the various maids, butlers, grooms and gardeners. (Mary had a simple solution for "the servant problem"; she kept the hired help happy by inviting them to watch home movies along with her other guests.)

"Mr. Fairbanks and I lead a very quiet existence," Mary said. "We don't have the time or desire to give lavish parties." Later things would change drastically, but during the first two years of their marriage, the entertainment at Pickfair was not very elegant. "Imagine my surprise," Mary commented, "when I came to dinner and saw three stock car drivers and a bunch of dusty cowpunchers sitting around the table!"

The guests at these early Pickfair dinners were a strange assortment of the trainers and playmates and yes-men who followed Doug nearly everywhere. Prominent in this retinue were two prizefighters, Spike Robinson and Bull Montana, who drew weekly salaries for sparring with their boss whenever Jack Dempsey or Gene Tunney weren't around. Robinson affected the tough-guy behavior expected of an ex-champion, but Bull Montana, in spite of his cauliflower face and caveman physique, couldn't have frightened a child. A gentle, lovable buffoon of Italian birth, the Bull fractured the English language and came up with so many dumb, inadvertent witticisms that he won a reputation as "Hollywood's only Shakespearean clown." (Later in the 1920s Montana was to have a successful career as a character actor and star of two-reel comedy shorts.)

Other members of the Fairbanks court included Tom Geraghty, a veteran reporter and film publicist who wrote several scripts for Doug; dashing William Wellman, an ace pilot for the Lafayette Flying Corps, who came to Hollywood for a small role in Fairbanks's last film for Paramount; directors Allan Dwan, Raoul Walsh, Victor Fleming and Howard Hawks. The last three were expert at "Doug," a game named after its inventor and champion player. A strenuous form of badminton (which then vied with minia-ture golf as Hollywood's favorite pastime), it was played over a high net, but with specially designed heavy shuttlecocks and standard tennis racquets. Though taken with the utmost seriousness at Pickfair and extensively promoted by the fan magazines, for some reason it never quite caught on as a na-tional sport.

One occasional guest at Pickfair dubbed Doug's buddies "the locker-room brigade." They were always ready to chortle whenever Fairbanks slipped under the dinner table and frightened guests by grabbing at their ankles; they roared with laughter when he pushed some poor boob into a chair wired to give its occupant an electric shock. Mary never openly ap-proved or disapproved of these shenanigans. Allene Talmey, who wrote a profile of Mary and Doug for *The Morning World,* described her as "a quiet and gracious woman whose adult mind looks with amusement upon the constant flow of Doug's practical jokes."

Often Mary was the only woman at the Pickfair dinner table. Occasionally Charlotte Pickford, Lillian Gish or Frances Marion were present, but Doug was intensely jealous and really didn't like people vying for Mary's attention. (Ap-parently he didn't look on his cronies as competition.) Soon after their marriage, Hollywood hostesses learned that Mrs. Fairbanks always sat next to Mr. Fairbanks and danced only with her husband, a breach of etiquette that once nearly led to an international incident when Mary refused to waltz with a member of the British royal family.

At the time Mary said that she thought it was improper "to

meet a man one minute and then the next to go into his arms and dance. Of course, I never dance in public. Occasionally we have a few people—six or eight—at Pickfair, but then I dance only with Doug, and then it's only the waltz or the two-step. We never 'jazz'."

Much later she admitted that she wouldn't have objected to changing partners for an occasional dance or dinner—it was Doug's law and she abided by it to keep him happy. But there is no evidence that she ever struggled against, or felt victimized by, Doug's possessiveness. "People sometimes said Doug built that big cement wall around Pickfair to keep Mary to himself," Lila Lee recalled. "And she had the reputation of being reserved and standoffish. But I think she and Doug were happy together and she really didn't need or want anyone else."

The Fairbanks brand of "I-only-have-eyes-for-you" marital bliss delighted the American public. "Everyone seemed to think they had been born and raised in convents, and spent all their evenings toasting marshmallows over a fire," recalled Allene Talmey recently. "And when I wrote my article which implied otherwise, there was a terrible stink. You have to understand that the fans were *willfully* innocent—they didn't want to hear the truth about the stars; they wanted to believe that Mary and Doug were the same offscreen as on."

Miss Talmey went on to say that in many ways there was no discrepancy between the Fairbankses' private and public personalities. "On first meeting, Mary was as demure and sweet as one would have expected. She stayed pretty much in the background, letting Doug answer most of the questions, even though she was by far the more intelligent of the two. But that was natural—wives were expected to walk in their husbands' shadows in those days. Of course, no one could have upstaged Fairbanks. He was the most alive man I ever met, but his energy made me very uncomfortable. It was as if his skin was too tight and he might at any moment break out of it and spatter you."

Mary and Doug's friends insist the couple never put on an

act for the press or public. "That's really the way they were," said Mildred Zukor. "I remember the time they came to see my father [Adolph Zukor] at our family home in New City, New York. We had a sun porch with a suspended couch hanging from the rafters, and one morning Doug shinnied up the chains and swung recklessly from one rafter to the next. It was child's play for him, but Mary shrieked, 'Oh, Doug, come down! Be careful!' "

But Mary and Doug also have their detractors, who claim that the cozy domesticity of Pickfair was only one side of the picture. There was a broad range of charges, everything from hypocrisy to stinginess. People said that one reason Mary and Doug chose the simple life was because they were both a bit tightfisted.

Mary was the first to admit that she was "thrifty," though never to the point of depriving herself of the material comforts of life. She liked Paris gowns and expensive automobiles, once purchasing a custom-built, glass-enclosed Rolls-Royce roadster which was, in her opinion, "the last word in daintiness." Doug also liked foreign clothes and big cars, and his concept of hospitality was more expansive than Mary's. In 1922 he invited Chaplin, Pola Negri and fifty other close friends on a six-month world cruise aboard a steamship chartered at a cost of $250,000. For weeks, the papers carried stories about the projected tour, but it was eventually·cancelled, probably because Mary or a Pickfair business advisor convinced Doug that there were more economical ways of getting publicity.

But while the Fairbankses lived well by any standard, they were noted for cutting corners whenever possible. Anita Loos recalls one occasion when a group of people were asked to dinner at Pickfair on the cook's night off. Following instructions, they stopped off at the local butcher and ordered thick, richly marbled steaks cut to their specifications. As they were leaving, they told the butcher to put the bill on the Pickfair account. "Oh, no!" he snapped. "No more credit!"

Miss Loos recalls that Mary had a bad reputation around

the Hollywood dress shops. She often bought a gown, wore it once and then returned it, saying it didn't fit properly. Doug also tried to economize on his clothing bills. One of his major extravagances was silk shirts which he began wearing at a time when they were virtually unknown in Hollywood. "Everyone was very impressed by those shirts," recalled actor Ben Lyon. "They were terribly expensive and Doug learned that he could have them made quite cheaply in Hong Kong. So he decided to order two dozen and told his valet to send along one of the old shirts as a model, with instructions that it should be copied *exactly*. Well, the valet accidentally chose a shirt that had been mended—Doug had burned a hole over the breast pocket and it had been patched with a piece of the tail—and when the twenty-four new shirts arrived from Hong Kong, they all had a little patch over the pocket. The shirt-maker had done as he had been told—he copied them *exactly*, down to the last detail."

Mary's thrift—or parsimony—was a heritage from her childhood, a hangover from the days when she paused and reflected before breaking a dollar bill. She never grew out of the habit and kept a careful watch over her income. Mary invested her money shrewdly, never speculatively, and refused to pay for services that had not been rendered to her satisfaction. In 1918 she went to court rather than pay an agent's fee to Cora Welkenning who claimed that in 1916 she had negotiated Mary's million dollar contract with Famous Players.

Mary told the press that Mrs. Welkenning had never acted as her agent, but this was not the whole truth: there may never have been a formal agreement, but in the early stages of the negotiations, Welkenning did act as intermediary between Zukor and the Pickfords. The suit dragged on for four years and went before three juries before there was a final decision in Mary's favor. Contesting the suit cost Mary in excess of $300,000—three times as much as the fee Mrs. Welkenning had demanded—but she considered it money well spent.

"If I had owed Mrs. Welkenning anything I would gladly

have paid it," she commented. "But I didn't. It's been an expensive victory, but I'd do it again. You see, it was the principle of the thing. . . ."

And money was one principle that Mary was always ready to defend to the death.

Penny-pinching was not, however, the main reason why so many people describe life at Pickfair as "dull" or "deadly." Mary and Doug felt it was their duty to live quiet, sober lives of respectability as a way of atoning for the scandal of their divorces and marriage. It was what the public expected of them, and though Doug sometimes chafed under the weight of the responsibility, Mary was determined she would never again disappoint her fans.

So Pickfair became filmland's leading embassy of middle-class virtue at a time when the rest of Hollywood was whooping it up and exploring the pleasures of flash success and sudden wealth. This was the beginning of the Hollywood era of "wonderful nonsense," a time when movie stars built gaudy mansions and called them Falcon's Lair or The Garden of Allah; when Tom Mix wrote his name in electric lights on top of his house, named his ninety-six foot yacht "The Miss Mix-It" and went to parties in a coach and four; when Charles Ray, the screen's leading country bumpkin, ate dinner off solid gold plates and tried to discuss the Orient with his imperious Japanese houseboy; when Gloria Swanson sat languidly by her swimming pool and took lessons in "it" from Elinor Glyn; when the epitome of "it" was the slave bracelet Natacha Rambova gave Rudolph Valentino as an engagement present.

It was a period when "it" was in the forefront of everyone's mind. "If you didn't take the young lady on your right upstairs between the soup and the entrée," producer Walter Wanger once said, "you were considered a homosexual." Mid-dinner sex was not unknown at Pickfair—John Barrymore once worked off a fit of sudden passion on a couch outside Mary's bedroom—but it was the exception and not the rule.

There were few escapades at Pickfair, no flowing wine, no cocaine, no nude cavorting in the pool. When Mary told the press that there was no "jazzing" in her home, she wasn't kidding.

Hollywood's live-wire set took a dim view of the Ovaltine and popcorn balls and dignity dished out by the Pickfair majordomo. While an invitation to one of Mary and Doug's "at homes" may have been welcomed in certain circles (in the words of one Pickford biographer) as "the ultimate achievement," in other circles it was greeted with about as much enthusiasm as a chance to have tea at the local chapter of the D.A.R. In fact, Mary was soon accorded the kind of respect that is usually reserved for a D.A.R. dowager. Once when she came late to a luncheon, all the women (most of them actresses) rose spontaneously at her entrance, and probably only lack of know-how kept them from curtseying.

But Mary was never as stuffy or saintly as her public personality sometimes suggested. With friends she trusted, she would open up and enjoy herself. Douglas Fairbanks, Jr. once said she had "a delicious sense of humor that is evident only at rare intervals. She adores the ridiculous. Although she appears shocked, one gets the idea that she appreciates a story that is just slightly shaded."

Louise Huff agreed. "Mary had a naughty, slightly wicked sense of humor. Once she gave me a photograph of herself with the inscription, 'Dear Louise, don't *I* look just like *you* in this picture?' Maybe it sounds bitchy, but it wasn't—by this time my days as a Pickford look-alike were long gone—and we both giggled a bit over it. I've kept the picture because it reminds me that Mary was not as sanctimonious as people suppose."

But Mary usually hid her sense of humor beneath a veil of propriety. Her enemies resented what they called her "self-importance." They claimed that her piety was pinned up and let down as easily as her golden curls, that she was all work and no play, that she spent too much time communicating with the Lord about the fate of her loose-living colleagues.

The hostile view of Mary was succinctly and forcefully summed up by Mabel Normand who had known Pickford since the Biograph days. "Say anything you want about me," Miss Normand instructed an interviewer, "But don't say I like to work. That sounds too much like that prissy bitch, Mary Pickford."

Pretty, fun-loving Mabel Normand might have been well-advised to take a leaf from Mary's book. In 1922 she and Mary Miles Minter (the most successful of the Pickford imitators) were implicated in the murder of William Desmond Taylor (the director of three Pickford films), and both their careers were ruined. Though pressed for a statement about the crime, Mary had nothing to say except that she was praying for everyone involved.

Mary had many other occasions to pray for her friends in the 1920s. Predictably enough the era of wonderful nonsense led directly into the era of the great Hollywood scandals. In quick and ugly succession came Robert Harron's mysterious death in a New York hotel room, Wallace Reid's death from drug addiction, Chaplin's affair with sixteen-year-old Lita Grey, the Taylor murder case, the Roscoe "Fatty" Arbuckle trials, director Thomas Ince's death on W. R. Hearst's yacht. Out of these unsavory chapters of film history grew the image of Hollywood as the new Babylon, a playground of dope and booze and free love for the rich and irresponsible.

Following each of these scandals, the self-appointed guardians of public morality would rehash past history to prove that Hollywood was a hotbed of depravity and licentiousness. Inevitably Mary and Doug would be pilloried for making divorce "respectable for decent people." (Which, indeed, to some small degree, they had done.) In 1922, shortly after Taylor's murder, Reverend Dr. John Roach Straton made headlines by denouncing them from the pulpit of his New York church for "demoralizing and corrupting the honorable institution of marriage." Hundreds of people rushed to their defense, but Mary and Doug wisely stayed silent except to hint that they were once again thinking of moving to London or Paris where no one cared about their morals.

But their best defense, as they both realized, was to steer clear of any kind of controversy or scandal, and mostly they succeeded, even though Jack and Lottie were a constant threat to their respectability. One of the first Hollywood scandals centered around Jack and his first wife, the incomparably beautiful Olive Thomas, who died a mysterious and horrific death in Paris at the end of 1920.

When Jack first met Olive, she was Florenz Ziegfeld's favorite show girl, both on- and offstage. On their third meeting, Jack gave her a $12,000 platinum cigarette case with the inscription—"To Ollie—the only sweetheart I will ever have." He proposed and she accepted. Mary and Charlotte objected to the match and begged the couple to wait, think it over, get to know each other, but Jack paid them no heed. Past experience had taught him that his mother and sister would forgive him practically anything, and there was no fuss when he married Olive in 1917. But the new Mrs. Pickford never got over her impression that her in-laws believed Jack had married beneath him.

To prove them wrong, Olive embarked on a film career, and while her acting ability was negligible, her dimples and vivacity took her straight to the top—by 1919 she was running a close second to Mary in many popularity polls. Jack's career had leveled off and was now on a fast decline. Not that he cared very much—egged on by Mary and Charlotte, he went through the motions of being an actor, but his heart wasn't in it. And he tried to play the dutiful husband, but for all his love for Olive, the role lay far outside his abilities.

The first quarrel came during their honeymoon. It was quickly patched up, but there were many more separations and reconciliations during the first three years of their marriage. In September 1920, when things seemed to be going pretty well, they decided to visit Paris on a combination second honeymoon and business trip—Olive wanted to order some dresses for her next picture and Jack was in the midst of negotiating a contract with a European producer. Their trip created an unusual amount of excitement and press comment because Jack was the second Pickford to visit Paris in 1920—Mary and Doug had just been there on their honeymoon.

Jack and Olive weren't interested in the Comédie Française or Sainte Chapelle or the other tourist spots Mary and Doug had so diligently visited; they spent most of their time in a Montmartre bistro called *Le Café du rat mort*. "The Dead Rat" had the worst reputation of all the Montmartre cabarets. "It was a dive, a low-down dive, run at top tourist prices," said a former Paris resident. "You could feed any vice there, but always for about twice what you'd pay anywhere else. A bottle of what passed as the best champagne—the local customers called it 'le piss Grand Cru'—sold for three dollars, a lot of money at that time."

After a late Saturday night at "The Dead Rat," Olive and Jack returned to their suite at the Ritz Hotel, looking bright-eyed and unsteady, but not drunk, according to a maid who saw them pass along a corridor. Inside their rooms, Jack went straight to bed, but Olive was wide-awake and too excited for sleep. A half hour later, she went into the bathroom and swallowed a full bottle of bichloride of mercury tablets. Screaming and clutching at her throat in agony, she ran into the living room where she was later discovered by Jack or a maid—there is some confusion about who came to her aid. Some say Jack wasn't in the suite at the time; according to this hypothetical reconstruction of the tragedy, he brought Olive home, went to his bedroom, waited a few minutes and then slipped out and went back to Montmartre.

Someone, Jack or the maid, called a doctor who rushed Olive to the American Hospital where she died five days later. The suffering was horrible—her throat and vocal cords had been permanently damaged by the poison, but before she died she managed to whisper, "Well, Doc, it looks like Paris finally got me."

The American press blamed France for Olive Thomas's death. The Hearst papers denounced the Paris cafés which enticed customers with "the glitter of priceless jewels adorning bare throats and bare limbs of women under cleverly shaded lights, langorous music, rivers of champagne, lascivious dances which turned the heads of young American girls unaccustomed to the lying attractions of such places." As a Ziegfeld chorine and Jack Pickford's wife, Olive Thomas hardly qualified as an innocent abroad, but surprisingly enough, the French press also denounced "The Dead Rat" and "those other dens of iniquity which not only crowd Montmartre, but also have invaded the residential quarters of the Champs Élysée and the Bois du Boulogne."

At this time the Paris police were investigating the activities of a certain Commander Spaulding, an American who was purportedly supplying *tout Paris* with hashish and cocaine. Reporters mentioned Spaulding and Olive Thomas in the same paragraph, but they never made a direct connection, and despite the description of the Pickfords's bright eyes when they returned to the Ritz, no one ever seemed to guess why they appeared "unsteady, but not drunk."

"We were very naive," says Allene Talmey. "We knew almost nothing about drug addiction—the people we interviewed had the money to support their habit, so there weren't any junkies, not in today's sense. So it all seemed very naughty until you died of it. And even then there was no correlation between cause and final effect. We edited ourselves. I would never have dreamed of saying someone was addicted to liquor or drugs, except perhaps John Barrymore, and everybody knew about him—he was always drunk on opening night."

After an autopsy and police investigation, a Paris coroner decided Olive Thomas's death was accidental—in his opinion, Olive had meant to take sleeping pills, not mercury capsules. But, as a French physician pointed out, had she swallowed the same amount of sleeping tablets, she would still have died, and without nearly so much suffering. Only a few days before her death, Olive had written a note to an English friend hinting at some "terrible reason" why she could no longer live with Jack. Was she implying Jack was in love with another woman? Some people thought so. Others, remembering that bichloride of mercury was then prescribed for venereal diseases, think Jack had given her syphilis. Either explanation leaves room for doubt: the act was in excess of the facts.

No one knows why Olive took the mercury tablets, but if her intention was to bring pain and remorse to Jack, she succeeded. Overcome with guilt-tainted grief, he was barely rational as he brought his wife's body back to the States on the Mauretania. Most of the voyage he spent locked in his stateroom, drinking and soul-searching with his close friend, actor Thomas Meighan. Jack had to be watched carefully; once when Meighan was sleeping, he straddled the railing of the first-class deck and was ready to throw himself overboard when a purser pulled him to safety. On arrival in New York, he collapsed in Charlotte's arms, and gasped between sobs, "I've never watched anyone die before."

Mary and Doug did not attend Olive's funeral at St. Thomas's Cathedral in New York. Their absence was not a sign of disrespect or indifference—they stayed away out of common sense. Even without them, the funeral was nearly turned into a three-ring circus by the fans who came to gawk and grasp at the celebrated mourners. During the recessional a riot broke out and the pallbearers (Meighan, Owen Moore, Myron Selznick and Florenz Ziegfeld, among others) barely managed to keep a grip on the casket. "Women fainted," *The New York Times* reported the next day. "Men who struggled either to free themselves or to check the onrush of others had their hats broken and were pushed to the floor. Then policemen came shouldering in and order was restored."

Jack's wake didn't end with the funeral—it went on and on until Mary, a staunch believer in the therapeutic value of hard work, hired him as her film director. This was a new career for Jack, one that he had talked about in the past, but directing soon bored him as much as acting. He co-directed two of Mary's films, including *Little Lord Fauntleroy*, one of her biggest successes in the 1920s, but his contribution was minimal. Both times he worked in tandem with an experienced director and by this time Mary didn't need much guidance—she knew as much about film production as anyone else in the business.

Still, she went through the motions of making Jack look important—once when he was sick, she suspended production until he returned to the set. She often tried to act the disciplinarian, and Jack always promised to mend his ways, but he never did.

Soon after Olive's death, Jack bought a plane and started practicing aerial feats over the Los Angeles canyons. One of his favorite tricks was a low nosedive over the roof of Pickfair. Mary made him swear he would give up aviation, and for a month or two he did. But one day, as Mary was talking to a reporter in her studio bungalow, a plane buzzed back and forth, drowning out the conversation. Finally Mary ran outside and screamed, "Oh, Jack, you promised! Stop! You'll kill yourself!" Jack dipped the left wing of the plane in acknowledgment of Mary's enthusiastic greeting.

Mary spoiled Jack, but merely tolerated Lottie. And while she tried to keep Jack out of the headlines, she went to court to gain custody of Lottie's daughter, Gwynne Ruppe. It was an ugly battle which ended with the court deciding Lottie was an unfit mother. Gwynne was placed under the joint guardianship of Charlotte Pickford and Douglas Fairbanks, but she spent more time at Pickfair than with her grandmother.

"We do not intend to push Gwynne into a film career," Mary said. A few months later she had changed Gwynne's name to Mary Pickford II and the little girl was making guest appearances in her aunt's films, much to the delight of the fans. Gwynne's small presence, the pitter-patter of her tiny feet, was the missing touch needed to complete the fan magazine's portrait of Pickfair as the ideal American home.

8

If there is one thing that separates Mary and Doug, especially Mary, from the stars of today, it was their willingness to share their lives with their fans. Assuredly they would never have subscribed to the fallacious, modern-day proposition that a star owes the public nothing but a good performance; stardom has never had much to do with acting ability, but rather it is based on a tenuous, elusive intimacy that can evaporate at any moment, any time the public grows weary (or begins to disapprove) of its current favorite. Mary and Doug enjoyed their fame and knew how to manipulate it to their own advantage: they were masters of the art of public relations.

They always impressed the fans as being open and spontaneous, and yet much of what they said in interviews reads as though it had been carefully planned, well rehearsed and possibly ghost-written. There were certain subjects they refused to discuss, the most important being their feelings for each other. "I'm superstitious," Mary explained. "It's bad luck to put affection into words."

But the fans felt they knew Mary and Doug as well as they knew their next-door neighbors. They were aware, for instance, that Doug was jealous, that he wouldn't let Mary bob her hair, that he disapproved of short skirts (Mary was still tripping over her hems when other women were flaunting their dimpled knees), that they called each other by silly pet names. (There were over fifty of these endearments, and they changed periodically, but for a while he was "Tiller" and she was "Hipper.") It wasn't much, but these few homey glimpses through the Pickfair keyhole were enough to create the illusion of intimacy, and that was really all the public wanted.

Never once during the good years of their marriage did Mary and Doug exchange cross words with the press and public, except on those occasions when they were mobbed and their lives were in danger. Even those incidents Mary accepted with that unnerving mixture of humility and noblesse oblige that is characteristic of her official self. After being nearly dismembered by a group of Japanese admirers, she turned to a horrified bystander and said, "This is cordiality, a great expression of friendship. . . . Stop and think what a remarkable tribute it is to the motion picture." This kind of self-abnegation is only one step away from talking about one-self in the third person. It's spooky, but there's no reason to believe Mary was insincere. She knew that behind her career there was more than talent, hard work and dedication—there was also an outstanding debt to the public, and she was conscientious enough to repay it as best she could.

There was, however, one wish Mary refused to grant her fans until the last years of her career. Shortly after the marriage, the American public let it be known through letters and fan magazine polls that their "favorite screen dream" was a picture starring Doug and Mary. "Perhaps in the near future we will play together," Mary replied, and when she announced that she would soon portray Shakespeare's Juliet, everyone jumped to the conclusion that her Romeo would be Fairbanks. But Doug knew his limitations—lyric passion wasn't his forte and he was a little long in the tooth for the role of an ardent teen-ager. (He did, however, have the makings of a good mute Mercutio.) Even before Mary abandoned the idea of filming Shakespeare, Fairbanks insisted that he would be drawn and quartered before he played Romeo.

There are several reasons why Mary and Doug never acted together at the height of their careers. First, it wasn't good economics—the public would be getting two stars for the price of one. Second, a co-starring vehicle implied some kind of a romantic plot, and Doug was always ill-at-ease in love scenes. Passion wasn't precisely Mary's specialty, either, and most of her leading men were as sexless as paper dolls—they looked as though their underwear was a part of their bodies. On the few occasions when she played opposite an actor who seemed capable of dropping his drawers—for example, the young John Gilbert in the 1919 *Heart o' The Hills*—she was peppery, a regular little spitfire. But the fans didn't want to see Mary's virtue compromised—they wanted her intact, wholesome, ignorant of the facts of life except as they applied to the domain of birds, bees and barnyard animals.

It is, of course, ironic that a woman who had grown up in the seedy, morally untidy world of the provincial American theatre, who had been twice married and the central figure in a sordid and well-publicized divorce trial, should end up as "The Patron Saint of Childhood." (The phrase, capitals and all, comes from a feature article in a 1921 issue of *Vogue*.) Mary had mixed feelings about her canonization. In public she bowed her head and gave thanks; in private she fought for the inalienable right of growing up and acting her age.

Suds (the film she was making at the time of her marriage) was a stab in this direction, and while not a bomb, it didn't go over as well as expected. Artist Max Ernst found "surrealist motifs" in the scenes in which the carthorse shares Mary's flat, but the regular critics weren't so impressed. "While it is the acme of artistry for Mary to shed her beauty, it hurt some-how," said *Photoplay*. "It was like seeing a lovely flower crushed."

Pickford ignored the warning signals and went ahead with the production of *The Love Light*, in which she played an Italian girl who is married, unknowingly, to a German spy. On learning his true identity, she is (according to a publicity handout) "torn between love for him and loyalty for her country"; predictably enough (a Pickford heroine being a Pickford heroine), she chooses patriotism over passion. In spite of the fact that he is the father of her *kleine bambino,* she shoots and kills her German husband.

This kind of junk plot was standard fare for the 1920s, and Frances Marion (who both wrote and directed *The Love Light*) had got by with a lot worse. So, for that matter, had Mary, but apparently both she and Miss Marion thought they had a winner in this stale story. The plot of *The Love Light* was worked out in Italy at the time Mary was honeymooning with Doug and Frances was vacationing with her third husband, former college athlete and divinity student, Fred Thomas. Marrying the twice-divorced Frances had ruined Thomas's reputation in clerical circles, so she decided he should take up acting as a career. Marion suggested he play the German husband in *The Love Light.* Mary was delighted —she liked Fred (who later became a leading cowboy star), she loved the idea for the film and she was so fond of Frances Marion that she announced that henceforth her former scenarist would direct all her films.

The Love Light, however, ended Pickford and Marion's director-actress relationship, though they remained friends and Marion was to write Mary's last film. Star directors have only one task: to make the star look good; anything else is a bonus. On this count, Miss Marion had failed both as director and writer. The film was a bust because, in the words of *Variety,* "Mary in motherhood is not Mary as the millions know and want her."

For her next film, *Through the Back Door,* Mary changed directors—brother Jack and Alfred Green replaced Miss Marion—but not direction: she went on playing a girl on the threshhold of maturity. This time she was a Belgian refugee maid privy to an upstairs-downstairs view of the American aristocracy. It was a pleasant little comedy, with a well-remembered scene—the maid glides across a greasy floor with scrub brushes attached to her shoes. But, despite a number of other amusing moments, *Through the Back Door* caused little stir at the box office.

A year earlier, in a review of *Pollyanna,* the critic of *The*

New York Times had placed his finger on the problem that was to plague Mary for the rest of her career:

> People have been asking recently, "Why doesn't Mary Pickford grow up?" The question is answered at the Rivoli this week. It is because she can make more people laugh and cry, can win her way into more hearts, and even more protesting heads as a rampant, resiliant little girl than anything else. She can no more grow up than Peter Pan. When she stops being a child on screen, she'll probably just stop. But that time is a long way off.

Pretty praise, but it had never been Mary's intention to spend her entire career in never-never land.

Nor would any perspicacious critic have wanted her to do so. Mary was an actress of limited range, but she could express depth of feeling, and once or twice, notably in *Stella Maris* in 1918, she proved that she was worthy of holding her head high in the company of Lillian Gish, Mae Marsh and the other great silent screen actresses. But Pollyanna and her other childhood roles, all written on two or three notes, asked for sentimentality, not sentiment; for whimsy and cuteness, not delicacy and refinement of playing. They utilized her skills as a comedienne, which were considerable, though not as considerable as some of her present-day admirers have claimed. Mary's gift for comic pantomime has often been compared to Chaplin's, and while there is a similarity, her flights of fancy rarely soared into visual poetry and are impressive mainly as an actress's valiant attempt to flesh out some very weak roles. Too many of her Chaplinesque "bits" were meant as nothing more than crowd pleasers, and while they do please, they're also slightly fussy and overly calculated.

Mary had hoped to break out of her pinafore roles with Juliet or Marguerite in *Faust,* and she had already fashioned a screenplay from Goethe's play when the disappointing returns for *Through the Back Door* forced her to drop the project.

"The character of Marguerite seems too tragic for me to attempt at this time," she explained. "People do not expect such a somber picture from me, and to jump at once from the parts I have taken to that of Marguerite is altogether too abrupt a change to make."

So, for her last film of 1921, Mary reluctantly agreed to film Frances Hodgson Burnett's classic *Little Lord Fauntleroy,* the story of a small American boy who inherits an English title and a huge baronial estate. The novel had often been proposed as a possible Pickford vehicle, but Mary had managed to avoid it by questioning whether the public would accept her as a boy. It was a flimsy excuse—Fauntleroy, who had golden curls and wore velvet suits with lace collars, was of almost indeterminate sex, and the part had always been played by a woman since the first dramatization of the novel in 1888.

Fauntleroy was nothing more than Pollyanna in pants, and there was no good reason why Mary's fans would object to her playing the role. Today *Fauntleroy* has unpleasant undertones, but it never would have occurred to the movie public of the 1920s that the little lord had inherited the wrong title, that he was really cut out to be queen of the realm. Nonetheless Mary loathed the part, and as a reward for undertaking it, she cast herself as the Fauntleroy's doting mother, Dearest. In short, she had worked out a compromise between her fans' wishes and her own ambitions—she would be both a child and a grown woman.

Dual roles were extremely popular in the early days of the feature film—they were considered the ultimate test of an actor's versatility—and Mary had already pulled off the stunt with great success in *Stella Maris.* But in that film Mary was not required to act with herself—the two characters she portrayed never met—as she would have to do in the many scenes between Fauntleroy and Dearest. These scenes would, of course, be created through trick photography, and while they demanded no special skill on Mary's part, they were tedious and time-consuming to film. But the hard work was amply rewarded—when Mary as Dearest kisses Mary as Fauntleroy (a shot that took sixteen hours to complete), audiences were awestruck by the marvels of movie technology. How was it done? Why did Mary/Dearest look so much taller than Mary/Fauntleroy?

The credit went to photographer Charles Rosher, who shot all the Pickford films between 1918 and 1928. He perfected the double-exposure process and came up with the idea of Mary as Dearest wearing ten-inch heels in her scenes with Fauntleroy. So that Mary could rest between takes, Rosher also originated the role of the stand-in, the first being a mannequin's head, dressed with golden curls, on top of a wooden frame; she was called "Maria."

Rosher has often been given credit for the pictorial elegance of the later Pickford pictures, and the credit is deserved as long as it is remembered that Mary, who had always recognized the importance of strong production values, was largely responsible for the look of her films. She never stinted when it came to presenting herself to the public, and when, in 1921, a trend started for longer and bigger and more expensive films, she was one of the first to jump on the bandwagon.

Movies had to keep up with the manner in which they were presented to the public. The days of the nickelodeons were over, the first movie palaces had started to appear around 1914 and only a few years later a theatre in Cleveland invited shoppers to stop by in the afternoon with this advertisement:

> When you come downtown to shop, we suggest a matinée at Loew's State . . . You'll find a wonderful structure, with its beautiful Grand Lobby adorned with elegant decorative murals, luxurious furnishings and priceless antiques; you can spend a few minutes listening to the string orchestra and singing birds, or chatting with the parrot; refresh yourself with tea on the mezzanine and then, in the magnificent theatre auditorium, enjoy a Deluxe performance of excellent pictures, presented with symphonic music.

All this for thirty-five cents, including Uncle Sam's war tax. And this was Cleveland! In New York, S. L. "Roxy" Rothapfel and Major Edward Bowes were wooing patrons into their theatres with promises of Wurlitzer organs, Arabian nights decor and stage shows that were a bizarre blend of Ziegfeld, pseudo-classic music ("In an English Garden" or "La Paloma" orchestrated for strings), shadow plays and pirouetting chorus girls who passed as ballerinas.

Amid these surroundings, movies had to get bigger and lusher and more "artistic" or they would get lost in the shuffle. By 1920 it was no longer possible for a director to call together a group of actors and ad-lib a film from a scratchy scenario. Now everything had to be carefully preplanned and shot according to schedule; some details could be left for last-minute improvisation, but the main line of the action had to be worked out far in advance. Location work was risky—it was safer to work in the studio, where there were no weather problems, where lighting and design could be carefully controlled. And so began the era of the "studio-look," the period when Hollywood started to recreate the world in papier-mâché.

Little Lord Fauntleroy was Mary's first "ten-reel superproduction." This meant it ran close to two hours, maybe longer (projection speed varied in the silent days), certainly much longer than the average six- or seven-reel picture. Today it seems endless; it's painstakingly designed and photographed, beautifully costumed, but rather lamely directed, and while Mary tries to give Fauntleroy some gumption, she looks foolish in the little lord's velvet knickers and frilly jackets. Fortunately, she partly redeems herself as Dearest. Mary rarely looked so handsome on screen as she does in the cinch-waisted, flowing gowns and flowery bonnets she wears in this picture. Maturity becomes her—it gives her a soft, womanly glow and allows her to dispense with all the fussy embroidery of the childhood roles. But, in all honesty, it's not a very exciting or interesting performance, and the critics of the day had some justification in ignoring Dearest in their rave reviews of the film.

Little Lord Fauntleroy was one of the biggest hits of 1921. After three so-so films, Mary was now back on top, which was good news, but she had made the comeback in a child's part, which was bad news. Uncertain of what she should do next, Mary played safe and remade her first great success, *Tess of the Storm Country*, in which she played one of her in-between roles, a character who was no longer a child and yet not quite a woman. The picture was nearly as big a success as *Fauntleroy*, and it gave Mary a sense of security. She felt the public might now be prepared to accept her in grown-up roles.

While Mary's career was moving along by fits and starts, Doug was forging ahead with a new screen personality and a new film genre that was virtually his creation—the swash-buckler. The mixture of swordplay and melodrama had literary and theatrical antecedents that dated back beyond Hugo, Dumas and Scott to Shakespeare, and probably there were cinematic precursors as well. But Fairbanks was the popularizer and master of the form. And none of the derring-doers who came after him—Errol Flynn, Tyrone Power, Gene Kelly, Burt Lancaster—ever matched the wit and exuberance Fairbanks brought to these roles, though Lancaster in *The Crimson Pirate* (1952) comes pretty close.

It was Mary who discovered the property that allowed Doug to set off in this new direction. On their honeymoon she had read a *Saturday Evening Post* story called "The Curse of Capistrano" and passed it along to Doug with the suggestion that he acquire the film rights. Doug shared Mary's enthusiasm, and on his return to Hollywood he announced that his next film would be *Capistrano*, later retitled *The Mark of Zorro*.

The hero of Johnston McCulley's story leads a double life—by day he is the foppish and foolish Don Diego de Varga; by night, Senor Zorro, a master swordsman who etches

"Z's" on the cheeks or chests of his enemies. Placed in the past and set against a slightly foreign background (Spanish California of the 1850s), the story was a far cry from anything Fairbanks had done before, but its hero (the inspiration for Superman and Batman, according to comic-strip historians) might well have been a distant ancestor of Doug's all-American screen character. All his mollycoddles and citified playboys turned virile adventurers were essentially dual roles. Vega/Zorro wasn't so much a departure as a variation on an old theme. A transitional role, it took Doug out of the modern idiom and into the realm of fantasy and myth where he was to stay to the end of his career.

In spite of this similarity, critics were puzzled by the new Fairbanks of *The Mark of Zorro*. One reviewer found it impossible to place the film "in a definite category. Unquestionably it is comedy drama. Yet there are occasional hasty flights into melodrama, and again, as in the flagellation of the wronged Franciscan priest, there is a stroke of pathos." *The Dramatic Mirror*, an influential theatrical publication of the time, also took exception to the priest-flogging scene in a strongly negative review: "*Zorro* is not up to expectations, and bears one of the most sickening scenes ever depicted upon the public screen, namely the beating of a priest upon the bare back by way of showing man's fiendishness and utter disregard for religion . . ." And a fan magazine noted that "teachers and civic groups are protesting Doug's lighthearted use of a sword point to carve a bloody Z on the face of a bad guy."

The public, however, knew a good thing when they saw it—and *Zorro* was very good, one of the best of all the Fairbanks films. It broke records at the Capitol Theatre in New York, and at the end of 1920, Fairbanks placed first in the popularity polls. He surpassed Chaplin and even upstaged Mary, who dropped as low as fourth position on some lists.

Long before the happy box-office returns for *Zorro* had begun to accumulate, Fairbanks had started work on *The Nut*, the next-to-last of his modern comedies, a parody of

American ingenuity. (Doug plays an inventor of Rube Goldberg-type conveniences.) While making the picture, Fairbanks had a bad accident. Jumping out of a window, he caught his foot on the ledge, and landed with his arm doubled under his full weight. He had splintered a bone and production was suspended until the fracture mended.

It was around this time that Fairbanks started using a double for his stunt work. There is a dispute as to exactly when he first took this precaution—some people say a double was used for certain scenes of *The Nut;* others insist Doug performed all his own stunts until the mid-1920s—but no matter when it started, it was to remain a closely guarded secret until long after Fairbanks's death. At first, it was not a question of Doug not having the stamina and dexterity to execute even the most demanding feat—he was to remain in top physical condition until nearly the end of his life. Rather, it was a matter of economics: if Doug happened to injure himself, the cast and crew would have to stand by until he recovered at a loss of several thousand dollars per day. So, in the really hectic scenes, Fairbanks was replaced by Richard Talmadge, the greatest athlete of all Hollywood stunt men, who resembled Doug closely in appearance and spirit.

After *The Nut,* Fairbanks took on a role he had often thought of playing and one for which *Zorro* had been a kind of dress rehearsal. This was D'Artagnan in *The Three Musketeers.* The French were initially upset at the idea of an American actor playing one of their great literary heroes, but Doug retorted that "the world would never have had a Hamlet if it had waited for the Danes." And most people agreed that no actor in France or anywhere else in the world was as well suited to D'Artagnan as Fairbanks. It was only fitting that "the best swordsman in Hollywood play the best swordsman of France."

The United Artists publicity mills ground out lots of copy about Fairbanks's mastery of the foil, most of it pure fabrication. For Zorro, Doug had hired Henry Uyttenhove, fencing coach of the Los Angeles Athletic Club, who showed him the correct method of parry and attack, the proper position for guards and lunges. On screen he looked as though he had been born with an épée in hand, but both Uyttenhove and Fred Cavens (fencing coach of the later Fairbanks films) have claimed he never acquired more than a modicum of technique.

But a little technique was all Doug really needed. When combined with his considerable gymnastic skills, it produced dazzling results, and in *Musketeers* he performed what has been called the "single most difficult feat of his career"—the left-handed handspring balanced on a short dagger with which he wipes out an entire regiment of the Cardinal's Guards. (Men who saw the film when they were boys still remember this moment with awe in their eyes.)

The Three Musketeers went into production at about the same time as *Little Lord Fauntleroy,* and for a while there was talk of filming these "ten-reel superproductions" in Europe—*Fauntleroy* in England, *Musketeers* in the south of France. Instead, England and France were constructed on the back lot of the Pickford-Fairbanks studio at great and much-publicized expense—*Musketeers* at an exaggerated $1,000,000 was said to be the costliest film ever made. Doug spent lavishly on the picture: Broadway playwright Edward Knoblock (best remembered as the author of *Kismet*) wrote the screenplay; Barbara La Marr (Milady de Winter) and Marguerite de la Motte (Constance) wore dresses of genuine antique brocade; Uyttenhove trained all the actors (even the extras) in swordplay; up-and-coming Fred Niblo, director of *Zorro,* was placed in charge of the production.

To insure authenticity, the architecture of sixteenth-century France was painstakingly duplicated by the studio carpenters, the stones used to build the sets were weathered and hewn into irregular shapes and Fairbanks invited the ridicule of his fans by growing a mustache. In America in the 1920s mustaches were worn only by silent-screen comics, elderly gentlemen, continental roués or, in the vernacular of the time, "poofs and powder puffs." Face hair was considered un-

American, and Mary and the fans urged Doug to return to his old clean-shaven self once *The Three Musketeers* was finished. But Doug liked his "lip-herbage" (as Mary called it) and the touch of aristocracy it brought to his moon-shaped face. And pretty soon many American men were ignoring their upper lip when they lathered up for the morning shave. Doug brought the mustache back into fashion just as, a little earlier, he had been partly responsible for the sunbathing fad that swept America at the end of the First World War. People had then started to toast themselves to a crisp in an attempt to achieve the coppertone complexion that was one of Fairbanks's natural characteristics.

By 1921 Doug was having weight problems—the excess poundage was muscle, not flab, but still it made him look heavy—and before shooting *The Three Musketeers* he slimmed down by fifteen pounds. And in spite of the fact that D'Artagnan's tent-sized culottes and plumed hats occasionally made him look like the tenor in a Shubert operetta, he cut a dashing figure in the film. He's at least twenty years too old for the part, but since there are few close-ups, the discrepancy is never bothersome. His physical agility and grace create the illusion of youth.

Reviewing the film for *Life,* Robert Sherwood wrote:

> When Alexandre Dumas sat down at his desk, smoothed his hair back, chewed the end of his quill pen, and said to himself, "Well, I guess I might as well write a book called *The Three Musketeers,*" he doubtless had but one object in view: to provide a suitable story for Douglas Fairbanks to act in the movies.

The fans agreed with Sherwood. *The Three Musketeers* was Doug's biggest hit to date.

It was superior to the earlier films in the professional polish of its photography and editing and set design. Knoblock's screenplay was chaste—he discarded the sexual indiscretions that pop up in the original story—but it was also a smooth résumé of the main action of Dumas's lengthy and very complicated novel. Like most film adaptations of good novels, this one is a Reader's Digest condensation of the original: skillfully done, and yet a bit plodding and tedious in its attempts to jam all the jumbled pieces into a smooth story continuity.

The Three Musketeers is actually something of a bore except for those sequences in which Doug picks up a rapier and starts bouncing off the walls. This is one of the reasons why *Zorro,* with its silly, comic-operetta plot, is so much more enjoyable than *Musketeers*—the earlier picture had no pretensions to art or to serious storytelling, but was content with providing Doug with a framework he could use as a trampoline for his exhilarating acrobatics. But the trend was toward more story, more art, more elaborate production, and as time went on, Doug was to have more and more trouble in getting his films off the ground.

The vogue for the ten- or twelve-reel superproduction presented a new problem to the product-starved United Artists Corporation. Early in 1920 the company had placed this advertisement in all the trade magazines:

UNITED ARTISTS

PICKFORD—CHAPLIN—FAIRBANKS—GRIFFITH

On the first day of each month, beginning September first, exhibitors are assured of at least one big picture from the screen's foremost artists.

That meant that each of the four founding members of United Artists were expected to produce at least three movies per year. Mary and Doug lived up to their part of the bargain in 1921, but Chaplin, a notoriously slow worker, made no contribution until 1923, and then it was *A Woman of Paris,* a film he produced and directed, but did not appear in. Two years later came *The Gold Rush* and in 1928, *The Circus—*

his only other productions for UA in the first decade of its existence.

D. W. Griffith contributed ten films between 1919 and 1925, including one genuine masterpiece, *Broken Blossoms,* and two near-misses, *Way Down East* and *Orphans of the Storm,* but of the ten only *Way Down East* was a financial success. Griffith blamed his failures on UA's weak distribution setup; the UA board of directors suggested that the failure was the result of a decline in the quality of Griffith's work. There was right on both sides, but the upshot was that Griffith left UA and went to work at Paramount in early 1925.

By then United Artists had acquired a new group of stars or star-producers, including Samuel Goldwyn, Gloria Swanson, Rudolph Valentino and Norma Talmadge, whose husband, Joseph Schenck, later became president of the company. But in the early years UA really meant Pickford and Fairbanks. They supplied most of the product and it was their popularity that enticed exhibitors into fitting the UA pictures into their programming schedule, a risky business since most film companies insisted on exclusive booking contracts. Since UA produced only a dozen or so films a year, the theatre owner who booked the Pickford and Fairbanks pictures had to fill out his yearly schedule with the output of independent or "poverty-row" producers.

Another drawback for the distributor was the United Artists policy of booking only on a percentage basis, not on flat rentals as was then customary. Paramount had tried this earlier with the Pickford/Artcraft films, and it had worked, though even at that time theatre-owners were unhappy. Now, faced with what could become a precedent (across-the-board percentage booking), they balked. McAdoo and Price couldn't handle the situation—they were figureheads, not experienced film men—so Hiram Abrams, a former Paramount executive, was called in to see that "the distributing company was able to distribute."

A former UA staff member described Abrams as "tough as nails and by no means an esthete." In short order, he locked horns with McAdoo and his "East Coast yes-men"; they fled, and he took control of the business end of the corporation. Abrams was able to persuade most exhibitors to book the United Artists movies, though in smaller cities the company had to resort to second-rate theatres, and was shut out of some areas completely. When he couldn't get distribution, Abrams rented theatres (a policy now known as "four-wall booking") and played his pictures on extended runs to show that the United Artists product was profitable.

Many industry people feel that Abrams has never been given due recognition for making United Artists a going concern, that many of his policies were credited to the flashy personalities on his board of directors—Chaplin, Griffith, Fairbanks and especially Pickford, who already had a reputation as an astute businesswoman. Probably this is true, but certainly he was not totally responsible for United Artists being called "The Tiffany's of Hollywood." Abrams set the prices, but Fairbanks, Pickford and company provided the goods. Mary and Doug's productions soon set new Hollywood standards for expense, polish and technical innovation. Sometimes the stories of their pictures were silly—but who noticed? Even a flawed diamond looks good in a fabulous setting.

9

After 1921 Mary and Doug sometimes spent as much as six months on each new picture. Their shooting schedules averaged out at about twelve to sixteen weeks, but production work was the last stage of a job that had been going on for months. Mary and Doug were producers as well as stars, and in their supervisory capacity, they were responsible for every phase in the development of a film—choice of material, writing, budgeting, selection of personnel, publicity and, finally, presentation. This was the heyday of the movie premiere, and no picture, certainly no Pickford or Fairbanks picture, was complete until it had been launched with limelight, squealing fans, celebrity guests and a theatre lobby refurbished in the style and period of the film.

Prior to the release of their films, Mary and Doug usually came East to supervise the opening and tend to other United Artists business. Their visits to New York were so frequent that the press called them "The Hollywood Commuters," and referred to their suite at the Ritz-Carlton as "Pickfair East." These transcontinental jaunts had a dual purpose: business came first, of course, but they were also a cure for Doug's recurring wanderlust. "Some men's vice is drinking and others are addicted to flirting, but Doug's vice is travelling," Mary said with a mock sigh. "I fully expect to die on a train or on a steamer in some unchartered spot of the globe . . ."

In early September 1921, with *Fauntleroy* and *Musketeers*

behind them, Mary and Doug boarded the Super Chief for New York with the usual retinue of family, friends, business advisors and personal servants. They traveled in their own car, but their privacy was disrupted at Chicago and nearly every other whistle-stop by reporters who came aboard to interview Mary or photograph Doug chinning himself on the baggage racks. Bennie Zeidman and the other UA publicists had made sure the Fairbankses would have plenty of snapshots for their family album. Whenever the train came to a halt, a society matron or a little girl rushed forward with a bouquet of American Beauty roses for America's Sweetheart, and there was always a group of local photographers ready to capture Mary's wide-eyed expression of gratitude.

This was standard procedure for any star on a cross-country trip. It was something the Hollywood elite expected as due recognition of their position within the industry. When it didn't happen, they were distraught. Leatrice Joy remembers a painful train journey taken at a time when her career was in decline. "At one stop, I was met by a photographer and one elderly lady holding a very wilted nosegay. It was so depressing. I refused to have my picture taken."

There was not much talk about invasion of privacy in 1920s Hollywood. Mary and Doug had decided to share their lives with the public, and other actors followed suit. They made no division between home and studio, between work and vacation—at least none that was apparent to their fans. And so it was on this trip. When she wasn't posing for the Sunday rotogravure sections, Mary was writing the titles for *Fauntleroy* with her directors, Jack Pickford and Alfred Green, who had come East only to finish up this job. (Jack, however, had an ulterior motive; he was then courting Marilyn Miller, "the dainty twinkletoes" star of Florenz Ziegfeld's *Sally*.) And once the work on *Fauntleroy* was completed, Mary started planning the production of *Tess of the Storm Country*. At the same time Doug was turning over ideas for his next picture, while winding up the publicity details of *The Three Musketeers*.

Arriving in New York, they threw themselves into an endless round of tantalizing interviews about their future plans. It was just barely possible, they suggested, that if the right property came along, they might return to the Broadway stage for a six-month engagement. No one took them seriously, but it caused a momentary flutter in the hearts of theatregoers who were also movie fans—and, of course, it kept the stars in the news.

Mary and Doug were masters of finding ways of keeping themselves before the public. One of their ploys was to announce a vacation months in advance, and then postpone it for weeks, sometimes months, after their scheduled departure. Sometimes there were legitimate reasons for the delay, but often it seemed that they were stalling only to build up suspense. And so it was in 1921. They were sailing . . . they weren't sailing . . . they might be sailing, and as an added fillip, they might not be returning. They hinted that they might stay abroad for a year or two, mainly vacationing, but also possibly making a picture or two in France or England. Once again, their expatriate leanings were inspired by the unresolved status of Mary's Nevada divorce, and again, they seemed intended as a warning to her public: support me or I'll desert you.

Doug and Mary sailed for Europe on October 1, 1921, only seven months later than the first date set for their holiday. On board the *Olympic* with them was Bennie Zeidman, Ma Pickford, little Gwynne (called Mary Pickford Ruppe at this time) and Robert Fairbanks (now chief of operations at the Pickford-Fairbanks studios). The ship docked at Cherbourg, and from there the Fairbanks party took the boat train to Paris, where they took over the royal suite at the Crillon. They stayed there only a few days, just long enough for Mary to fill twelve trunks with new Lanvin frocks. Then, for a day, the party separated, as Doug and his male companions flew from Paris to London while Mary and the ladies traveled by land and sea. Mary had flown previously (once in the 1915 film, *The Girl from Yesterday*), but hadn't taken to it, and at this time flying was still a masculine sport: it wasn't until the late 1920s, when Lady Mountbatten and Princess Emmeline de Broglie started hopping over the Channel for a Paris lunch, that air travel became truly fashionable for ladies. Besides, Mary was feeling and looking peaked—her weight was down to eighty-eight pounds—and therefore she decided not to risk the excitement of crossing the Channel by air.

A few days later she collapsed in London. For over a week, her breakdown was headline news on both sides of the Atlantic, with speculative diagnoses ranging from pregnancy through overwork to "complications stemming from a nervous disorder." Through a spokesman Doug confirmed reports that Mary might need a long convalescence and that they were looking for a flat in Mayfair, but went on to deny that there was anything seriously wrong with his wife. To show his lack of concern, he kept up with his social engagements, surprising and delighting crowds as he strutted through Piccadilly in spats, top hat and a morning suit.

Mary made a quick recovery. One day papers reported that she was "in seclusion and in need of constant rest"; three days later she was out on the town. She and Doug saw the new English plays; dined at London's famous theatrical restaurant, The Ivy; and were lavishly entertained in the best homes in England. Starting in 1921, the Pickfair European tours became a dizzying blur of famous places and famous faces—not just show-business celebrities, but dukes and duchesses, princes and kings, all the rich and beautiful and clever people who made up the international set known as "café society."

Their first encounter with royalty occurred at a party in Mayfair. Among the other guests was the Duke of York, second in line to the throne, who asked Mary for a dance. She refused, explaining politely that she danced only with her husband. The shy and stammering Duke took no offense, but the British press was outraged. For days the episode was debated in the papers, some claiming Mary had insulted the royal family while others praised her loyalty and wifely devotion. Privately Mary was deeply embarrassed by the incident, and wished she had accepted the Duke's request. And Doug, the incarnate snob, might also have had second thoughts had he known that the Duke of York would eventually reign as George VI.

While in London, Mary and Doug were taken up by the Duke and Duchess of Sutherland, Mayfair's leading host and hostess, and by Lord Louis ("Dickie") Mountbatten and his wife, the vivid and spirited Lady Edwina. The Mountbattens lived in a Park Lane mansion, filled with "eight hundred tons of Italian marble and malachite," where they entertained the so-called "Bright Young People," a pack of pace-setters whose acknowledged leader was the Prince of Wales (Lord Mountbatten's cousin). Of all the bright young people, Lady Edwina was perhaps the brightest; certainly she was the most controversial. Handsome, witty, intelligent, she had no patience with the narrow, autocratic conventions of the British aristocracy, and was totally fearless about offending her more conservative peers. Mixing and mingling as she pleased, she was the personification of a new type of British woman—the emancipated, slightly bohemian socialite. (Noel Coward used her as a model for several of his heroines, including Amanda Prynne in *Private Lives*.)

Despite the patronage of the Mountbattens and the Sutherlands, Mary and Doug discarded their plans for an extended stay in London and took off for the continent. They stopped a day or so in Paris, staying just long enough to hire a car and chauffeur to drive them to Switzerland, where they visited the lion of Lucerne and tramped through the countryside near Basel. (The chauffeur and car followed at a discreet distance.) After two days at Lake Como and Lake Lugano, they crossed over into Italy, inspecting it from top to bottom, seeing in breathless succession all the sights of Venice, Rome, Naples and Sicily. One of their best evenings, Doug later wrote in an article for *The Boston Post*, was spent in Rome "looking for the 'plain folk,' those who, when they enter America, are classified as 'wops.' "

Through the courtesy of the Italian government, they were

allowed to go through the newly excavated portions of Pompeii, including sections that were not open to the public. Then they steamed out of Naples harbor for Sicily, spent three hours in Palermo and sailed on to Tunis. "A visit there is like stepping into Biblical times," Doug commented in his *Boston Post* article. After touring and being disappointed by the ruins of Carthage, they went on to Algiers and Biskra, where Mary took her first and last camel ride. Doug wanted to send one of the baby humpbacks to Chaplin as a souvenir, but the local customs officials were not amused.

After inspecting "all the romantic places made famous by Robert Hichens's *The Garden of Allah*," they sailed from Algiers to Marseilles, which Mary found less "colorful" than she had imagined. They drove to Paris for the Longchamps races, and then crossed the Channel to London, spending ten days playing with the Mountbattens and the Sutherlands before boarding the S.S. *Paris* for New York.

It had been the grand tour to end grand tours—England, France, Switzerland, Italy, Africa and the Middle East, all visited in less than two months. The Fairbankses traveled in the same way that they produced films—on a superspectacular scale. Their vacations were really an extension of their work, another way of keeping themselves in the headlines while they were "between pictures." It was a highly successful stratagem; in fact, as time went on, their European tours often surpassed their films in stirring up public excitement.

But it was an exhausting form of relaxation. As one Hollywood wag put it, "Mary and Doug have to go back to work to rest up for their next vacation." And indeed, as soon as one of their trips was finished, they were ready to jump immediately into their next production. Arriving in New York on the *Paris* in December 1921, Mary told reporters she would soon start work on the remake of *Tess of the Storm Country*, and Doug announced that he was toying with three projects, Owen Wister's *The Virginian*, Booth Tarkington's *Monsieur Beaucaire* and the legend of *Robin Hood*, of which the last would probably be the first to go into production.

At first, Doug hadn't been enthusiastic about playing Robin Hood. "I don't want to play a flat-footed Englishman walking through the woods," he had said. But Robert Fairbanks, convinced that his brother would make an ideal bandit of Sherwood Forest, dreamed up a clever way of changing Doug's mind. He bought bows and arrows and set up a target on the grounds of the studio. Always eager to acquire a new athletic skill, particularly one that could be used to advantage in his films, Doug was soon a devotee of the art of archery. And in short order he began to see the possibilities of a film about Robin Hood.

It would be the biggest picture ever made in Hollywood, outranking Griffith's *Intolerance* and his own *Three Musketeers*. Its major set, a twelfth-century Norman castle, would be the largest ever constructed in Hollywood, bigger, in fact, than any castle that had ever existed in England. It would also be historically authentic—experts were hired to check on all details of set and costume design.

Doug's old friend, Allan Dwan, was called in as director, and the screenplay was prepared by an unknown writer with the upper-crust British name of Elton Thomas. It was not long before Elton Thomas was recognized as Fairbanks's pseudonym, though it was never widely acknowledged that "Thomas" had considerable help in preparing his scenarios. On *Robin Hood*, his collaborators included Tom Geraghty, Dwan and whoever else happened to be hanging around the Pickfair set at the time. (One of Doug's collaborators was Lotta Woods; her major contribution, someone later said, was "rolling the paper into the typewriter.")

According to Dwan, there never was much of a script for *Robin Hood*, though there were plenty of script conferences. These meetings, usually held in Fairbanks's studio gymnasium with such famous literary lights as Jack Dempsey in attendance, were goof-off time, a period when Doug could relax and work off his taste for practical jokes. Most of the humor sprang from a massage table wired to give an electric shock to anyone who sat on it. "Sit down there and listen to this," Doug would say; then, just as his cronies were about to make contact with the upholstered mat, he'd push a button that frazzled their behinds.

Often as they were settling down to work, Doug would remember that it was time for his afternoon workout, or decide he needed a steambath. Dutifully the collaborators (excepting Miss Woods) would strip off their clothes and follow Fairbanks into the vapors where they sweated out a few more ideas for the script, mainly suggestions for the stunts Doug would perform in the picture. He was more interested in these bravura set pieces than in plot continuity, so it is no surprise that *Robin Hood* has a very lackadaisical structure.

The sets created another problem. They were designed by Wilfred Buckland, a specialist in monumental reconstruction; for a Belasco stage play, he once slavishly duplicated the interior of a Child's restaurant, and for De Mille's film version of *Carmen*, he built a huge *plaza de toros*, authentic to the smallest detail. But *Robin Hood* was bigger and better than anything he had done before—highly stylized and occasionally reminiscent of Maxfield Parrish's illustrations, the designs were overpowering in their grandiosity. Once the walls of his castle had been constructed (under Dwan and Robert Fairbanks's supervision) on a twelve-acre lot on Santa Monica Boulevard, Doug stared up at them and murmured, "Gosh . . . I can't compete with those . . . that's not me."

He was right. To show off the sets, Dwan had to photograph much of the film in long shot and looking at it is often like watching a parade through the wrong end of binoculars. Dwan, however, argued that the sets provided ample opportunity for showy stunts, including what was to become the film's most memorable moment; Robin's descent along the crease of a billowing tapestry nearly the size of the famous gold curtain of the old Metropolitan Opera house. Doug was enchanted with the stunt; he rehearsed it a few times, it worked, and he invited friends to watch it a few more times.

Soon the *Robin Hood* sets were the major tourist attraction in Hollywood. (Pickfair was relegated temporarily to second place.) Jim Thorpe, Somerset Maugham, Sir and Lady Arthur Conan Doyle came to visit, and Doug showed them around the set with all the beaming pride of a small boy with a new and very expensive Christmas toy. Chaplin, one of the first to be given the guided tour, was amused by Fairbanks's childlike glee with his oversized erector set, and enlisting the aid of a studio accomplice, he worked up a little surprise for Doug.

Once Fairbanks was showing a distinguished guest around the outside of the castle and the drawbridge unexpectedly descended. A small figure, dressed in a nightgown and tasseled cap, crept out of the entranceway and ambled sleepily across the bridge. It was Charlie, with a tiny kitten under his arm. Reaching solid ground, he put down the cat, picked up a milk bottle and wearily retraced his steps to the castle, the drawbridge slowly closing behind him.

Prior to *Gone With the Wind, Robin Hood* probably received more production publicity than any other picture in American film history. Fan magazines and the Sunday rotogravure sections of the nation's papers were filled with pictures of the sets and gossip about production. It was, the papers claimed, at $1,000,000, the most expensive movie ever made, and the sets were, according to the dimensions cited, the largest ever constructed in Hollywood. The magnitude and cost were exaggerated—*Robin Hood* cost about $750,000 and it seems doubtful that the dining hall of the castle was really larger than the atrium of Grand Central station—but certainly it was a big and costly film, maybe the biggest and costliest of all films up to that time.

To dwell on this is only to emphasize that cost had become synonymous with prestige, even for those United Artists who had joined together not only for a larger share of the profits of their films, but also to have artistic control over their careers. Mary and Doug played a part in educating film audiences to expect the best production values, the best acting, all the latest technical advances, but their films for UA—this is truer of Mary than of Doug—might have been made at any other studio, though never on so lavish a scale.

And except as producers and stockholders in the distribution company that released their films, they would never have been so generous about promoting their films. As soon as *Robin Hood* was ready for release, they came to New York, checked in at the Ritz-Carlton, and immediately went up to the roof, where Doug posed for photographs, bow and arrow in hand. "Don't shoot," he had been warned, but the practical joker won out over Doug's saner self and he shot an arrow all the way across Madison Avenue, where it landed in the shoulder or chest or backside—there was controversy about the precise point of penetration—of furrier Abraham Seligman.

Seligman went into shock, and though he was only superficially wounded, he was rushed to the Fifth Avenue Hospital. Bearing a bouquet of roses and looking contrite, Doug visited Seligman the next day, and after about twenty minutes in the hospital room he and his attorney emerged with smiles and assurances that the furrier bore no grudges. Details about the meeting were scant, but it was (correctly) assumed that Seligman's good will hadn't been bought with a dozen roses; there was also a small cash settlement, something in the neighborhood of $5,000.

Ending as smoothly and cheaply as it did, the Seligman incident could be written off as publicity for the late October 1922 opening of *Douglas Fairbanks in Robin Hood*. (This was the full title of the picture, as it appeared in all advertisements; Doug wanted to discourage other producers from rushing their versions of the public-domain Robin Hood story into release at the same time as his, and on the whole he succeeded, though a picture called *Robin Hood, Jr.* went into distribution only a few weeks later.) But, as it turned out, the Fairbanks production didn't need this or any other kind of publicity to put it across—it was an immediate, unqualified success with both the critics and the public.

It isn't, however, a very good film, or more precisely, it's only half a good film. Part of the problem is the sets, which get in the way of action, and the other part is that there is no action to speak of until the second half of the film. Nearly six reels are gone before the Earl of Huntington becomes Robin Hood and takes to Sherwood Forest with his band of merry men—though in this case "band" is an inadequate word; there seem to be close to a thousand bow-and-arrow revolutionaries. The early scenes of the film belong to Wallace Beery (King Richard) and Sam de Grasse (Prince John) who ham up a storm and supply the film with its only forward momentum. Although he has a couple of good comedy scenes, Fairbanks has little to do beyond looking indignant or playing the bashful, backward (almost prepubescent) beau to Enid Bennett's purse-lipped Maid Marian. And he does it badly; watching him in these opening moments, one is painfully aware of how little an actor he was, acutely aware that any second-rate leading man could have played most of these pedestrian scenes far better than Fairbanks.

Later, when he starts scaling battlements and plunging down tapestries, he redeems himself, and the movie becomes a feast of physical exhilaration. In these sequences, Fairbanks is wit in motion—his acrobatics have all the comic flair that his mimed romantics so often lack. He makes no attempt at playing Robin as anything other than a modern-day American, and as he flies about the battlements, he suggests a rugged, all-American Peter Pan, a Pan with (to put it delicately) definite sexual characteristics. And therein, perhaps, lies the secret of his appeal. The original Peter Pan refused to grow up and consequently was forced to live in never-never land with the other "lost boys" and fairies. Doug's solution to the threats of manhood were less drastic. He told all the little men who adored him that they could be boys forever. All that was needed was a sense of adventure, a brawny physique, a healthy mind and a nice girl like Wendy or Maid Marian who wouldn't push a fellow into the bedroom until he was good and ready.

Nineteen twenty-two was a very good year for Pickford and

Fairbanks. After a slight decline, Mary's career was again in high gear and Doug's popularity was greater than ever; the divorce suit finally ended in victory for Mary, and their hobnobbing with the English aristocracy brought them new prestige. Suddenly, almost overnight, the delicate state of health that had plagued Mary for the previous two years disappeared, and she and Doug settled down to a gratifying routine of hard work mixed with pleasant domesticity. For a brief while, they were free of censure or scandal, except when Lottie or Jack acted up and cast a shadow over the Pickford name.

The younger Pickfords were soon to be involved in a major Prohibition scandal, and at the end of the year Jack was threatened with a subpoena to explain why he had given so many chits and checks to a well-known bootlegger. The police were called to Lottie's house one day, and the actress was found, bruised and dazed, wandering aimlessly down the street. Afterward, Lottie had a brief spell of good behavior, marrying in 1922 the most durable of her four husbands, Allan Forrest, a handsome actor whose biggest break came two years later when Pickford chose him as her leading man. Mary did not, however, look so favorably on Jack's new bride, Marilyn Miller, the "Look for the Silver Lining" heroine of Florenz Ziegfeld's *Sally*. She once called Miss Miller "the most ruthlessly ambitious woman I've ever met," and coming from Mary those are strong words.

Marilyn Miller, who had been on stage since she was four, had been groomed for stardom by her stepfather, a martinet who favored Prussian methods of discipline. "As a young girl, Marilyn danced through a hoop of lessons," said one former colleague. "Singing lessons, ballet lessons, acting lessons—that was her life. And when she was sick or for some reason missed a lesson, Mr. Miller beat her." Before she was out of her teens Marilyn was a major Broadway star; she had also managed to escape from her evil stepfather by marrying juvenile musical comedy lead, Frank Carter. The marriage ended tragically a year later when Carter was killed in a car accident. "Marilyn was never the same after that," says her former friend. "It was then that the partying began."

At a house party on Long Island, she met Jack. He was not yet over the loss of Olive Thomas; Marilyn was still recovering from Carter's death. Neither was emotionally prepared for a serious romance, or so their friends advised. Mary and Mama Charlotte weren't the only ones who disapproved—Flo Ziegfeld made a rumpus about the romance, thereby making headline news out of an affair that might otherwise have stayed in the gossip columns.

Ziegfeld's position was understandable. He didn't want to lose his biggest star to the movies and Jack Pickford; history would then be repeating itself—he had lost Olive Thomas in exactly the same way. But this time it was worse. Ziegfeld had created a show, *Sally,* to prove that Marilyn could act and sing as well as twirl on her toes (her specialty), and now that the New York engagement was ending; he wasn't about to let her run out on an exclusive contract that assured him of road tours and future Broadway bonanzas.

So he hit back at the lowest level. While *Sally* was on tour in Boston, the local police raided a party given by two show girls for a crew of wealthy Harvard jocks. Marilyn wasn't on the premises at the time, but for reasons that were never clear, her name was dragged into a case that allegedly involved party-girl prostitution and bathroom gin. Marilyn told reporters she was being framed. By whom? She wouldn't answer, but the implication was that Ziegfeld was behind the whole thing. He resented Jack Pickford. Why? Again, Marilyn avoided answering the question, though she did say she refused to let Ziegfeld into her dressing room unless her mother was present. "Flo Ziegfeld can choose my shows," she added, "but not my husband."

Ziegfeld struck back. Why did he disapprove of Jack Pickford? Look at his military record; look at Olive Thomas's suicide, and consider whether the facts printed in the papers were the true facts. His concern for Marilyn was fatherly: he did not want to watch her make "a tragic mistake." The innuendos were too much for Charlotte Pickford. There was a coroner's report to prove that there had been nothing underhanded about Olive's death, she claimed, and other documents that showed an honorable Navy discharge for Jack. She went on to suggest what many people were thinking: Ziegfeld's concern for Marilyn was perhaps more than fatherly.

Next, Billie Burke (Mrs. Ziegfeld) entered the fray. There was nothing between her husband and "Miss Miller." (A reporter noted a slight "touch of ice" in her voice as she mentioned Marilyn.) The diamonds Flo had given Marilyn were nothing more than "opening night baubles." Her husband went on with this distasteful matter only to protect Miss Miller from "young Pickford" who had already destroyed "unhappy, defenseless Olive."

The attacks and counterattacks continued until Marilyn finally promised to honor her contract for the road tour of *Sally*. This meant that her ambitions for a film career had to be set aside for at least a year and that her life with Jack would be catch-as-catch-can for an equal period of time. The détente was far from ideal, but it got Ziegfeld off everyone's backs, even persuaded him to give a quiet, succinct blessing to the marriage ("If Marilyn is happy . . .").

Once the engagement was official, Mary buried her qualms, and insisted Jack and Marilyn be married at Pickfair. It was a small affair—about forty guests and twenty photographers—held in front of an orchid-laden, improvised altar in the Pickfair living room. The string quartet from the Pickford-Fairbanks studio provided the processional as Mary, the matron-of-honor, walked down a staircase, followed by Marilyn, a vision in Georgette crepe. Only one sour note disrupted the harmony of the occasion—Marilyn had invited her former mother-in-law, Mrs. Frank Carter, but not her own mother, and Mrs. Miller was extremely open in admitting her bitterness at not being asked to the Pickfair wedding.

The next day, there were additional mother-in-law problems. For weeks the press had wanted to know where Marilyn and Jack would spend their honeymoon. Mrs. Pickford insisted that Jack report for work the Monday after the wedding—he was then filming *Garrison's Finish* (for which Mary wrote the titles), his first important role in almost two years. But, while there was no honeymoon, there was a honeymoon cottage, and on the threshold, Jack and Marilyn pecked at each other for the fan magazine photographers, as he rushed off to the studio. Two months later, when she returned to Chicago for the opening of *Sally*, the roles reversed; she rushed off to the theatre and Jack lounged about their hotel suite and the local speakeasies.

Juggling careers was only one of the problems that beset their marriage. Only a few weeks after the wedding, director James Young initiated divorce proceedings against actress Clara Kimball Young on charges of infidelity, naming as corespondent Jack Pickford, who had allegedly been intimate with his wife several times at a hotel on Catalina Island. Marilyn stood staunchly behind Jack, and since the infidelity had happened long before their courtship, she had no cause for jealousy. Still, it was a messy business, blown out of all proportion by the press, which clearly had reservations about the durability of the Pickford-Miller marriage. If the press can influence the outcome of a private affair, then certainly Jack and Marilyn never had a chance. Every squabble, every rift and reconciliation was played up until the spring of 1927 when Marilyn, after a lengthy red tape battle with French bureaucracy, divorced Jack in Paris.

10

At the end of 1920 an unheralded picture called *Passion* opened at the Capitol Theatre on Broadway. Though made in Germany, the film was advertised as "a continental production" since it was feared the American public was not yet ready to forget the war and forgive the Germans. Sauerkraut was still called "victory cabbage," and Brunnhilde, Tristan, Hansel and Gretel remained taboo at the Met. The American Legion was waging war against those Americans who were ready "to forgive and forget." In reviewing *Passion*, a historical pastiche about Madame du Barry and Louis XV, a few critics casually mentioned (usually in a concluding paragraph) that it had been made in Germany, but film fans took no notice. They flocked to see it, and the picture became one of the big hits of the year.

Overnight director Ernst Lubitsch was catapulted from obscurity to within inches of D. W. Griffith's throne. There was extravagant praise about the "masterful way" in which he combined "Reinhardt spectacle with a telling, intimate detail that brings remote history-book figures to full-dimensioned life." Lubitsch was hailed as "a genius," the picture was a "milestone," and sultry Pola Negri, its leading lady, was compared to Theda Bara, Duse and Bernhardt. The success of *Passion* opened the way for other foreign imports, and suddenly the public became aware that not all films were made in Hollywood—something that had been forgotten during the war—and that Hollywood films were not necessarily the best in the world. Foreign movies were more sophisticated in story and psychology, and technically the German productions were the equal, sometimes the superior, of those made in America.

Passion broke box-office records at the Capitol, including some set by Pickford and Fairbanks films. But it was a fluke—few foreign imports duplicated its success. They were too stylized, too arty, too "foreign," to find large audiences outside the big cities. The major Hollywood companies, namely First National and Paramount, which were responsible for the distribution of foreign films in America, soon lost interest in them as a commercial venture, but remained envious of the critical acclaim they received. So they decided to combine the best of two worlds. They would bring European film artists to Hollywood and set them to work on projects that would have appeal for the mass American audience. And so began the so-called "foreign invasion of Hollywood," though it was actually more of a raid than an invasion.

Mary and Doug, always attuned to the movie fashions of the time, were among the first Hollywood citizens to recognize the artistry and prestige of the foreign film. And it was Mary who was responsible for bringing Ernst Lubitsch to America. She paid his passage and gave him a nonexclusive, three picture contract. In doing so, she knew she was inviting the wrath of the superpatriots, and was ready to plead for total amnesty. Much to her surprise, there was not a peep of protest. Apparently, Mary Pickford, the Liberty Bond heroine, was immune to attack.

Preceded by a flurry of publicity, Lubitsch arrived in Hollywood in December 1922 with an entourage that included his wife; his Danish set designer, Sven Gade, and his secretary and first assistant, Henry Blanke. He traveled in a style befitting his reputation as Europe's foremost director, but in most other ways he suggested a Seventh Avenue furrier. A pixie of a man, with a thatch of black hair oiled down over his forehead, Lubitsch spoke heavily-accented English and continually chewed on a huge, foul-smelling cigar, scattering ashes wherever they happened to fall. German fried potatoes were the main staple of his diet, and he ate them with gusto, apparently with his fingers. Mary admits she was repelled when, after one of their early conferences, she discovered greasy fingermarks all over the freshly painted, dove-gray walls of her studio bungalow.

Lubitsch's first idea for Mary was an adaptation of *Faust,* but she was still uncertain whether her fans would accept her as an unwed mother. She suggested *Dorothy Vernon of Haddon Hall,* a once-popular novel and play about a sixteenth-century girl who is caught up in the intrigue between Queen Elizabeth and Mary Stuart. The vehicle was a warhorse of the stock-company repertory, but Mary saw Dorothy as "a contemporary woman, a modern-minded girl," and thought the story would spotlight Lubitsch's flair for combining spectacle with intimacy.

Lubitsch read the script she had had prepared, and turned thumbs down. "Der ist too many qveens and not enough qveens," he said cryptically. What he was trying to express was his feeling that the roles of the two queens overshadowed Dorothy and yet weren't powerful enough to maintain audience interest for an entire film. Mary wasn't convinced, but she didn't want to force him into working on a project he didn't like. So, as a compromise, they decided on *Rosita,* a comedy loosely based on a nineteenth-century French play about a Spanish king who loves a street singer who loves a penniless nobleman. It was far more sophisticated than anything Mary had played since her Biograph days, and undoubtedly she looked on the title role, a soubrette, as something of a challenge. Not only would she be playing a woman, but a naughty, non-WASP woman, something she hadn't attempted since *The Love Light,* and beyond that, *Madame Butterfly,* both flops. To herald her emancipation, she posed in mantilla and flouncing skirts for the studio photographer. "Yes," read a caption under one of the pictures, "Little Mary is growing up with the aid of lace and ribbons and woman-length hems and a wee coquettish fan . . . there's a hint of sex, a laughing lure in her eyes. . . ."

Mary looked charming in the photographs, but she bore only a meagre resemblance to "America's Sweetheart." Industry insiders began to question whether she had been wise to team up with Lubitsch: his films were worldly and tinged with cynicism, hers were sweet and homespun; he was an autocrat, she was known to be singleminded in her pursuit of perfection. It did not seem the best of all possible actress-and-director combinations.

Lubitsch wasn't the whipping crop and jodphur kind of director—nearly all his actors adored him—but he was always the star of his own films (unlike Marshall "Mickey" Neilan, one of Mary's favorite directors, who never tried to upstage a star, particularly when the star was Mary Pickford). He left fingerprints on his pictures as well as on dressing room walls, and was soon renowned for "the Lubitsch touch," a vague, studio-coined phrase that defies definition. If anything, it meant that Lubitsch had a distinct artistic personality that could be perceived by even the dullest member of the American public.

There was also, however, a "Pickford touch," and too many fingerprints can smudge even the best of films. It was inevitable that there would be problems, and they weren't long in surfacing. Most of the fighting took place off the set. Actress Marian Nixon, who played a small part in *Rosita,* remembers no altercations before the cast and the crew. But Hollywood was full of gossip and some of it was leaked to the press. Charles Rosher, Mary's favorite cameraman, walked off the picture, explaining that he wanted "to avoid the flying crockery." A few weeks later, a Hollywood columnist commented, "What with Ernst Lubitsch tearing up scenarios and pulling down sets at the Pickford studio and Pola Negri wrecking the morale and general proprieties at Paramount, it looks as though the German Menace will ruin Hollywood yet."

Pola Negri had arrived in Hollywood several months before her mentor, Lubitsch, and promptly set out to prove that she was, as advertised, a tempestuous femme fatale. Men flocked around her, and Pola chose the biggest catch of the lot, Charles Chaplin. Then she took on the reigning queen of the Paramount lot, Gloria Swanson, in what was to become the most highly publicized feud in American film history. Both women today claim the rivalry was a total studio fabrication, and possibly they did get along beautifully—as they imply—by ignoring each other completely.

There can be no question, however, that Pola tried to start a feud with Pickford. When Paramount assigned her Mary's old bungalow for dressing quarters, she immediately threw out all the furniture, and told the press that Mary's decor had been too frumpy for her taste. Pickford refused to be drawn into a battle. Pola could redecorate as she saw fit; there were no bad feelings; in fact, Miss Negri was a frequent guest at Pickfair. Negri did indeed come to Pickfair with Chaplin, but Mary has also hinted privately that she received many of Charlie's girl friends out of courtesy rather than affection. There was more labor than love in the Negri-Pickford relationship, particularly by mid-1923, when Pola started work on *The Spanish Dancer,* based on the same play as Mary's *Rosita.* Intentionally or not, she had placed herself in competition with Pickford.

The contest ended in a draw. In her memoirs, Pola Negri says her Spanish dancer got better reviews than Mary's Spanish singer, but overall, it didn't. *Rosita* was favorably received by the critics and did good business in its first metropolitan engagements; then it bombed out. Maybe, as film historians claim, *Rosita* was too sophisticated for provincial America, but Mary, in characteristic fashion, blamed herself. "I admire Mr. Lubitsch and his work," she told a *Photoplay* interviewer. "I had come to know and understand his kind of sophistication, but I didn't realize that he was at one extreme end and I at another extreme end of the modern social scale in the public mind. It was my own mistake. . . . Oh, *Rosita* isn't so very bad—but I might have known I am not the Spanish or Latin type. I am essentially Nordic."

Over the years Mary's opinion of *Rosita* has altered drastically. She now considers it the worst picture of her career. Lubitsch was "a director of doors," all right for certain actors (like Emil Jannings), but incapable of directing women. Considering Lubitsch's success with Negri, Pauline Frederick, Claudette Colbert, Kay Francis and Greta Garbo, this is an astonishing judgment, but understandable in the light of Mary's confession that she never saw a Lubitsch film after *Rosita*.

Today Mary refuses to allow the picture to be shown. This is unfortunate since *Rosita* is a jewel, one of the best of Lubitsch's silent films. That, of course, is the problem—it's *his* film, not Mary's. She is charming, but any one of a half-dozen other actresses could have done as well—or better. Bebe Daniels, for instance, or Gloria Swanson, Constance Talmadge, Lila Lee or Bessie Love.

The box-office failure of *Rosita* ended all plans for future collaboration between Pickford and Lubitsch. She announced that her next production would be *Dorothy Vernon of Haddon Hall* with Mickey Neilan as director. For a while Lubitsch was afraid that his Hollywood career might end with *Rosita*, but Doug, undeterred by Mary's experience, was still interested in working with the director. "If I ever direct you," Lubitsch told Fairbanks, "when you're jumping from roof to roof, I'll give you something to do on those roofs!" For a while they talked of making a pirate film, to be filmed on location at Catalina Island, but there were script problems and the production was shelved temporarily. With no immediate projects waiting for him at the Pickford-Fairbanks studio, Lubitsch decided to move on, first to Warner Brothers, then Paramount.

Mary and Doug were always most diplomatic in speaking publicly about Lubitsch, and he was guarded in his opinion of them. As near as he came to an open confession of his feelings was made many years later. "Mary is the most practical woman

I know. She talks money, discusses contracts and makes important decisions with disconcerting speed. And yet nothing of this prevents her from playing scenes filled with sweetness and passion."

Doug had wanted Lubitsch to direct "his pirate picture," a vague title for a glimmer of an idea, something Fairbanks kept turning over in his mind as he rejected earlier projects. The rights to Booth Tarkington's *Monsieur Beaucaire* were sold to Paramount for Rudolph Valentino, and *The Virginian* was abandoned when Mary decided Doug would be miscast in the title role. "You see," Fairbanks told a reporter, "it's a question whether people will accept me as the Virginian, that slow-moving, soft-speaking, easygoing hero of the plains that Owen Wister made all America love. Temperamentally, I am just the opposite . . ."

There was nothing definite about Doug's next film except its leading lady. In 1922 he saw *The Spanish Jade,* a British film produced by his friend, Tom Geraghty. The title role (Manuela, "a daughter of Old Spain") was played by an American actress who had made a small splash in English films, a striking and sultry beauty named Evelyn Brent (best remembered today as "Feathers" in von Sternberg's *Underworld*). Fairbanks was so taken by her that he brought her to Hollywood and placed her under contract for his next picture.

Arriving in California, Evelyn discovered that Doug was still undecided about his next film. While he delayed, she posed for photographers and talked to reporters who hailed her as the star of tomorrow. None of Doug's earlier leading ladies had ever been given such a buildup, and soon rumors spread that there was more than a professional bond between Brent and Fairbanks. According to gossip, he onced tried to scale the wall that surrounded her home, much to the distress of her husband, film producer Bernard Fineman, whom she had secretly married soon after her arrival in Hollywood.

In June 1923 Brent broke her contract because, the press was informed, she was weary of waiting for her big break.

The explanation is suspect since by this time Fairbanks was working on an Arabian Nights fantasy, *The Thief of Bagdad*. And before leaving the Pickfair studios, Evelyn posed for publicity stills in Oriental costumes that were clearly intended to suggest the setting of the forthcoming Fairbanks production. Consequently her departure caused a good deal of speculation around Hollywood.

A few months later, *Screenland,* one of the most popular of the fan magazines, told its readers what all Beverly Hills was whispering about. According to the article, Mary had gotten wind of the romance and had immediately ordered Evelyn Brent off the Pickfair lot. Doug meekly obeyed and then hired a new "discovery," vaudeville dancer Julanne Johnston to play his leading lady in *The Thief of Bagdad.*

Shortly after the article appeared, Mary and Doug instituted a $100,000 libel suit against *Screenland.* Evelyn Brent and her husband were also ready to seek legal redress, but before they could do so, Mary and Doug dropped the suit. Many people regretted their change of heart since there was a growing resentment about the fan magazines' lack of journalistic ethics. Doug and Mary never explained why they withdrew their suit, and so one can only presume that their primary goal had been to call public attention to fan-magazine scandalmongering. Still, their sudden about-face lent support to rumors that there was more than smoke behind the Brent affair.

Doug's friends insist that there was nothing between him and Miss Brent. The majority don't recall the incident at all, while those with longer memories refuse to give it much credence. "I would doubt very much if it were true," said Anita Loos. "Doug was too much in love with the idea of being Mary Pickford's husband. I don't think he would have done anything to endanger his position as the king of Hollywood."

In 1923 Fairbanks celebrated his fortieth birthday. He was remarkably fit for his age, but still he was forty, a trifle mature for the swashbuckling heroes he played on screen. For his fans, however, he was as youthful as ever, an illusion Doug carefully nurtured with photographs of his strenuous physical activities: sparring bouts with Jack Dempsey, hurdle-races with acrobat-actor Fred Stone, tennis matches with Wimbledon champions. Who would believe he was forty? No one perhaps, if his thirteen-year-old son had not unexpectedly achieved national prominence.

Young Doug had never figured importantly in the publicity about his father, and after the divorce he was rarely mentioned. Since then, his mother had gone through one husband and almost all her divorce settlement. Beth had played the stock market and lost; then, ostensibly for young Doug's schooling but really to take advantage of the favorable exchange rate, she moved to Europe. She was pawning her jewels when producer Jesse Lasky decided Doug, Jr. had the potential of becoming the next Jackie Coogan. Desperate for money—she was also supporting her father—Beth accepted Lasky's offer.

Unaware of his ex-wife's financial problems, Fairbanks was sharply outspoken about what he called "the exploitation" of their son. He was right, of course; young Doug was being pushed into a career solely because he happened to bear the Fairbanks name. And he brought it no honor. Young Doug's first picture, *Stephen Steps Out,* was a flop. Even worse, in the picture Doug, Jr. is a pudgy kid whose mealy body discredited all his dad's ideas about physical fitness.

In a few years, Doug Jr. lost his baby fat and gained an androgynous David Bowie-type elegance. (In the 1929 *Woman of Affairs* he and Garbo make the most glamorous brother and sister team in film history.) Later still, he was to surpass his father in both looks and acting ability, though never in sheer magnetism. But young Doug was a slow starter—his career did not get off the ground until the late 1920s—and it was some time before his father accepted his choice of profession.

These were rough years for Beth and her son, but they

never requested financial support from Fairbanks. Young Doug occasionally visited Pickfair where he found a friend in Mary. His father, however, continued to regard him with a reproachful eye.

There was an obvious reason for his resentment. Shortly after young Doug's arrival in Hollywood, a trade columnist wrote, "Thus far Douglas Fairbanks, Sr. has essayed the role that was essentially boyish, the role that wasn't conspicuous for its gray matter either on the outside or the inside of the head. But with Doug Jr. in the game, will not the very fact of his existence be an ever-present reminder that Doug Sr. is past the first flush of youth, and will it not induce him to forego the juvenile for the more mature?"

Fairbanks's answer to this question was a resounding no. He went right ahead with his plans to play *The Thief of Bagdad,* the most dashing and exotic role of his career. Previously Doug had kept his wiry body under wraps, but in *Bagdad* he would strip to the waist for several scenes. To get in shape, he wrestled daily with a trainer named Abdullah until his musculature would have been the envy of a twenty-year-old Olympic gymnast. To accentuate his steely chest, he wore a pair of sheer harem pants, designed to suggest those worn by Michael Fokine in the Diaghilev-Baskt ballet, *Scheherazade.*

Diaghilev and Fairbanks sound like a startling combination, but *Bagdad* was a very art-conscious movie. Budgeted at $2,000,000 (nearly three times as much as *Robin Hood*), it was in fact the most ambitious and daring production of Doug's career. In part it owes a debt to Fritz Lang's *Der Müde Tod (Destiny),* which Fairbanks purchased and withheld from American distribution until he had copied many of its special effects, including a flying carpet, a winged horse and a magic army that appears and disappears at the thief's command. Maxfield Parrish, the famous illustrator, was hired to create the sets, but his designs were considered impractical, and none of his work was used except in a striking advertising poster.

Parrish was replaced by William Cameron Menzies who worked in the tradition of the German studio productions. The world of the film was totally artificial: trees were painted, objects and architecture were built out of human proportion and a highly-polished floor was devised to reflect buildings which had been painted darker at the top so that they appeared to float. Thus, Bagdad was turned into an Art Nouveau dream city, exotic, overripe and otherworldly.

These stylized trappings caused Doug to alter drastically his style of performance. About all that remains of the old Fairbanks is the film's simplistic message: "Happiness must be earned." The jumping-jack vigor of the past has been replaced by a gliding and graceful dancelike movement that seems to have been inspired by Nijinski. Doug seems at ease with it, but still, it doesn't sit right with the viewer; somehow it's too flossy for Fairbanks. Even worse, the picture doesn't give him much opportunity for stunts; the portions of the script usually given over to acrobatics are here taken up by trick effects, and they are of variable quality. The magic carpet is smashing, but the winged horse is a real disappointment—instead of flying, he gallops through the skies in all-too-apparent superimposition.

As a result, *The Thief of Bagdad* has nearly as many dead spots as moments of genuine enchantment, very few of which are supplied by Doug. Half-nude, he is the personification of masculine glamor and more than holds his own against the imposing sets; but when he puts on a Sultan's jacket and turban, he fades into the decor. Here, as in *Robin Hood*, he is upstaged by supporting cast members, especially Anna May Wong and So-Jin, a wizened Japanese actor with an uncanny resemblance to Joel Grey.

Doug, however, was confident that *Bagdad* would be the crowning achievement of his career. Determined to make it the leading event of the 1924 movie season, he took it out of the regular UA program and set up a separate distribution unit to book it. This maneuver distressed the United Artists board of directors, and the resulting tension spawned rumors that Mary and Doug were thinking about leaving UA and returning to Paramount.

The fracas over *Bagdad* was not the only basis for these rumors. Mary and Doug, it was said, were finding their dual capacity as producer and star more taxing and less financially rewarding than they had expected; according to this argument, they could have earned nearly as much money and with one half the headaches if they worked for an established studio. Mary, in particular, was spending more on her productions (between $300,000 and $600,000) than was justified by their box-office returns, something that would never have happened at Paramount or First National. And if they did sign with a studio, it seemed inevitable that it would be Paramount, not only because of past ties but also because Zukor owned the rights to *Peter Pan,* a property Mary was eager to film.

But in the spring of 1924 they were too occupied with launching *The Thief of Bagdad* to think about future plans. The opening was held in New York, and they arrived two weeks early to work out the final arrangements. As usual, they stayed at the Ritz-Carlton and as usual they were given a royal welcome. Nearly every night, there was a dinner party in their honor, one of the most glittering hosted by playwright J. Hartley Manners and his actress-wife, the incomparable Laurette Taylor. Laurette had met Mary and Doug a year earlier when she went to Hollywood to film her greatest stage success, *Peg O' My Heart.* For a time, there had been talk about Mary playing Peg on screen, and Laurette had generously approved this casting; she was a dedicated Pickford fan. Later, when through a complicated set of circumstances, she got the opportunity to recreate the role for film, she was genuinely grateful that Mary and Doug made her feel at home around the Pickfair swimming pool. Doug even dropped by the set of *Peg* and improvised a little scene for Taylor and her beloved canine co-star, a mutt named Michael.

Laurette's way of reciprocating was to give a dinner party in Mary and Doug's honor at her neo-Gothic town house on Riverside Drive. The guest list, which included Nazimova, two Barrymores, the very young (pre-*Vortex*) Noel Coward and half-a-dozen good society names, was so glamorous that it merited mention in the society columns of *The New York Times*. Mary and Doug were all over the front pages of the Manhattan tabloids. A few days after Laurette's party, they were again in the spotlight as guests at a special matinée of Max Reinhardt's *The Miracle,* the theatrical event of the 1924 season.

For the presentation of *The Miracle,* Reinhardt and his flamboyant producer, Morris Gest, had transformed the inside of the old (now demolished) Century Theatre into a Gothic cathedral, extending the decor beyond the proscenium arch and into the auditorium and the theatre lobby. One doubtful critic said the only thing miraculous about *The Miracle* was its scenery, and according to individual taste, Reinhardt's production could be seen either as an early example of "environmental" or "total theatre" or a vain attempt to duplicate onstage the scenic splendors of film. Doug's response to *The Miracle* was unreservedly enthusiastic, so much so that he immediately hired Morris Gest to oversee the premiere of *The Thief of Bagdad.*

Gest was a master showman in the tradition of his father-in-law, David Belasco. His eclectic taste ranged from Eleanora Duse and the Moscow Art Theatre to *Chu Chin Chow* and the *Chauve-Souris* revues, all of which he imported from Europe. He breathed and talked art, but frequently confused it with kitsch; in other words he (like Belasco before him) was the Broadway equivalent of a Hollywood producer. So it seems only appropriate that Fairbanks chose him to mastermind the *Bagdad* premiere.

The picture opened at the Liberty Theatre, a legitimate house which charged advanced prices for its two-a-day screening. This kind of "special engagement" booking was not unusual even in 1924, but then as now, it's tricky business, dooming those films that don't live up to the advance publicity to half-empty houses while the public waits for second-run engagements at regular prices.

For the opening, Gest turned the Liberty into an Arabian Nights *Miracle*. According to *The New York Mirror,*

> the theatre fairly dripped atmosphere, much of it coming out of censers. The stage settings were most lofty and miraculous in its (sic) workings. The walls of the auditorium were hung with painting by Pagany—enlargements many of them of his exquisite illustrations for the Holt "Arabian Nights." In the lobby, there were tapestries, incense, rugs and silks, Turkish coffee and a caravan of Oriental singers who chanted songs of welcome. . . .

Outside, a crowd of 5,000 had gathered, and when Mary stepped out of her limousine, she was nearly crushed. Doug grabbed her and carried her into the theatre on his shoulders, a protective and spontaneous gesture, perhaps, but still one that was now a ritual of every Pickford and Fairbanks public appearance. Laurette Taylor was there as were two of the Barrymores and at least a quarter of New York's social four hundred.

The first reviews backed up Fairbanks's opinion that *Bagdad* was his greatest achievement to date. And the box-office returns at the Liberty and other first-run theatres were also encouraging. It wasn't until several months later, when the picture started its second-run engagements, that it became evident that *Bagdad* wasn't going to duplicate *Robin Hood*'s success. It was too slow-moving for children, too dreamy and epicene for Doug's regular fans. *Bagdad* grossed almost as well as *Robin Hood,* but since it cost three times as much, the net profit wasn't nearly as impressive. As a result, this was to be Fairbanks's only attempt to combine European artistry with the vitality of the American action film. From here on, he played safe.

11

Once *The Thief of Bagdad* had opened, Mary and Doug took off on another European tour. With Charlotte in tow, they sailed on the *Olympic* at midnight on April 12, 1924. Their departure was mentioned in the papers, and to prevent riots, the White Star Line barred all visitors and ordered passengers to be on board at least two hours before sailing time. This put a crimp in the plans for bon voyage parties, and caused considerable disappointment to the throngs of fans who arrived too late to see the Fairbankses walk up the gangway. But Mary and Doug made amends by appearing on deck as the ship moved out to sea, waving and blowing kisses to the crowd on shore.

The first-class passenger list was a glitter of celebrity names, including Pablo Casals, D. W. Griffith and the young Noel Coward, still a few months away from his first great theatrical success, *The Vortex*. In *Present Indicative* Coward admits that he was then "a bad celebrity snob," and that he went after Mary and Doug with all "the calculation and practised aim of a lion hunter." Aboard the *Olympic* the three formed a close friendship. They spent most of the voyage together, many hours wiled away on parlor games, at which Coward was especially adept, and on conjuring tricks, Doug's latest passion.

Also on board were two or three "Bright Young Things,"

including The Hon. Richard Norton and his wife, Jean, who, before landing, invited Mary and Doug to a dinner party for the Prince of Wales. Could they bring Noel, they asked? They could and did, and Noel was exceedingly grateful, though he paid for his supper by playing the piano for most of the evening. He was not the only performer, however; Doug closed the party with a few magic tricks.

Partying with the aristocracy was, of course, no novelty for Mary and Doug, but on this occasion they may have had reason to believe they would not be welcomed in the better Mayfair drawing rooms. During the past year, the Mountbattens had visited Pickfair, and taken part in one of Doug's home movies. Stills of Lady Edwina being molested by a trampish Charlie Chaplin appeared in several fan magazines. On returning to England, the Mountbattens were severely reprimanded by their uncle, King George V. But the incident had no repercussions—Mary and Doug were still welcome in the homes of their upper-crust British friends.

After visiting Warwick castle, Kenilworth and Haddon Hall (a publicity jaunt for Mary's forthcoming film), they moved on to the continent, visiting Paris, Madrid, Aix-les-Bains, Interlocken, Berne, Lucerne, Zurich, Munich, Berlin, Oslo, Copenhagen, Amsterdam and Brussels before returning to New York less than three months after they had sailed on the *Olympic*. It was a spectacularly successful tour, yielding hundreds of photographs of Mary and Doug shaking hands with international personages, all of them rushed back to the States and printed in the rotogravure sections of the Sunday papers. The only ticklish moment came in Copenhagen. Mary and Doug arrived expecting to meet King Gustave, but were informed by an embarrassed press attaché that the King had never heard of them. A day later, after being told that only a nincompoop could be unaware of Mary and Doug, Gustave graciously granted them an audience.

It was after this tour that the following joke began to circulate around Hollywood:

Q: Why does Doug Fairbanks go to Europe every year?
A: To book his royal visitors for the next year.

And indeed this was the beginning of the invasion of Pickfair by aristocratic visitors. For the next seven years there was a seemingly endless succession of dukes and duchesses, earls, marchese, diplomats, even a minor king or two—a jumble of illustrious sounding names that can be sorted out only by consulting the *Almanach de Gotha*. And even there one may draw a blank for the good reason that Mary and Doug were sometimes taken in by a phony title. According to one story (possibly apocryphal), an elegantly clad young woman drove up to Pickfair in a chauffeured Rolls-Royce and announced that she was the Princess Vera Romanoff. Mary and Doug entertained her regally for a weekend and then, after her departure, discovered she was really a secretary from Santa Monica.

On another occasion, a countess of doubtful authenticity asked if she could spend three days at Pickfair on her way to Hawaii. Eleven months later, she was finally persuaded to continue her journey. By that time she had gone through over three hundred bottles of champagne, having insisted that she had to have a glass or two every morning as an eye-opener.

These anecdotes made the rounds of Hollywood and caused a lot of merriment, nearly all of it at Doug's expense. Mary was not immune to the splendor of her important guests —she admits in her autobiography that she was once staggered by the thought that the King of Siam was sitting in her bathtub—but she always kept a sense of proportion. She liked people for what they were, while Doug could forgive them anything if they had a title attached to their name. His snobbishness had never been exactly a secret, but now it was out in the open and even his closest friends ribbed him good-naturedly. Charlie Chaplin once greeted him with the question, "Hello, Doug, how's the duke?"

"What duke?" Fairbanks asked.

"Oh . . . any duke," Charlie replied innocently.

Above left, Mary and her mother, Charlotte Pickford. *Above right,* Mary and her first husband, Owen Moore.

Right, Mary, in a typical "little girl" costume.

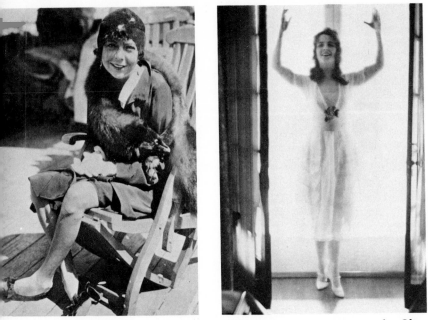

Above left, Lottie Pickford, in a demure moment. *Above right,* Olive Thomas, Jack Pickford's first wife. *Below,* Jack Pickford and Marilyn Miller on their honeymoon.

Above, Frances Marion and Mary, in a story conference. *Below,* Chaplin signs his first United Artists contract, as (from left) D. W. Griffith, Pickford, H. T. Benzhopf, Dennis O'Brien and Doug look on.

Above, Mary promotes Liberty Bonds. *Below,* A composite publicity still, showing Mary in her roles in *Stella Maris.*

Above, Doug clowning in front of his pre-Pickfair Hollywood home, Spaulding Manor. *Below,* Pickfair as refurbished in the early 1930s.

Left, Doug and Mary sailing away on the *Lapland* for their honeymoon (1920).

Below, Mary and Doug on their honeymoon in England. *Right,* Doug and Mary on their wooden (fifth) anniversary (Mary gave Doug a Douglas fir).

Top, Mary visiting Doug on set of *The Three Musketeers. Center,* Fooling around on the United Artists lot. *Left,* Photographer Charles Rosher adjusting Mary's first stand-in, "Maria."

Top, Mary with the Duchess de Penaranda and the Duchess of Alba (Catalina Island). *Center,* Mary hosts a meeting of "Our Club." *Right,* Place setting at Pickfair.

Above, Maurice Tourneur and Mary on set of *The Poor Little Rich Girl* (1917). *Below,* Cecil B. De Mille and Mary on location for *A Romance of the Redwoods* (1917).

Above, Mary, Charles Rosher and Sam Taylor mugging for the cameras, during shooting of *My Best Girl* (1927). *Below,* Doug and Mary confer with Ernst Lubitsch on set of *Rosita* (1923).

Above, Doug as the Thief of Bagdad (1924). *Below,* Doug as Robin Hood (1922).

Above, Doug as D'Artagnon in *The Iron Mask* (1929). *Below,* Doug as the Black Pirate (1926).

Above, Mary, Jack, Mrs. Pickford and Doug attend a Hollywood premiere. *Below,* Mary and Doug giving the fascist salute in front of the Arch of Titus. *Right,* Mary as Katherine in *The Taming of the Shrew.*

Left, Doug, Jr.

Center, Lady Sylvia Ashley and Doug. *Bottom,* Mrs. and Mr. Harold Lloyd congratulate Mary and Buddy Rogers after the wedding.

But this much can be said in defense of Doug's infatuation with royalty: it was one he shared with a good number of people in Hollywood. This was the era when it was fashionable for movie actresses to return from Europe with a titled husband as a souvenir: Mae Murray wed a Georgian prince named David Mdivani and Pola Negri married his brother, Serge. Gloria Swanson married the Marquis de la Falaise de la Coudrey, who after their divorce married Constance Bennett. (There were catty remarks that Pola had married Serge only because, as a princess, she would outrank Gloria, her arch-rival, who was only a marquise.) When Swanson and Coudrey returned to Hollywood, Paramount gave its employees a holiday to meet the newlyweds' train; they were joined by Mary, Doug and other figureheads of the industry, and the carryings-on at the station might have seemed excessive even as a welcome for the King and Queen of England.

By this time, a new era in the history of Hollywood society was beginning. As Mary had pointed out long before, the movies had allowed the actor to escape from bohemianism into middle-class respectability; having taken that step, he was now becoming a real social climber. And it wasn't just the actor who was status crazy; it was also the producer, the director, the entire front rank of the industry.

Inevitably, this status-seeking crept into the American film, starting with the bon ton society comedies Cecil B. De Mille produced in the late teens and early twenties. These overdressed fantasies had about as much to do with high life as window shopping along Fifth Avenue, and were equally voyeuristic, until Lubitsch (after his *Rosita* fiasco) took up the genre and added some continental wit and savoir faire to the De Mille formula. But Lubitsch was the exception; on the whole, Hollywood's infatuation with royalty, wealth and high birth was heavy-handed and double-edged. All those penthouse dramas in which the likes of Pauline Frederick and Joan Crawford and Constance Bennett suffer gallantly in diamonds and satin end on the same moral note: poor is rotten, rich is rottener. Or, to phrase it the other way round, money and rank aren't everything, but nothing's worth much without them.

The films about royalty, which fall roughly into three categories, show the same ambivalence. First, in pictures like *Orphans of the Storm, The Patriot* and *The Scarlet Empress,* kings and queens and their courts are depicted as corrupt, frivolous or simple-minded, and while the overall tone is disapproving, there is a lot of lip-smacking over the lavish decadence. Then there are the string of naughty comedies (running from *The King on Main Street* in 1925 to *The Prince and the Showgirl* in 1957) about a royal playboy with a letch for a plebeian glamor girl; here the message seems to be that beneath their britches all men are brothers. Finally, there are the romances like Molnar's *The Swan* (filmed three times) and (to pick a recent, well-known example) *Roman Holiday,* in which (usually) a princess falls in love with a commoner, only to renounce him when she learns duty comes before affection.

Of the lot, the last group is the least amusing, but also the most revealing about Hollywood's attitude toward royalty. In none of these pictures is there any indication that the hero or heroine has the ability or wisdom to rule; the only qualification for kingship is a pretty face. And they are motivated by nothing more than a sense of noblesse oblige toward their subjects who are yet ever-present as a threatening moralistic force.

Glamor; noblesse oblige; an unknowable, censorious public —as interpreted by Hollywood, kingship was akin to stardom, particularly Mary and Doug's brand of our-duty-is-to-our-fans stardom. And, indeed, by 1924 the references to Mary and Doug as the King and Queen of Hollywood were beginning to lose their metaphorical quotation marks. A Hollywood aristocracy was being born, and Doug and Mary were the crowned leaders.

Like the kings and queens who capered through Hollywood comedies, there were moments when Mary and Doug set aside their scepters and acted like the common folk. "Do

You Know How They Play?" the *Los Angeles Examiner* asked its readers:

> Just the way you do—if you have any love for the outdoors at all. They adore a day's outing which pauses at noon on the top of a mountain where, in their old clothes, they can make a fire and Doug can fry bacon and eggs while Mary makes toast on a long stick.

Well, there were long tramps by horseback through the canyons around Los Angeles, but when Mary and Doug and their guests paused for lunch, the meal (maybe steak and eggs and Florida grapefruit) had been prepared by the kitchen staff of Pickfair, some of them sent out in advance to set up picnic tables.

Probably not all the lords and ladies who visited Pickfair liked being awakened at dawn for a trip to the canyons or the beach, and at least one took a dim view of the Pickfair accommodations. "Tell me," asked an English duke, "do you still live in that quaint little cottage?" Doug was at a loss for an answer. Pickfair was growing more elegant each day, and now, when the guests sat down to dinner the majordomo placed a printed menu before each gold place setting. Still, it was a cottage compared to San Simeon, the Nymphenburg of the West Coast. A weekend invitation to San Simeon was even more prestigious than a party at Pickfair, and Hearst's folly might have become Hollywood's royal residence had it not been so damp, had Hearst not been so moody and teetotaling a host . . . had his relationship with Marion Davies been more orthodox.

The Hearst papers had once promoted Marion Davies as a Mary Pickford challenger, but the two actresses were friends and there was never any social or professional rivalry between them. Mary was the Queen while Marion, God bless her, was the royal wench. She was pretty and sharp and witty, but no one ever mistook her diamond and blood-red ruby bracelets for the crown jewels.

Davies would never have been capable of striking (in

Allene Talmey's words) "the necessary air of dignity, sobriety and aristocracy" that Mary and Doug brought to their monarchal roles. The comment was not intended kindly, but as Mary's friends point out, she deserves credit for what she achieved. "It's really remarkable, considering her background, that Mary was able to entertain kings and presidents with such ease," says Leatrice Joy. "I don't think anyone else in Hollywood could have managed it nearly as well."

How much Mary enjoyed it is another matter. Miss Joy remembers an occasion when she and her husband, actor John Gilbert, came to Pickfair for an afternoon of tennis. While the men were on the court, Miss Joy joined some other guests at the pool. Mary sat apart from the others, speaking to no one until she called out, "Come here and talk to me, Leatrice. You're one of the sunshine people."

There are other anecdotes that suggest Mary felt somewhat remote from the life around her, that for her taste there was too much starch and not enough sunshine at Pickfair. Once Jack Pickford and his current leading lady, Beatrice Lillie, dropped by for one of Mary and Doug's Sunday tea-and-swim parties; as they strolled across the back lawn, Jack and Bea were lost in deep conversation, and they never paused or looked around, not even on reaching the edge of the pool; descending the steps, they swam to the far end, fully clothed and never interrupting their tête-à-tête. The guests around the Pickfair pool watched them in dead, disapproving silence until Mary broke the tension with a peal of laughter. Everybody joined her, but some of the amusement was noticeably forced.

Mary occasionally ribbed Doug about his snobbishness. "She laughed at his pretensions," recalls Anita Loos. "Not nastily, but still it hurt, because she was right and he was wrong." Here was the beginning of a gulf that would soon widen and bring friction to their marriage.

After the disappointment of *Bagdad*, Doug retreated to less pretentious, more familiar terrain in *Don Q, Son of Zorro*, a sequel to his first swashbuckler. It's an enjoyable picture, crammed with action and graced by the presence of its porcelain-pretty leading lady, Mary Astor; but like most sequels, its charms are slightly faded. Still, the critics welcomed it with genuine enthusiasm, a particularly interesting tribute coming from Iris Barry of the London *Spectator:*

> . . . . this rapid, almost Mozartian picture is very closely akin, in another medium, to those newer ballets, like *Les Matelots,* which the Diaghilev company has invented. The patterns which the slender black figure of Fairbanks makes in the unbounded scene of the cinema are as rhythmical as the equally, practically, almost everyday movements of the Diaghilev dancers . . . he is no longer the purely-athletic film star he once was, any more than ballet-dancers are pure athletes. His movements are almost poetically graceful, and what is more they are infused with a light spirit of comedy.

There is more to this review than initially meets the eye. First of all, the high-flown comparisons, while not inappropriate, are pretty heavy baggage for a picture as slender as *Don Q.* But they are typical of the time; by 1925, film had achieved respectability, and critics were overselling it as an art form. (The same is true today.) And it's also fascinating that Doug is praised for his physical grace and comic flair at the very time when these gifts, fully expressed in even his earliest films, were beginning to lose their spontaneity. This, too, is typical of modern-day film criticism, and it always signifies a certain turning point in a star's career: when an actor is lavishly praised for jumping through the same old hoops, he's no longer an actor, he's an institution.

By no means was Doug worn out, but signs of fatigue and age did creep into *Don Q.* In the picture, he plays two roles— the fifty-year-old Zorro and Zorro's son, Don Q. Using as few close-ups as possible, Fairbanks manages to create the illusion of youth, and his dexterity with a whip (a skill he picked up for the film) is far more exciting than any of the stunts in *Bagdad*. But there's a bad moment when he uses the whip as a rope and descends from it with perceptibly unsteady footing. In that split second as he flounders for a safe landing, it's apparent that Fairbanks has seen better days. And all the talk about Mozart and Diaghilev would never persuade his fans otherwise.

Age was also a problem for Mary, though unlike Doug, who had his bad angles and bad days, she was extraordinarily photogenic, and in 1924 looked nearly as fresh and youthful as she had when she first walked through the door of the Biograph studio. Her problem was that the public wanted her to be even younger than she was in her Griffith films. The failure of *Rosita* had been followed by the fiasco of *Dorothy Vernon of Haddon Hall*, a lavishly produced spectacle, which was nearly as stuffy as its title suggests. Opening to lukewarm reviews in the spring of 1924, the picture did well in its early advanced-price bookings (*Variety* implied the gross receipts were padded), but business fell off drastically when it went into general release.

The taste of failure always put Mary on her mettle, and she was determined to follow *Rosita* and *Dorothy Vernon* with a smash success. For a while, it looked as if James M. Barrie's *Peter Pan* would be her next picture. The choice of the actress to play Peter caused almost as much studio-inspired public controversy as the search for Scarlett O'Hara a decade later: every "winsome" actress in Hollywood was suggested for the part, including Lillian Gish, May MacAvoy and Marguerite Clark. Defying the stage tradition that the role be played by a woman, actor Gareth Hughes campaigned for the assignment with the quip, "Why must it always be a peterless Pan?"

Hughes never stood a chance. The leading contenders were Gish and Pickford, and possibly if Paramount had met her demands, Mary would have won the role. Adolph Zukor wanted Pickford back on the Paramount lot, and aware of her recent difficulties with United Artists, he told her she could play Peter only as part of a multipicture deal. But by this time the troubles had been solved—it had been agreed that every UA producer had the right to choose the form of distribution he wanted for his films, and could set the rental fees he thought best. Once this was settled, Mary and Doug were content to stay at United Artists.

With Pickford out of the race, Paramount started a talent search for Peter, with James M. Barrie serving as the final judge. Barrie chose Betty Bronson, a young actress with only a few minor screen appearances to her credit. It was a good choice: even *Pan* haters have to admit that the film version is engaging, and that Miss Bronson makes an enchanting Peter. But her big break never led to major stardom. Paramount launched Bronson as "the new Mary Pickford," and many years later she ruefully confessed that she thought Zukor and his colleagues would have preferred the old Mary Pickford.

The difficulty was that there wasn't enough room for two Mary Pickfords in jazz-age America. The bathtub-gin generation went to the movies to see dimpled knees and Clara Bow, dancing daughters and Erich von Stroheim—they didn't want Pickford *or* her imitators. Maybe they would have taken to Mary if she had bobbed her hair and bee-stung her lips, but probably not. She belonged to a generation that believed in valentines and vanilla ice cream. And if she had pleased the flapper set, she would have lost her diehard fans, the women, children and family audience that made a ritual of attending the neighborhood movie once or twice a week. This was the audience that rejected *Rosita* (too spicy) and *Dorothy Vernon* (too "antique"), that looked for reassurance in the loose moral climate of Prohibition, that wanted Mary to remain as child-like and innocent as they no longer were.

The backward expectations of her fans must have become depressingly clear to Mary early in 1925 when *Photoplay* asked its readers to name the roles they most wanted her to play. The list started with *Cinderella* (which she had filmed in 1911); next came *Anne of Green Gables* (made with Mary

Miles Minter in 1919); and then *Alice in Wonderland* and *Heidi*. Young as she looked, Mary was now past the age of making a believable Heidi, and while *Alice in Wonderland* intrigued her as a producer, she wasn't interested in playing the title role. And with good reason—Alice is continually upstaged by the weird beasts of Carroll's phantasmagorical menagerie.

Just in case Mary missed the message, *Photoplay* awarded a special citation to a woman who wrote pleading that "Miss Pickford never abandon an illusion that there are such little girls and that we have one before us: an illusion that [she is] a little girl in spite of the fact we know [she is] a grown woman." In other words, for her fans, Mary was the female, real-life Peter Pan, the little girl who shouldn't grow up.

To oblige her public, Mary chose as her 1925 film, *Little Annie Rooney,* based on a popular song of the 1890s. It tells the story of a girl who sets out to avenge the death of her father, a New York cop. Annie was one of Mary's halfway roles: she was little, but big enough for puppy-love feelings toward the ruffian who is falsely suspected of killing her dad. Eventually she not only proves him innocent but also consents to a blood transfusion that saves his life. No petting, no kissing, just the intermingling of body fluids—one wonders what Freud would have made of it.

Little Annie Rooney is one of Mary's dampest films. There are so many tearjerking scenes that director William Beaudine once alerted the crew, "Man the lifeboats, boys! Mary is going to cry!" Those tears turned into box office gold: *Annie Rooney* was Mary's first substantial success in three years.

12

One day during the filming of *Little Annie Rooney*, Mary returned to Pickfair from the studio and received a phone call from Doug. "Where are you?" he asked anxiously.

A dumb question deserves a dumb answer, but before Mary could say she was in the Taj Mahal, the anxiety in her husband's voice called her up short. "Stay where you are," Doug barked. "I'll be right home. Don't let anyone in."

There were a raft of kidnappings in the mid and late 1920s, and as Mary was soon informed, she was scheduled as the next victim. The plot, which had been leaked to the police, called for sandbagging her chauffeur, followed by the gagging and blindfolding of Pickford who would be held captive in a Santa Monica hideaway until a $100,000 ransom was coughed up. Mary was not the only target; Jackie Coogan, Pola Negri and oil millionaire E. L. Doheny III were also on the kidnappers' list.

The police insisted they had to wait for the kidnappers to make the first move. So Mary was asked to follow her regular schedule, though certain precautions were taken to guard against accident. When her Rolls-Royce left Pickfair each morning, her stand-in, not Mary, was in the back seat. And at the studio, she was protected by a plainclothesman and a pearl-handled Colt .45 that Doug taught her to use in case of emergency.

But it never went that far. Within a few weeks, the kidnappers were apprehended before they had time to put their plan into action. There were three conspirators—a butcher, a car salesman and a Wells Fargo delivery man; one was acquitted, the other two sentenced from ten years to life imprisonment in San Quentin.

This was not Mary and Doug's first or last brush with crime. A few months before, burglars had tried to invade Pickfair and a few months later there was another kidnapping plot involving Mary. A convict in the Oklahoma State Prison at Muskogee confessed that he and three friends were planning to abduct Mary, Jackie Coogan, Aimee Semple MacPherson and two Oklahoma heiresses, Maud Lee Mudd and Hattie Dickson. The confession was suspect, but Doug took precautions anyway. Soon, Pickfair was guarded by watchdogs, plainclothesmen and an alarm system that sounded in the local police precinct.

The alarm system did not, however, scare off the parasites who used legal action to get a share of the Pickfair fortune. There were plagiarism suits, including one against Mary's next film, *Sparrows*. And shortly after winning her court battle with agent Cora Welkenning, she was again sued for back wages by Edward Henmer who claimed to have acted as her manager between 1915 and 1918. As verification, he told of Charlotte's objections to the Fairbanks alliance and then went on to speak of an incident that allegedly took place just before Mary met Doug.

According to Henmer, one morning at 3 A.M., he and Mrs. Pickford had "rescued" Mary from the Manhattan apartment of a "prominent movie director" and returned her to her home in the Hotel Knickerbocker. Then, the next morning, Zukor and Charlotte sent Mary to California "to separate her from the director." (No name was mentioned, but according to gossip, Henmer's mystery man was James Kirkwood, who directed all the films Pickford made in New York in 1915.)

Mary got a court order restraining Henmer from talking to the press, but she needn't have bothered. The public chose to ignore Henmer's stories—as did the court; the case was eventually dismissed in Mary's favor. Neither flop films nor salacious gossip could ever alter the devotion of Mary's fans. For them, she would always be a shining symbol of uplift and propriety. At the time Henmer was telling tales out of school, the director of The Cleanliness Institute of New York suggested that bathtubs be renamed "Beauty Parlors of Mary Pickford" to interest young girls in feminine hygiene. Within the same month, a political commentator predicted that if the American people were forced to elect a woman President, they would undoubtedly choose Mary. And a year later, when a group of celebrated actresses formed an organization (informally known as "Our Club") to advise and protect newcomers to Hollywood, they unanimously elected Pickford as their president.

"Our Club" was little more than a glamorous coffee klatch, but Mary took her duties seriously. For "the young hopeful," she prepared a list of what she called "The Ten Film Commandments." Some of her suggestions were eminently practical—"have another vocation to fall back on"; "get professional experience"; "bring a large and diversified wardrobe"—while others were vague and elusive—"see if you have talent"; "be sincere and ambitious."

It's surprising that Mary didn't advise the girls to follow her example and salt away something for their old age. No one knew how much Mary and Doug were worth, but by 1925 everyone knew they were rich, which may have been one of the reasons why they attracted so many kidnappers and con artists. There was too much publicity about their wealth, some of it exaggerated. Pickfair, for example, was said to represent "an investment of $500,000," but on the market it probably would have brought no more than $50,000. (Today, when all but three of its original fourteen acres have been sold off, the estate would bring about $1,500,000, according to Beverly Hills real estate agents. They are willing to add another $500,000 "for sentimental value.")

Besides Pickfair, the Fairbankses also owned a beach camp near Laguna, a beach house at Santa Monica (called "Fairford" by their circle) and in 1926 Doug bought a 3,000 acre ranch outside San Diego for $500,000. This property, soon rechristened Rancho Zorro, was steeped in the history of Spanish California, a period that had fascinated Doug since his first trip to the West Coast. The land had once belonged to Pete Lasardi, an early "sheep king" of San Diego, and the ruins of an eighteenth-century hacienda were still standing on the estate. Doug planned to restore it as a "combination museum and barbeque headquarters." But the ranch was intended as more than a showplace; Fairbanks also meant to raise livestock and Valencia oranges. Unfortunately, no one informed him that it takes years for transplanted orange trees to fructify, and once, when he told his European friends about the quality of his citrus crop and offered to send them samples, he was forced to buy fruit from a rival farmer.

Doug often said that Mary had all the business brains in the family, but in fact he made many shrewd investments. Both he and Mary were farsighted enough to realize that some day Los Angeles real estate would skyrocket in value. For a while they had some joint holdings, but in 1925, for tax reasons, they were advised to separate their business interests. As the final stage of a very complicated maneuver, Doug transferred to Charlotte ("Mrs. C. Smith") forty deeds of property, "estimated to be worth $1,000,000." At about the same time, there was an announcement that "the Pickford-Fairbanks studios are to be operated by United Artists, which plans to completely rebuild them and make most of its pictures there." In other words, Mary and Doug had shoved the upkeep and management of the studio onto corporate shoulders; they did not, however, yield the deed of property. The land on which the UA plant stood was now their only joint holding.

In 1926 Mary and Doug made two of their most highly regarded films: Mary turned in *Sparrows* and Doug finally got around to his much postponed pirate epic, *The Black Pirate*. These are among the very best pictures they made at UA.

Sparrows in fact is arguably Mary's most satisfying picture since her Paramount/Artcraft period.

In the film, she plays another of her in-between roles. She is "Mama Mollie," the teen-aged guardian of a flock of unwanted or illegitimate children living on a farm in "the southern swamplands." Mollie believes God will care for them just as He looks after the sparrows. But in protecting the children from the sadistic guardians of the baby farm, she eventually has to play God herself. Mollie, being Pickford, is up to the task—at the very moment when her devotion flags, she dreams of Christ, surrounded by angels, and awakens refreshed, newly inspired and ready for action.

Obviously *Sparrows* has its cloying moments, but the saccharine is cut with some cracking good melodrama, notably a hair-raising sequence in which Mollie and her charges must ford a creek by walking on the backs of some very lively alligators. Director William Beaudine insisted the shot couldn't be faked, so Mary gamely agreed to play it for real. For days, she practiced creeping over the beasts, carrying a weighted doll under her arms. (When the cameras turned, she would be toting a real child on her back.) The alligators had been drugged, but some showed signs of vicious animation, and Mary was terrified.

One day Doug dropped by the set, took one look at the yawning jaws and twitching tails, and ordered Beaudine to finish the shot in superimposition. By then Mary had braved the alligators six or seven times, and decided to go on as planned. But she never again worked with Beaudine. (Probably Mary would have been wiser to fake the shot. It is so realistic that it terrified young children, and as a result, the picture did not do as well as expected at the box office.)

Mollie was one of Pickford's warmest and most engaging characterizations, eliciting a much deeper level of identification than had Annie Rooney. It must have been a tricky role, since she is surrounded by young children who are supposed to be the same age as she, though actually they were twenty to twenty-five years younger. The illusion is far from perfect, but it's surprisingly good, certainly good enough to allow the audience to suspend disbelief.

Sparrows was a deluxe production, though not nearly as grand as *The Black Pirate*. On the other hand, Doug's newest picture wasn't as elaborate as *Bagdad,* though in some ways it picked up where the latter left off, namely in the area of technical exploration. *The Black Pirate* was one of the first films shot in a crude two-color process, the forerunner of Technicolor. Originally Doug had planned to make the picture on location, but color photography demanded the controlled conditions of a studio. So, abandoning the great outdoors as an inspiration, Fairbanks began "studying the paintings of the great masters," and for a while it sounded as though *The Black Pirate* would be as stylized as *The Thief of Bagdad*. But Doug had learned his lesson—there's nothing painterly about the pirate picture. It's free of the kind of photography that elbows the audience into gasps of admiration.

The script (based on a story by Elton Thomas) is disjointed and confused, but it's also lively and good-natured. The spirit of the film is established in a printed prologue:

> A Page from the History and the great writers as well as the great painters. Lives of the most Bloodthirsty PIRATES who ever infested THE SOUTHERN SEAS —Being an account of BUCCANEERS and the Spanish Main, the Jolly Roger, Golden Galleons, bleached skulls, Buried Treasure, the Plank, dirks and cutlasses, Scuttled Ships, Marooning, Desperate Deeds, Desperate Men, and—even on this dark soil—ROMANCE.

Many of the recent Fairbanks films had been weighed down with the niceties of plot continuity, but *The Black Pirate* made its points in capital letters, and the capital point is ACTION. It seems as though there's more swashbuckling in the first reel of this film than in the entirety of *The Thief of Bagdad,* and it's wonderful swashbuckling. There are two memorable sequences. One involves a band of pirates swimming underwater with daggers between their teeth. The other shows Doug performing his most renowned feat: he slides down a sail with his weight on a dagger held at a forty-degree angle to the canvas, slitting it as he goes along.

Some cheating went into both shots. The water ballet of the pirates was performed without water: over one hundred men, holding blades between their teeth, hung by wires as they went through the motions of the breaststroke. And in the other sequence, Fairbanks used a double, far more obviously so than in any of his earlier films. He hoists himself over the sail, and turns his back to the camera; then there is a cut. Next, he (really his double, Richard Talmadge) skims down the sail on the dagger. It's superb trick work, but when you know it's not on the up-and-up, it's easy to spot the fakery.

But in 1926 not many people noticed it. Doug, though not quite as svelte (but every bit as firm) as in *Bagdad,* still looked good in the sparing close-ups he allotted himself. (This time his chest is covered, but he shows off his legs by wearing nothing but a doublet and ragged, thigh-length trousers for most of the film.) His acting, as usual, is no better than not-bad, and as usual, he's occasionally upstaged by the scenery-chewers in his supporting cast, this time Sam de Grasse and Donald Crisp. (De Grasse deserves, at the very least, a parenthetical acknowledgment as one of the most accomplished scene-stealers of the silent screen.)

Fairbanks finished *The Black Pirate* in January 1926; *Sparrows* went on for a while, but by summer Mary and Doug were ready for another European tour. This time they were planning a two-year around-the-world holiday, though they might take some time off for work. They talked about making a film in Germany with *The Miracle* man, Max Reinhardt, and there were also invitations from France and England. Nothing was set but their itinerary. From Europe they would travel on to Russia, China, Japan, and finally Hong Kong where they would board a steamer for California.

This time Mary and Doug had really earned a long vacation. Besides legal battles, brushes with criminals and pursuing their careers, they had also contended with difficult family problems during the preceding two years. Fairbanks continued to be irritated by his son's acting career, soon to go into high gear with his performance in a West Coast production of John Van Druten's play about English school life, *Young Woodley*. Even more exasperating were newspaper reports that young Doug (aged seventeen) was about to marry actress Helene Costello (six years his senior). The stories were inaccurate, but that was cold comfort to Doug, Sr., who couldn't get used to the idea of having a son old enough to court the girls.

A more serious hardship for Doug was the failing health of his half-brother, John, who had suffered a severe stroke three years before. John—or "Jack" as he was called—virtually lost the power of speech, but one day while driving with Doug, he pointed to a cemetery and mumbled, "Jack there." Doug's blood turned to ice, and for days he was unable to shake a fit of black depression. A short time later, he remarked that he hoped, when his time came, he would go quickly. "I can't think of anything more horrible than being ill," he said.

Mary's family upsets, as usual, centered on Lottie and Jack, who were then on the brink of shedding their current spouses. Lottie no longer got much press coverage, but Jack's troubles with Marilyn Miller were reported blow by blow. This was very distressing for Mary. Jack, she told an interviewer, was her "favorite hobby," and she was always trying to find him "the right girl." Knowing his taste for Ziegfeld chorines, she once asked show girl Peggy Fears, "Why don't you marry Jack?" But Miss Fears was looking for bigger fish. Later she married a millionaire and became a Broadway producer.

There was one bright spot in Jack's life. In the mid-1920s, his career picked up, and he gave two good performances in two good films, *The Goose Woman,* with Constance Bennett, and *Exit Smiling* with Beatrice Lillie. But just as Mary was feeling encouraged about her brother, there was bad news about her mother. Charlotte's health began to decline in 1925. At first there seemed no cause for alarm, but only a week after Mary and Doug announced their plans for a world tour, Charlotte entered a Los Angeles hospital for a tumor operation. The trip was cancelled, then reset for the spring when Mrs. Pickford might be well enough to accompany them.

Finally, at the end of March 1926, Mary, Doug, Charlotte and Mary Pickford, Jr. (or Gwynne, as she was now called) left by train for New York. Charlotte looked chipper and steady when she boarded the Super Chief, but five days later, arriving at Grand Central, she was carried off in a wheelchair. Nothing to worry about, the United Artists publicists said, just an attack of indigestion.

On April 3, still suffering from "stomach trouble," she was wheeled aboard the S.S. *Conte Biancmano,* and on reaching Genoa six days later, she was wheeled off. Mary and Doug took her to Montecatini, a fashionable spa outside Florence, famous for its restorative waters, elegant cuisine and international clientele (which always numbered a few film celebrities, including Anita Loos and director Clarence Brown). Assured that Charlotte was in good hands, Mary and Doug started off on the first leg of their journey.

Mainly they were revisiting familiar spots—Paris, London, Venice, Rome, Berlin. But along with the old friends and beloved landmarks, there were also new experiences, one being the European premiere of *Little Annie Rooney* in Berlin. For the first time since the war, a German orchestra played "The Star-Spangled Banner" as Mary and Doug walked down the aisle and took their seats. It was an emotional moment, interpreted by the press as a final burial of wartime animosities.

Mary and Doug returned from Berlin to Italy expressly for a half-hour audience with Benito Mussolini at Chigi Palace in Rome. Il Duce and the Fairbankses exchanged autographed photos and formed a mutual admiration pact. The next day Doug told reporters he was "enthusiastic and impressed by the progress and modernity of Italy"; then he and Mary executed the fascist salute before several famous Roman landmarks. And on their return to Hollywood they taught the salute to a group of friends (including Betty Bronson and Doug Jr.) at a beach picnic in Laguna. (Photographs of the "lesson" appeared in American newspapers in 1927.)

Mary's infatuation with Mussolini lasted until at least 1934, when, according to *The New York Times*, she and Primo Carnera "shared a platform and the applause of 300 Italians" at a celebration in the Hotel Ambassador for the fifteenth anniversary of fascism. Mary Pickford gave the fascist salute and cried, "Viva Il Duce!" Carnera just smiled and bowed from the waist, but Mary had prepared a speech. As the *Times* goes on to report:

> Miss Pickford was less concerned with the historic significance of the celebration than with her "affection for Italy." "I am very happy to be here because I feel very much at home among Italians . . . the last time I visited Italy I found a different spirit there than on my earlier trips. That was because Mussolini had taken it over. Italy has always produced great men and when she needed one most Mussolini was there. Viva Fascisimo! Viva Il Duce!"

Not surprisingly, this incident has been omitted from most accounts of Mary's life, and many people refused to believe it happened until they are handed the *Times* clipping for verification. Then they go into shock. One screenwriter, after examining it, began sputtering about "the poor kids who come to Hollywood, make a killing and promptly deny their roots and allegiances by turning arch-conservative." And it is true that Mary was staunchly behind the Republican party—by the mid-1920s she was chummy with Calvin Coolidge and in the 1940s offered to tutor Wendell Willkie in personality and public speaking.

It's also true that in the early 1930s she told a group of

juvenile inmates at Welfare Island in New York that their imprisonment was "a spiritual exercise":

> I look on the Depression and on setbacks such as you boys and girls have had here as a privilege. It brings out the finer things. Napoleon and Lincoln were made by hard times. You're getting spiritual exercise for your muscles. . . . Remember that for me, will you, and thank God for this experience.

Today, if she made the same speech, the kids would probably stone her—not undeservedly so. There is something repellent about Mary, who had grown up under adverse circumstances, telling a later generation of poor and underprivileged young people to "thank God" instead of urging them to go out and do something constructive to right their wrongs.

The inmates of Welfare Island in 1932 did not, however, throw things; they guffawed a few times and then gave Mary a polite hand. She had said nothing they hadn't heard before—she was following the establishment line of Hoover America. To understand Mary's political statements, one has to remember that she thought of herself as an unofficial, roving ambassador of a country that made her rich and famous, and out of gratitude and a sense of duty she expressed the prevailing, middle-of-the-road position. That position included the optimistic thought that the Depression wasn't an economic disaster, but rather a testing of moral fiber; that Mussolini wasn't a dictator, but a genius who got the Italian trains rolling on schedule.

It seems unlikely that Mary ever gave much deep thought to her political convictions. Her politics were probably colored by her finances, and her admiration for Mussolini was, as the *Times* implied, mainly an emotional response. Mussolini possessed certain qualities she admired: power, efficacy, charisma—he got things done and he knew how to manipulate people to support his regime. Including Mary and Doug:

their testimonies in his behalf certainly played some small part in helping isolationist America underestimate the threat of fascism.

That Mary and Doug respected leadership, no matter what the ideology, is clearly shown by their 1926 tour. They ran through the entire palette of political colors. At the same time they were visiting Mussolini, Doug was having trouble with the Spanish government. *The Black Pirate* had just opened in Madrid, and some critics attacked it as an insult to Iberian culture. Fairbanks immediately shot off a telegram to the Spanish people assuring them that it was all a huge misunderstanding, and since he was a close friend of Alfonso XIII, a big movie fan, the whole affair was quickly forgotten.

Once the Spanish problem was solved, Mary and Doug moved on to Central Europe, stopping first in Prague. There Mary was known and loved as Maria Pickfordova, and she was officially welcomed by President Jan Masaryk. The meeting was so pleasant that Masaryk invited her to visit him the next time they passed through Prague, which was to be, as he knew, only two weeks later.

In the meantime, Mary and Doug went on to Russia, the high point of their tour. Long before leaving America, Doug had announced that he and Mary might make two movies in Russia, but the Soviet officials were less than cordial in their response. A Moscow professor named I. Vsevo condemned Mary and Doug as "too bourgeois for Communist Russia" and asked that they be refused visas.

But their entry permits were granted without any trouble. Mary—or Marushka—was adored by the Russians, and American films were the basis for a burgeoning Soviet school of cinema. As late as 1920 the U.S. State Department was shipping films to Russia to counteract the effect of Soviet propaganda. Besides the capitalistic vision of life, American movies provided Soviet directors with a crash course in film technique, and at the same time, the Russian people with some badly needed entertainment. The pro-American taste of Soviet audiences disturbed pro-Marxist American journalists.

In 1925, Paxton Hibben sadly reported to the readers of *The Nation* that Mary and Doug and a child star called Baby Peggy drew the biggest crowds at the film showings in a Moscow workers' club.

Thousands of people turned out to stare at Mary and Doug as they arrived in Moscow in July. They were escorted around the Soviet studios and introduced to a number of prominent directors, including Sergei Komarov, who asked to make a film record of their visit. Mary and Doug were so obliging that after their departure Komarov used his footage as the basis of a short screen comedy (unreleased outside Russia). The Fairbankses were shown several new Russian films, and officials were distressed when they left a screening of *Three Thieves* without a word. There had been great expectations for this picture, but once Mary and Doug rejected it, *Three Thieves* was relegated to obscurity.

Things went differently when they were shown Eisenstein's *Battleship Potemkin*. They asked to meet the director, pictured by Doug as "old, very serious and wearing eyeglasses and a beard," and were surprised to confront a kinky-haired, impish man in his late twenties. (Looking at the brilliant but austere *Potemkin*, one can understand Doug's original impression of the director.) After a few minutes of pleasantries, Fairbanks asked Eisenstein, "How soon can you pack your bags?" Or so says Ivor Montagu in *With Eisenstein in Hollywood*. It wasn't a very tactful remark, but Doug wasn't always tactful; it's also a questionable quote, since Montagu is always patronizing about the Fairbankses.

There is, however, no doubt that Doug promised to secure an American release for *Potemkin* and that he also implied that Eisenstein might be brought to the States by United Artists. Returning to New York, he told the press that "Eisenstein and the other Russians are now the leaders of world cinema." His endorsement was largely responsible for the American distribution of *Potemkin*.

On the other part of the bargain, Fairbanks reneged. Eisenstein's biographers claim he waited eagerly for a message from United Artists, but none ever came. Possibly Eisenstein misinterpreted a casual remark; perhaps Doug had second thoughts; perhaps shrewder minds tempered his enthusiasm. But the big mystery is why Eisenstein wanted so desperately to come to America; his biographers give various explanations, none very convincing.

Leaving Russia, Mary and Doug returned to Czechoslovakia where they were welcomed by Masaryk and hundreds of Prague citizens. Then, just as they were setting off for the Orient, they received word that Charlotte was seriously ill. They rushed to Montecatini and a few days later were on their way back to the States. Charlotte was dying of cancer. She knew but never told Mary, and Mary knew but never told Charlotte. They started to play a civilized charade that would last for the next two years.

These were the worst months of Mary's life, but she went ahead with her work, starting production on what is today the most widely circulated of her films, *My Best Girl*. This was the first of her United Artists releases that did not qualify as a superproduction. A modest little comedy, it's the standard, lightweight story about the shop girl who falls in love with the boss's son, mixes up the dinner spoons and drinks the finger bowls, but still winds up with her wealthy beau. As shop girl Maggie Johnson, Mary grows up a bit: there's a real Betty Boop bounce to her performance. She's good, but not very individual. Here, as in *Rosita,* she does nothing that a half dozen other actresses couldn't have done as well.

If *My Best Girl* holds a special place in Mary's heart, it may be because her leading man, Charles "Buddy" Rogers, would later become her third husband. Eleven years younger than Pickford, Rogers had been spotted by a talent scout in his home town, Olanthe, Kansas. Coming to Hollywood in 1925, he was groomed for stardom at an acting school run by Paramount. Boyishly attractive and extremely likeable (both on- and offscreen), Rogers was pushed by the studio into leading roles in a series of minor comedies, finally winning a major part in Paramount's 1927 aviation spectacle, *Wings*, directed by Fairbanks's protégé, William Wellman. When Wellman heard Mary was looking for a leading man, he recommended Rogers, and Mary having seen and liked his work in earlier films, agreed to meet him.

Buddy was thrilled. Mary wasn't his top favorite—that honor belonged to Norma Shearer—but he had never missed a Pickford film while he was growing up. ("She was," Rogers diplomatically told an interviewer, "one of my favorites while I was going to college.") He was "very nervous" at their first meeting in her studio bungalow, but Mary quickly put him at ease, and soon assured him that the part was his.

Years later Rogers said he first became infatuated with Mary during the making of *My Best Girl*, but Pickford remained aloof, friendly and yet never encouraging. Doug, however, went into a funk when he sat on the set and watched Mary kissing Buddy for the camera. He wasn't suspicious that anything was going on in private; still, the sight of Mary kissing a younger and handsomer man was a blow to his ego.

According to the fan magazines, Mary was always just outside camera range when Doug embraced a film heroine. If so, she must have had an insatiable appetite for boredom since few of Fairbanks's co-stars appeared to have much red blood in their veins. The only major exception was Lupe Velez, the "Mexican spitfire," his leading lady in the 1927 *The Gaucho*. The Fairbanks film was in production at about the same time as *My Best Girl*, and if Doug wanted revenge for Mary kissing Buddy, he had ample opportunity with Lupe. But their on-screen love scenes are tame and their offscreen relations were just as tepid. If anything had been happening, Lupe would certainly have broadcast it to the world—in later years, she was notorious for discussing the sexual prowess and proportions of her leading men. But there was no chemistry between them; Lupe was possibly just a little too vulgar for Doug.

She is, however, one of the few good things about *The Gaucho*, which is certainly Doug's most peculiar film; also, arguably, his worst. In it, he plays an Argentine bandit with a Robin Hood complex, who tries to save a holy shrine from capitalistic desecration. In the process, he falls victim to leprosy, goes through conversion and is healed by the waters of the shrine. He regains his faith when he sees a vision of the Virgin Mary, "a cameo role" played by Mary Pickford. Except for some unbilled extra work, this was the first time Mary had acted with Doug, and some fans were disappointed that she made such a fleeting appearance. But no one questioned the appropriateness of America's Sweetheart playing the Virgin Mary.

Despite the droopy atmosphere of religious uplift, *The Gaucho* has its genuinely vigorous moments—Doug does some fine tricks with a bola, and near the end, there's a superbly edited sequence of a cattle stampede—but on the whole, neither critics nor public liked the picture very much. Robert Sherwood, the movie reviewer for *Life,* bemoaned Fairbanks's decision to include "religion, lust or loathsome disease" in one of his productions: ". . . There is no place for anything but Douglas Fairbanks—all the beautiful, preposterous qualities that Douglas Fairbanks represents in a Douglas Fairbanks film."

The Gaucho and *My Best Girl* did pretty well at the box office, but for the first time there were comments in the press that Mary and Doug were "slipping." And neither seemed to have any idea of how they could bring new life to their careers. For the first time since they entered the movies, an entire year passed without a new Pickford or Fairbanks picture going into release.

13

There were two reasons for the hiatus in their careers—one professional, the other personal. The first was brought about by a recession that hit the film industry late in 1926. Suddenly and quite unexpectedly box-office receipts began to drop all over the country. Some Hollywood insiders blamed the emergence of a new entertainment rival, radio; others cited spiraling admission prices; still others thought the decline was caused by a new sophistication on the part of the public. Since the end of the First World War, when America first went movie-mad, the public seemed willing to watch virtually anything, and practically any moderately budgeted film was assured of gaining back its cost. Now moviegoers were becoming picky; they stayed at home and listened to the radio unless there was something really special playing at the local Bijou.

Nearly all the studios were affected, including UA, which ended the year with a deficit of over a million dollars. And none of them had any practical solution to the problem of luring the public back to the theatres, except the lowly, nearly bankrupt Warner Brothers, which in October 1927 released *The Jazz Singer,* thereby opening the era of the sound film. "A fluke!" said one industry spokesman of the success of *The Jazz Singer.* "Talking pictures are a novelty that won't last out the year," claimed another. These dire predictions were no more than wishful thinking. Studios didn't want the talkies to succeed, simply because making them would cause an expensive, time-consuming and heartbreaking revolution in motion picture production: sound stages would have to be built, theatres would have to be wired for sound, actors and other film craftsmen would have to master an entirely new form of movie storytelling.

Actors were especially alarmed by the coming of sound. Some Hollywood stars—Vilma Banky, for instance—could barely speak English; others were (to borrow a phrase from director Clarence Brown) "strictly dese, dem and dose guys." A few ultrafeminine leading ladies spoke in a truck-driver baritone; a couple of he-men sounded as though they had been caponized. Mary and Doug were luckier than most: they had a stage background and there was no reason to believe their voices would cause any problems. (As it turned out Doug did have some trouble—his voice recorded higher and lighter than it actually was.)

Still, neither was thrilled by the idea of talking pictures, though they were not dead set against them like their friend, Charlie Chaplin. Mary feared that sound would prove to be a second tower of Babel; abandoning the universal language of silent-screen pantomime was tantamount to abandoning the international allure and persuasiveness of the motion picture. "Differences in language make for all sorts of prejudice," she explained. "Even the English and Americans—there's a barrier between them when they hear each other speak."

Doug's attitude toward the talkies changed frequently, but in the beginning he was doubtful whether his essentially romantic screen character was adaptable to the new, more realistic medium of sound pictures. The silence (more precisely, the lack of spoken words) of silent pictures created a dream world, far removed from the logic and actualities of everyday life; add sound, and the artifice begins to crumble. It could be done, of course, but fantasy and romance are not so easily created in sound film as in the silents.

Mary and Doug decided to wait and see whether the talkies would maintain their popularity, and to wait until some of the kinks had been ironed out in the early process of sound recording. In the first year of sound, no one knew what they were doing, least of all the technical engineers, who destroyed several actors by failing to master the intricacies of treble and bass. And in these early days, the camera was enclosed in a soundproof glass booth; it couldn't be moved to follow action, an enormous disadvantage for actors as physical as Doug and Mary.

There was a second, more personal reason for Mary and Doug's absence from the screen during 1928. Charlotte Pickford's condition became critical, and near the end of 1927, the Fairbankses moved into her home. They stayed there and watched over her until her death on March 21, 1928. When her mother passed on, Mary became hysterical, slapping Doug full on the face and lashing out verbally at Jack and Lottie. Her hysteria lasted, according to her own admission, four or five days; according to other recollections, it went on much longer. For a while she tried to stay in communication with Charlotte through ESP and spiritualism (though she thought her mother would disapprove), and for years, she refused to drive past Mrs. Pickford's home in Beverly Hills, even though it was in a direct line from the studio to Pickfair and avoiding it meant going several blocks out of the way.

The Beverly Hills house was willed to Mary, as was the bulk of her mother's $3,000,000. In making this bequest, Charlotte had stipulated that "it be [Mary's] and her assigns forever, because whatever property I possess at the time of my death has come to me through my association with my said beloved daughter in her business and through her unusual generosity to me." Mary's share of the inheritance was estimated at $1,144,972. Jack, Lottie and Gwynne each received trust funds of $200,000.

Some people—Adolph Zukor was one—claim that Mary lost interest in her career after Charlotte's death. And for a while, this seemed to be true. "There is no question about the darkest moment of my life," she later said. "It was my mother's death." Spiritualism brought her only fleeting solace, and because of her marriage to Fairbanks, she couldn't turn to the Catholic Church for support. But there were other faiths, and Mary chose Christian Science: it pulled her through, and in gratitude she later wrote a little book called *Why Not Try God?*, which was designed to guide people through the kind of crises she had faced.

The title is the message: faith in God and belief in man's ability to overcome, Mary says, will give anyone the incentive to live a richer life. Alternately chirpy and maudlin, the book mixes Christian Science maxims with ectoplasmatic visions; dear departed spirits turn up in Mary's dreams, sometimes in her room, whenever she is blue and needs a few words of encouragement. When published in 1934, it sold over 50,000 copies, and though it's hard to believe, apparently some readers did find inspiration in it. *Liberty Magazine* (which had printed an early draft of the book under the title, "Why I Can Be Happy In Spite Of It All") claimed "its effects here and there were amazing. A condemned man carried a copy to the gallows with him. A woman in Boston, on the point of shooting two children and herself, read the article and was saved."

These testimonies may well have been true. Leatrice Joy tells of meeting a woman who believed Mary's book had played an important role in her life. During the late stages of pregnancy, Miss Joy's friend had contracted pneumonia, and doctors feared she would lose the baby and possibly die herself; medication couldn't be administered without harming the unborn child. To keep her mind off her problem, a nurse read aloud the article Mary had written for *Liberty,* and suddenly the woman realized that her breathing was less constricted. Within a few hours, her fever had dropped and she was taken off the critical list. She asked Leatrice Joy to thank Mary for the birth of her "beautiful son." The message was passed along, and Mary sent her a warm note of acknowledgment.

The restorative powers Mary found in her belief in God emerged slowly. In the spring of 1928, Doug was so concerned about her low spirits that he took her off on a short European vacation. This, the least publicized of their transatlantic holidays, was also one of the shortest: sailing in late April, they were back in New York before mid-June. It wasn't one of their happier homecomings—U.S. customs inspected their bags and imposed fines for undeclared goods—but otherwise, it had been a good trip, and seemed to have had a therapeutic effect on Mary. Before returning to Los Angeles, she took a decisive step, one that only a year earlier she had sworn she would never take; she went to Charles Bock's beauty salon on East 57th Street, and had her hair bobbed.

A few months earlier, she had told *The Pictorial Review* that, "despite the epidemic of haircutting sweeping the country," she was going to hang on to hers. "My curls have become so identified with me that they have almost become a trademark . . . a symbol, and I think that shorn of them I should become almost as Samson after his unfortunate meeting with Delilah."

But by 1928 her curls had lost their attraction for the public, so why not get rid of them? Now that Mama Charlotte was dead, she was a grown-up woman, an independent agent, and though Doug protested, Mary went right ahead and got her bob. To record this historic moment, she invited photographers to the haircutting, and her expression as the barber snips away at the curls suggests that she is losing something more personal than a hank of hair.

The rape of the Pickford locks made headlines around the world. There was no outrage, little disapproval, just a nostalgic awareness of an era coming to an end. An editorial in *The New York Times* commented:

> They [the curls] should, by rights, be deposited in the National Museum at Washington . . . Miss Pickford is of no age and of all. She is part of our American

civilization; she is an exemplar on which a generation
has been founded . . . Not for one moment would
she be taken as a Great Moral Influence; there is too
much humor and sound sense in her. She is, first of all,
a remarkably able business woman who does nothing on
impulse. She has cut off her curls because she has come
to the conclusion that it will be a good thing for business.
. . . The outstanding charm of Mary Pickford has been
her friendliness. It is amusing to hear about Hollywood's
insistence on sex appeal—a quality that in Mary is very
much minus. She is the living refutation of the Elinor
Glyn claptrap, which bases feminine allure on "It." She
is the greatest single figure in motion pictures and is as
comfortable as an old shoe. . . .

A museum piece, no sex appeal, an old shoe—Mary didn't
need enemies when she had eulogizers like this. But she
wasn't discouraged. Having bobbed her hair, she was now
ready to play a new kind of role (one with "It") in a new kind
of picture: she was going to make her sound debut in
Coquette, an adaptation of a play that had starred Helen
Hayes. Lillian Gish saw it on Broadway and urged Mary to
buy the film rights. Mary did, though it was miles away from
anything she had played before. The coquette of the title is
Norma Bessant, a teen-aged Southern vamp, torn between
two men, her father and an illicit lover. When Mr. Bessant
learns Norma is a shame to Southern womanhood, he shoots
her boyfriend and then kills himself.
    To prepare for her first talkie, Mary hired as dialogue coach
Constance Collier, a distinguished English actress who later
helped Katharine Hepburn on her Shakespearean and
Shavian stage roles. It was a peculiar choice, since Norma
Bessant had a Southern and not an English accent, and one of
the many problems with Mary's performance is her sad
attempt at an Alabama drawl. The unfamiliarity of sound
production unnerved Mary; in a rare moment of tempera-

ment, she fired photographer Charles Rosher. This was a mistake, because here, for the first time in her career, Mary looks much older than the character she is playing.

Though well received in 1929, Mary's portrayal of Norma Bessant has not aged well. Her coquetry goes far beyond the demands of the role, and there are moments when the audience hopes Mr. Bessant will kill Norma, not her suitor (Johnny Mack Brown). Perhaps Pickford's performance was never that impressive. She won an Academy Award for *Coquette,* but the citation stirred up the first of the great Oscar controversies.

The Academy of Motion Picture Arts and Sciences was conceived by Louis B. Mayer who felt that such an organization would bring status to the movie industry. Mayer enlisted the support of Mary, Doug and other prominent members of the film colony, and in May 1927 the formation of the Academy was formally announced at a black-tie dinner at the Biltmore Hotel in downtown Los Angeles. The primary goal of the Academy was "to foster technical research and the exchange of artistic and scientific views." An annual presentation of awards for achievement in various fields of the industry was devised primarily to focus public attention on the organization, but from the beginning the Oscars overshadowed the Academy's other activities.

Some of the early Academy meetings were held at Pickfair and Doug was elected president. Therefore, when Mary got the Oscar for *Coquette,* more than one critic wondered whether she had won votes for acting or for serving tea to the right people. "It gives the impression," wrote a columnist for the *Los Angeles Times,* "that the Academy is handing out its statuettes on a political or social basis." Two of Mary's competitors—Ruth Chatterton in *Madame X,* Jeanne Eagels in *The Letter*—had done better work; in fact, Eagels's performance is one of the very best of the early sound era. So presumably, Mary's award was less for *Coquette* than for cumulative excellence over a period of years.

Doug moved into sound more cautiously than Mary. His first film for 1929, *The Iron Mask,* was originally conceived as a silent, and only near the end of production were two or three reels reshot with spoken dialogue. Despite its hybrid nature, *The Iron Mask* is a fairly entertaining picture, lavishly mounted and skillfully directed by Allan Dwan, but it was largely ignored by the audiences of 1929. Partly this was because the public wanted all-talking films, partly because of the role Fairbanks chose for himself.

The Iron Mask picks up the story of D'Artagnan twenty years after the close of *The Three Musketeers.* Age hasn't taken all the vim and vinegar out of D'Artagnan, but he and Doug aren't what they were in the past. The swashbuckling is tired stuff, and a fast eye will catch the use of a double in several shots. D'Artagnan dies at the end, and it's a moving moment mainly for its iconographic connotations. Doug seems to be saying farewell to D'Artagnan, to the Black Pirate, the Thief of Bagdad, to all the rash and romantic heroes of his past.

The film contains another scene that can be interpreted in the same way. Midway through the movie, D'Artagnan loses his beloved Constance, and here again there is a melancholy, a depth of feeling that is rare in Fairbanks's films. It seems possible, as many critics have suggested, that Doug was reflecting on the declining state of his marriage as he shot this sequence.

The problems didn't seem so serious at first—nothing more than a nagging sense of malaise on both their parts. Mary was still depressed about her mother, and now that Charlotte was gone, she had to shoulder many duties—Jack, Lottie, certain business chores—that formerly Mrs. Pickford had shared. And Doug was also causing Mary some worry. There had always been a black undercurrent to his hyperactive exhilaration, but recently he was more tense and irritable than usual. And for good reason. Fairbanks had overtaxed his body—he was muscle-bound. His doctors warned that he was exerting himself beyond the limits suitable for someone his age, and that unless he cut down on his exercise, his circulation would be seriously impaired. Doug paid no attention. He maintained his usual schedule at the gym, and to ease his nervousness, started smoking and drinking a highball before dinner. And sometimes, aping his English friends, he had a nightcap before bed.

Doug was now the complete Anglophile. Sometimes he laughingly referred to his highborn British friends as "Burke's Steerage," but there is no doubt that he hankered after their style of life. Nearly all his clothes were imported from London, and often he talked of settling permanently in England. When he wasn't dreaming of an English manor, he was talking about roving the seven seas. His old wanderlust was reasserting itself with a vengeance. Mary, on the other hand, was content with an occasional European holiday; she wanted to stay in Hollywood and work.

For a while she managed to keep him at Pickfair. Early in 1929 he agreed to play opposite her in *The Taming of the Shrew,* the first sound production of a Shakespearean play. Fairbanks later said this was Mary's idea; she said no, the credit belonged to director Sam Taylor, although Doug was also enthusiastic about the project. "There's one thing I'm sure of," she added. "I know I was talked into it against my better judgment."

Making *The Shrew* was a bad experience for everyone involved. The script was based on Garrick's eighteenth-century "acting edition" of the play, "with additional dialogue by Sam Taylor." (After the film opened, a cartoon in a New York paper showed a bust of Shakespeare at the Library of Congress being replaced by one of Taylor.) Constance Collier was again hired as Mary's dialogue coach, but Taylor didn't want any high-flown Shakespearean acting; the important thing, he said, was "the Pickford bag of tricks." Mary was furious, and as filming progressed she lost confidence in Taylor and in her mastery of sound acting. The shrewish Katharine was not so very different from some of the headstrong heroines Mary had played in the past, but she felt uncomfortable in the part, and this may explain her lackluster and surprisingly genteel performance.

Some people, however, insist she held back in a calculated attempt to throw the picture to Fairbanks. If so, he was either oblivious to her generosity or resented it as a condescending gesture. Or perhaps he was just plain bored. Whatever the reason, he was thoroughly uncooperative. Every day he lingered a little longer over his calisthenics and morning sunbath, sometimes not arriving on the set until nearly noon. Meanwhile Mary and the crew had been waiting since nine, and as the hours passed, tempers grew noticeably shorter. Mary in particular found it hard to keep up a show of good humor; she estimated that the delays were costing upward of thirty dollars a minute.

On reaching the set, Doug had rarely memorized his lines and read them from blackboards that were hurriedly set up all around the set. This required constant adjustment of lighting and blocking in what was already a very complicated production. Worst of all, he refused to do any retakes, and whenever Mary requested one, he'd snap at her and walk off the set. She felt humiliated, and the rest of the company was embarrassed for her.

When *The Taming of The Shrew* opened in November 1929, it got some fine reviews (*The New York Times* critic put it on his ten best list), with Doug's Petruchio outranking Mary's Katharine. Today neither star looks very good and the picture seems hopelessly old-fashioned. (William Cameron Menzies's sets—the best part of the production—are exceedingly handsome, but bear little resemblance to the Padua of Shakespeare's imagination.) Probably the critics of 1929 were generous out of reverence for Shakespeare and affection for Mary and Doug, but their enthusiasm didn't impress the public. The picture was a box-office bomb, partly because it went into release just after the stock market crash. That was one of the two official explanations for its failure, the other being that film audiences just weren't interested in canned

Shakespeare. Unofficially, though, some industry commentators hinted that audiences weren't interested in Mary and Doug, either.

To recover from *The Shrew*, Mary and Doug went off on their seventh transatlantic tour. Their first stop was Switzerland where Gwynne was attending a private school; then, according to their itinerary, they were off for Egypt, Greece, India, China, Hong Kong and Japan, where they would board a steamer for San Francisco.

This, then, was the world tour they had so often planned but somehow never got around to completing. Traveling with them was Karl K. Kitchen, an Alexander Woollcott-ish columnist for the *New York Evening World* who wrote on everything from Hollywood ("the celluloid colony") to Mussolini ("the greatest man in Europe"). First meeting Mary and Doug in a professional capacity, Kitchen struck up a friendship, and by the late 1920s he was a frequent guest at Pickfair.

With a little help from Kitchen, Mary later described her impressions of this trip for *The Saturday Evening Post*. "In Africa and the Far East," she wrote, "we thought we could go as we pleased, unobserved and free-willed," but it wasn't so. Everywhere they went they were mobbed. In Alexandria their car was nearly wrecked by stevedores who jumped on the running board, screaming for autographs or mementos of any kind. (Someone explained to Mary that they wanted their ears autographed so they could have the signatures permanently tattooed.) In Athens, crowds blocked their view of the Parthenon, and when they sailed for the Greek Islands, their boat had to turn back because a reporter had stowed away under the bed in their stateroom.

Their trek through the Orient was, according to Kitchen's articles for *The World*, "a succession of luncheons, teas and dinners, all held in Mary and Doug's honor." He singles out for special commendation a reception given "at the home of Mrs. Edward Ezra, one of the great hostesses of Shanghai."

Two hundred guests of different nationalities sat down to a "fifteen course Chinese meal (including thrush heads)," which was followed by "a European dinner of almost as many courses." Chinese musicians played during the Chinese portion of the banquet and were replaced by a jazz band during the international section of the meal. All in all, a dinner to remember . . . and digest.

And all in all, it was a highly successful trip. By the time Mary and Doug returned to the states in January 1930, there was so much excitement over their travels that it seemed as if they were as popular as ever. But it wasn't so: the stars people want to read about are not necessarily the stars people want to pay to see on screen. By 1930, it was no secret that Doug and Mary's days as top box-office draws were over. Around this time, *The New York Times* told readers:

> Incredible as it may seem to oldsters, Mary is slipping as a box-office attraction. The mere setting down of that assertion may seem impious, but the truth must be told. A public that once was hers entirely is now following strange new goddesses and a generation has arisen that is forgetting—never knew—what her career has meant to the topsy-turvy world of amusement. . . . [This sophisticated public] has "outgrown" her artless comedy and tomboy humors—and done itself little credit in the growth. . . . A grown-up Mary—alas, perhaps too well grown!—has taken the place of what seemed inexhaustible youth incarnate, and a Katharine the Shrew storms ladylike where once a gamin frolicked. . . . Thus do relentlessly passing years exact their toll alike upon the just and unjust . . .

Rumors began to circulate that Mary and Doug were about to withdraw from the screen. Both stars denied the report, and Mary was sincere: she was already preparing her next production, a remake of a Norma Talmadge silent called *Secrets*.

Doug, however, was definitely considering retirement. "Aw, Mary," he said, "nobody cares about us anymore. Let's sell Pickfair and move to Switzerland and just get old." On another occasion, he told her, "When a man finds himself sliding downhill he should do everything to reach bottom in a hurry and pass out of the picture."

"A man doesn't have to slide if he's willing to climb," Mary replied. But Doug wasn't in the mood for climbing. Instead, he went off to Scotland for the Walker Cup Golf Tournament with Tom Geraghty. It was the first time since their marriage that he had left Mary at home, and rumors flew about an imminent separation. "You mustn't listen to talk in Hollywood," Fairbanks warned a reporter. "The idlers have nothing to do but spread stories, and busy people can't spend all their time denying them." Denying them did no good, anyway: the idlers went right on talking about the trouble at Pickfair.

Secrets made the making of *The Shrew* look like a picnic. Mary put one of her favorite directors, Mickey Neilan, in charge of production—a mistake, since Neilan was now drinking heavily. As leading man, she chose Broadway actor Kenneth MacKenna—another mistake since MacKenna photographed ten years younger than Mary. There were also script problems: Pickford spotted them, but as filming went along, she realized they were far worse than she had anticipated. Halfway through the film, after looking at the footage, she halted production at a loss of $300,000.

No explanation was offered for discarding *Secrets*. Instead, Mary announced that she would soon return to the stage and was disbanding her UA production staff. Her career as an individual producer was over; from here on, all her pictures would be supervised by Joseph Schenck, the president of United Artists. Before Hollywood had time to digest this news, Mary was off to Europe to join Doug. It wasn't the happiest of reunions. She was still smarting from the *Secrets* fiasco and he felt guilty about letting her live through it alone. After several heart-to-heart talks, he agreed to return to Hollywood and start work on a new picture.

Perhaps this was his way of doing penance; maybe he had had second thoughts about giving up the movies. Probably it was a bit of both. Fairbanks was prone to conflicting emotions at this time. Arriving in England six months earlier, he told a reporter that he doubted whether his "gifts were suited to talking pictures" and then, in the next breath, talked about his plans for making an English film with Eisenstein. Along with Disney and a few other animators, Doug felt Eisenstein (who was then adapting his theories of montage to sound) was one of the few film artists who had recognized the potential of talking pictures.

It was an impressive statement, but how much Doug really knew or understood about Eisenstein's theories is debatable. According to one report, he learned them from Ivor Montagu who got them from H. G. Wells who heard them first-hand. On his return to Hollywood, Fairbanks made no attempt to collaborate with Eisenstein (a mind-boggling combination); nor did he talk about starring with Mary in a projected screen version of *Caesar and Cleopatra*. (Another mind-boggler. After seeing *The Shrew*, Bernard Shaw refused to release the film rights to his play.)

Instead, Doug sailed with the commercial winds and made a musical, the most popular genre of film in the first two years of sound. The title, *Reaching for the Moon*, was borrowed from an earlier Fairbanks comedy; the songs were composed by Irving Berlin on an off-day; the other leading players included Bebe Daniels and Edward Everett Horton. Since none of the stars were endowed with musical talent, a young crooner from the Coconut Grove was brought in to sing the best Berlin songs. His name was Bing Crosby but *Reaching for the Moon* did nothing much to further his screen career.

A satire on American tycoonship, the picture is pretty much of a mishmash: a shipboard romance, a few tunes, long stretches of flat dialogue, a couple of sequences to show off

Doug's athletic prowess. Not surprisingly, *Reaching for the Moon* laid a huge egg at the box office. Once again, there were extenuating circumstances: it was released at a time when audiences were tiring of musicals, and because of the Depression, were in no mood to laugh at the inanities of big business. But Fairbanks accepted most of the blame for the picture's failure. At one time his name had been enough to put any picture across, but no longer.

With Doug back at Pickfair, the separation rumors were no longer so persuasive. There were family gatherings around the pool—Gwynne (back from school in Switzerland), Robert Fairbanks and his wife, the four Fairbanks girls (Doug's nieces) and occasionally Doug, Jr. and his wife, Joan Crawford. Fairbanks Sr. had fought hard against this marriage—his son (age nineteen at the time of the wedding) was too young, and Joan's background was not as upper-crust as Doug would have liked. Mary as usual tried to mediate between father and son, but in her autobiography, Miss Crawford implies that she never felt at ease with either of the senior Fairbankses. Perhaps she, like many people, mistook Mary's reserve for haughtiness.

Mary was now becoming increasingly reclusive. Doug was still occasionally seen around town or at the Riviera Country Club, playing golf with "Jayar" (his pet name for Doug, Jr.), but he too was staying close to Pickfair or the Santa Monica house, where he spent weekends during the making of *Reaching for the Moon*. One night at the beach, as he came downstairs to leave a note for the butler, he bumped into a prowler. "Douglas Fairbanks!" the man gasped. He had planned on robbing Fairbanks, and Doug had enough presence of mind to take advantage of his surprise. Reasoning quietly with the intruder, Fairbanks persuaded him to accept $35 in cash instead of ransacking the house for its cache of jewels and valuables.

The attempted robbery wasn't reported to the police or the press, but the story got around and was picked up by the papers. In the ensuing coverage, Fairbanks emerged as a foxy protector of hearth and home, a loyal and protective husband.

The impression was false. At the end of the year, Doug again took off for faraway places. This was a trip for boys only—Tom Geraghty, man's man director Victor Fleming, and Fairbanks's trainer, Chuck Lewis, went along, but Mary stayed in Hollywood and fretted. And with good reason. From here on, Doug returned to Pickfair only for Christmas and other special occasions.

14

Now that he was too old to play boyhood heroes on screen, Fairbanks started acting out his adventures in real life. In the early 1930s, he saw himself as a second Marco Polo, exploring parts of the world that were romantic and remote—even unknown—to most Americans. The first of these exotic voyages took him to Honolulu, Manila and Japan, and then on to French Indochina. After seeing the Taj Mahal and bagging a couple of Bengal tigers, he was off to Cambodia and the ruins of Angkor Wat. Then, just as he was leaving for Manchuria, civil war erupted, and he put Manchuria aside for another trip.

Returning to the States, Fairbanks decided to share his travels with his fans. "I am now completing *Around the World in Eighty Minutes,* a travel picture of my experiences in my recent tour of the world," he said. "I believe it will be far superior in entertainment than any fictional romance I could make. As to the future, I plan to appear only in films recording my travels."

Whether Doug had always intended to use his tour as the basis of a movie isn't known, though the presence of Victor Fleming suggests that he did. Home movies were one of Doug's favorite hobbies, and he had filmed many of the memorable moments of his life, including the world tour he made with Mary in 1929. But these movies were intended only for the Pickfair screening room, and even there they were not always warmly received. Some people who were forced to look at Mary and Doug's moving picture albums still rankle at the memory, recalling them as the ultimate in flagrant self-glorification.

Around the World is little more than a glorified extension of these home movies, but it's not so charming. Doug comes across as the epitome of the boorish American tourist— Babbitt inspecting the seven wonders of the world. His primary interest on reaching a new city is to try out the local golf course, and when he does get around to sight-seeing, his heart isn't in it. Climbing around Angkor Wat, he stops and wonders "if all this exercise really gets you anywhere." (The dialogue was written by Robert E. Sherwood, still writing *Life* prose, though he had already won some renown as a Broadway author.) Doug's premise is that "the world is essentially funny"— this at a time when millions of Americans were suffering because of the Depression—and to prove the point, he stoops to cheap laughs: the background music for his visit to the Taj Mahal is "Little Gray Home in the West." (Perhaps this was Doug's interpretation of Eisenstein's theories about the dialectic juxtaposition of sound and image.)

Critics were generous in giving faint praise to *Around the World,* and a small portion of the public showed their faith in Fairbanks by paying to see it. The picture just got by at the box office, never grossing enough to justify Doug's going ahead with more travelogues, but he went ahead anyway. In the fall of 1931, he started off on another world tour—this time traveling in the opposite direction, across the Atlantic—with director Lewis Milestone and writer Robert Benchley as his companions. According to news reports, they intended to "see some of the high spots of Prohibition-free Europe, then go over the Trans-Siberian railway to Manchuria"; there they would film "the bewhiskered Bolsheviks at play and work," and "top off these scenes with views of the Japanese and Chinese in hand-to-hand rounds of mah-jong."

Considering this description, it's probably fortunate that the film was never made. Doug's party got as far as Rome when civil war once again broke out in Manchuria, and instead of reworking the itinerary, Fairbanks called off the rest of the trip. By this time, the disappointing returns for *Around the World* forced him to reconsider the advisability of foisting more home movies on the public.

At the end of 1931, Doug was back in Hollywood. Mary had bought him a very special present, one that was far too large to fit under the Pickfair Christmas tree. It was an authentic Western saloon with a mahogany bar that once "sailed around Cape Horn to decorate the Union Saloon in Auburn, California, in 1854." Mary had hired "two pioneers from the California gold rush days" to find it, and along with Doug's collection of Remington and Russell paintings, it was intended as the basis of "a museum of western relics." This was one of Fairbanks's dream projects, but the timing was all wrong. A few years earlier, he might have been thrilled by Mary's extravagantly thoughtful gift, but in 1931 it was nothing more than another way of tying him to Pickfair.

Pickfair was something Doug was trying to escape. The upkeep was tremendous, and he was feeling the pinch of the Depression; by no means a pauper, he still felt the need to cut corners. And, Lord knows, there were a lot of corners in Pickfair. He didn't need a little gray home in the West; he didn't need Hollywood. "Why should I work?" he said. "I have enough money and I've worked all my life. Now I want to go places."

Once again there were rumors of trouble at Pickfair. Mary did her best to check them. Asked why she didn't join Doug on his tours, she replied, "I love to travel, but I love Pickfair better. It's thrilling to watch one's home grow and grow." In other words, she was a homebody, true to America, Hollywood and her career. This self-portrait isn't entirely inaccurate, though by this time she was beginning to lose interest in her work. Her sole release in 1931, *Kiki,* was, as she well knew, the worst picture of her career.

This was the first non-Pickford production Mary had made in over a decade. The producer was Joseph Schenck, the head of United Artists. Schenck was a good administrator—taking control of UA in 1926, he had pulled the company out of the red by the early thirties—but his qualifications for producer were not impressive. Crude, often crass, he lacked vision and often used strong-arm tactics. When his wife Norma Talmadge was carrying on an affair with Gilbert Roland, Schenck let it be known that he had given orders for Roland's emasculation. And for years Hollywood believed that Schenck had carried out his threat, until Constance Bennett mentioned over the bridge table that her new husband, Gilbert Roland, had everything a man wanted—with something to spare.

Kiki, a remake of a Norma Talmadge silent, was Schenck's idea. Talmadge's career ended with the talkies (she had a Brooklyn accent), but for a time in the mid-20s Norma vied with Mary for top place in popularity polls, and there are people who contend that Talmadge was a more subtle silent screen actress than Pickford. Certainly she was more versatile. Norma could play Kiki, a French chorus girl desperately trying to lure her lover away from his adulterous wife, but Mary couldn't. She was too "Nordic."

In Kiki's apache skirt and pancake beret, Pickford looks like a Los Angeles matron whooping it up for a charity masquerade. Now approaching forty, a critical age for any woman star, Mary hadn't wrinkled or sprouted crows-feet; instead she had become drawn, pinched, dowdy. And while she still had her good days, few of them occurred during the filming of *Kiki.*

"Where has Mary been hiding all this fire?" asked *Photoplay.* It wasn't a question worth answering. As the critic for a Los Angeles paper put it, "Kiki is a role better suited to the talents of Clara Bow or Nancy Carroll or Miss Pickford's daughter-in-law, Joan Crawford." Mary never fooled herself about the quality of her work. She knew *Kiki* was bad and that she was bad in it.

On top of these professional woes came a great personal grief—Mary learned that Jack was dying in Paris. The official diagnosis was "progressive multiple neuritis," a euphemism for too much too soon. He had been warned, but was ready to end his life as he had always lived it, full speed ahead. Doug had seen Jack in Europe only a few months before, and reported to Mary that her brother looked good, had some pink in his cheeks and she shouldn't worry. But Fairbanks was overly optimistic. Early in 1933, Mary was informed that Jack couldn't last much longer. She wired that she was on her way, and that in the meantime, Jack should try Christian Science healing techniques.

The next day, January 3, Jack Pickford died in the same hospital in which Olive Thomas had died nearly thirteen years before. Mary was now alone except for a philandering husband; a wayward sister, who was no comfort—Lottie never really recovered from Jack's death; and teen-aged Gwynne, who had become both a daughter-substitute and a younger sister.

To keep herself occupied, Mary started work on a new picture, another attempt to remake *Secrets*. Considering her troubles with the earlier version, returning to this property may seem like an act of self-destruction, but *Secrets* offered Mary a good part, and she was certain she could capitalize on her past mistakes. As director she chose Frank Borzage, winner of two Oscars (for Janet Gaynor's silent *Seventh Heaven* and Sally Eiler's sound *Bad Girl*), and as her leading man, she wanted Gary Cooper, who was then involved with one of Mary's closest friends, the American-born Countess Dorothy Di Frasso.

Cooper was tied up, so Mary settled for Leslie Howard, an improbable choice for the role of a rugged California frontiersman. (Though miscast, Howard managed to squeak by on his acting ability.) Borzage was sick for much of the production, and there were other minor problems, but when the picture was completed, Mary was satisfied. And rightfully so. While no masterpiece, and a great box-office disappointment, *Secrets* is the best of the Pickford sound films.

Doug in the meantime had sailed for the South Seas on Joe Schenck's yacht, *The Invader*. With him were Chuck Lewis, Tom Geraghty, director Edward Sutherland and Spanish actress Maria Alba, Fairbanks's latest "discovery." The starlet's presence on the yacht raised some eyebrows, but Mary managed to look unperturbed. Miss Alba, she explained, was an actress who was playing a role in Mr. Fairbanks's latest movie, *Mr. Robinson Crusoe*."

The picture was ostensibly the reason for the South Seas cruise. It was another one of Doug's travelogues, this one fleshed out with a slender plot, an update of the Daniel Defoe classic. The major modernization is the transformation of Friday into a native girl (Maria Alba)—a clever twist, but one that caused unseen complications. While ridding the Defoe story of any hint of homosexuality, it raised the taboo question of miscegenation. Somebody, maybe Tom Geraghty, came up with a clever solution: after introducing Friday to civilization, Crusoe resists the temptation of marriage and puts her to work as a hula dancer in a Broadway revue.

Mr. Robinson Crusoe is crude both in tone and technique, but it's more enjoyable than *Around the World*, mainly because of Doug—he's jolly and appealing and looks dashing in Crusoe's beard and rags. But it's for Fairbanks addicts only, and in 1932 there weren't enough of them to make the picture a hit.

The film was released in both sound and silent versions; there isn't much dialogue, just sound effects, background music, an almost continuous monologue by Fairbanks. The sound recording and a couple of scenes were finished in a studio, which meant Doug spent several weeks in Hollywood in the early summer of 1932. Pickford met him when *The*

Invader docked at a San Francisco pier, and even managed a bright smile when photographers asked her to pose with Maria Alba.

Mary had prepared a surprise for Doug. During his absence she had overhauled Pickfair—the outside was now smooth white, the inside redecorated by the legendary Elsie de Wolfe in what was described as "Georgian" furnishings. (Judging from photographs, the style was Waldorf-Astoria French Empire.) A room had been set aside to exhibit the samurai swords and other Oriental knickknacks collected by Mary and Doug during their Far East travels; in later years, cocktails were served here by servants dressed in Kabuki costumes. The renovations weren't to everyone's taste—David Niven described it as "overfurnished" and Anita Loos thought there were too many "Cosmopolitan-cover portraits" of Mary.

The cost of the Pickfair renovations (which included the construction of a guest house) was high and not to Doug's liking, but Mary argued that the expenditure was necessary at this time, the opening of the Olympic games in Los Angeles. The countryside would soon be crawling with international celebrities, all hoping to visit Pickfair, which had to be refurbished to live up to their expectations. And, after all, this had been done for him—athletics were his favorite pastime, not hers. So Doug stayed around for the Olympics, and figured prominently in the coverage given the games, though he was somewhat upstaged by a top-hatted Louis B. Mayer who seemed to have a front box (and front-page coverage) for every event.

Once the games were over, he left Mary alone to wander through the Georgian splendors of Pickfair. Again, rumors started to circulate. Mary dealt with them in two ways. Either she deigned to deny them with faint ridicule ("Oh, really?" "How silly!") or she ignored them and carried on as though Doug would soon be home to carry out his duties.

In his absence, she went on opening "Santa Claus" drives for indigent children and laying cornerstones wherever cornerstones had to be laid. In New York, she served supper to a group of Depression-poor actors to inaugurate the opening of the Actor's Dinner Club, a glorified soup line. She presided as (the first woman) Grand Marshall of the Tournament of Roses in Pasadena. She appeared at charity masquerades, once costumed as Delores Del Rio (the theme was "Your Favorite Movie Stars") and once, with Marion Davies, as a lady from the court of Louis XIV. And sometimes she went to a dance or a night club, but her escort was always above suspicion, someone like Charles Farrell or Johnny Mack Brown who was Fairbanks's friend as well as hers.

Finally, at the beginning of 1933, Mary decided to join Doug in Europe. It was to be a gala reunion. All arrangements were in the hands of the Countess Di Frasso, who was planning a café society houseparty at her Roman villa, the guest list including her "friend," Gary Cooper; Mary; Elsa Maxwell; screenwriter Donald Ogden Stewart and his wife Beatrice. They would sail on the S.S. *Rex* to Genoa where Mary would meet Doug, and after a few days with Dorothy Di Frasso, they would go over to Saint Moritz "for the winter sports."

As it turned out, the trip was one of Dorothy Di Frasso's social fiascos. First, Gary Cooper cancelled out—he had a picture commitment; then Donald Ogden Stewart suffered a nervous breakdown; Elsa Maxwell remembered a previous engagement; and Dorothy Di Frasso decided to stay in Los Angeles and nurse her ailing father. The party had dwindled to two—Mary and her friend, Mildred Zukor Loew (Adolph Zukor's daughter); they sailed on the *Rex* in February 1933, and arriving in Genoa, were met by Doug who whisked Mary to St. Moritz for a winter holiday.

Pickford's plans were indefinite. She would be abroad for at least six weeks, maybe longer if she accompanied Doug on his forthcoming trip to the Far East. It all depended on the starting date of her next movie.

Precisely six weeks later she was back in New York, even though there was no forthcoming movie. During her vacation, *Secrets* had opened in New York to pretty good reviews and indifferent business. Mary, who had never blinded herself to hard facts, now recognized that she was working on borrowed time, capitalizing on the indulgent affection of her longstanding fans. Many years later, in one of the most revealing statements of her life, Mary told English film historian Kevin Brownlow, "I left the screen because I didn't want what happened to Chaplin to happen to me. When he discarded the tramp, the tramp turned around and killed him. The little girl made me. I wasn't waiting for the little girl to kill me. I was pigeonholed. . . . I could have done more dramatic performances than the ones I gave in *Coquette* and *Secrets,* but I was already typed."

At first Mary made no public announcement of her decision to end her film career, but she did say she would burn the negatives of all her movies so that "future generations will not have the chance to laugh at me." Then she started buying up the rights to her early Biograph and IMP films with this purpose in mind. Eventually Lillian Gish talked her out of destroying her pictures, but Mary didn't allow them to be shown commercially until 1970.

On her return to New York in 1933, Mary said she had no film projects, but was thinking about returning to the stage. Lots of film stars were traveling the same route, particularly the ones that hadn't had much luck with sound. On the vaudeville circuit, they could earn $1,000 a week for a couple of songs, a comedy routine and a little dancing—chicken feed compared to their former salaries; still, it was better than oblivion.

Mary was not so lighthearted about her return to Broadway. She knew that Belasco was passé, and that since her appearance in *A Good Little Devil,* a new American theatre had arisen—O'Neill, The Theatre Guild, Ina Claire, the Lunts, Laurette Taylor. The Broadway stage had grown up and Mary wasn't coming back in pinafores. She told interviewers that she would go into training until her vocal and technical skills were up to legitimate standards.

Mary returned to Pickfair and supposedly began her

studies. There was no news until July 3, 1933, when *The New York Times* announced in banner headlines:

MARY AND DOUG PART

Practically every other major American paper gave the separation the same kind of coverage. Mary apologized for ruining the Fourth of July for her fans. "I'm sorry it had to come at this time, but it did—that's all. I'm still at Pickfair and my plans for staying there are indefinite."

This was not strictly the truth—she was in seclusion at Marion Davies's beach cottage. And she hadn't intended to break the news at this time. A few weeks earlier she had told Louella Parsons about her problems, swearing the columnist to secrecy. Parsons kept her word until she learned that another columnist was about to break the story; then she printed most of Mary's confidences. At last the problems of Pickfair were out in the open, which was probably Mary's intention in speaking to Louella. Pickford was too wise in the ways of Hollywood to expect a gossip columnist to keep a secret for very long.

When the news broke, Doug was in London, and talked to reporters only through a press representative. His message was brief: "No comment." Their friends, on the other hand, had lots to say, all of it encouraging for Mary and Doug's fans. Robert Fairbanks termed the whole to-do "a tempest in a teapot," and Karl Kitchen was sure the "misunderstanding would soon be patched up."

Press commentators played it both ways: they were optimistic about an "imminent reconciliation" and pessimistic about the "insurmountable problems" separating Mary and Doug. If there was a divorce, Pickford said, the grounds would be incompatibility, and immediately reporters began to talk about "a division of opinion on how they should live." Louella Parsons reported that a few weeks before the separation, Doug had sent Mary a telegram saying she must either sell Pickfair or bear sole responsibility for its upkeep. Louella was outraged, as were Pickfair fans around the world. But Fairbanks may have been using the sale of Pickfair as a way of prying Mary out of Hollywood and into the international life he wanted to lead.

Louella went on to mention Mary's "friendship" with Buddy Rogers. She reminded readers of how Mary had gone straight from the *Rex* to Chicago where Buddy and his orchestra were appearing at a World's Fair pavilion. (Buddy's career as an actor had declined in the early 1930s, and since he had some small musical talent, he started out on a new track.) But Parsons never referred to Doug's companion, though she knew Fairbanks was dashing around London with "a mysterious woman of the nobility."

It was several months before Lady Sylvia Ashley's name was known to the American press, and then, the reaction was, in the words of a Sunday supplement article, "Who is Sylvia . . . What is She?" According to the article, she had been born Sylvia Hawkes, the daughter of a footman or a greengrocer or a groom (no one knew for certain how her father made his living) . . . at 15, he started a career as a model . . . she looked good in lingerie . . . was called "Silky" . . . had crashed the chorus of "The Midnight Follies" . . . became a favorite of London's titled stage-door Johnnies . . . was introduced to Lord Edward Ashley by the Prince of Wales . . . married Ashley . . . was annoyed when she was not presented to the King and Queen . . . became famous for "her collection of expensive jewelry and lavish scale of living" . . . grew bored with the life of an English gentlewoman . . . left her husband in 1928.

Today Sylvia Ashley lives as a recluse in Southern California, seeing only close friends who report she still bears a grudge against the American press for casting her as a golddigger. She has a legitimate cause for complaint, but to some extent she looked the part. "She was glamorous rather than beautiful," says actor David Gray. "Her best feature was her long, silver-blond hair. She was a type of woman I call 'the lady-slut'—I'm referring to her appearance, not her character; Carole Lombard and Joan Crawford are other examples of what I mean. Today it no longer makes sense because we don't pigeonhole people anymore—nowadays, any lady can be a slut. But in the 30s and 40s the combination was very provocative."

Asked if Sylvia had anything to offer beyond glamor, Anita Loos (who gave her a small role in the London production of her 1923 play, *The Whole Town's Talking*) replied, "Not much—some charm, perhaps." And Mrs. Howard Strickling, who knew Sylvia as Mrs. Clark Gable, describes her as "a Dulcy," a reference to the well-meaning but scatterbrained flapper created by humorist Franklin P. Adams. On one point nearly everyone agrees—Sylvia knew how to catch a man.

For several weeks, there was no further word on the separation. Mary stayed at Pickfair and said nothing, except to deny rumors that she was thinking of divorce. Quite probably, Mary had intended the separation as Doug had intended his demand that she sell Pickfair—both were trying to force the other's hand. But he called her bluff as she had his—he did nothing. Weeks passed, and there was no indication that Doug would return to Hollywood, not even for Christmas. Mary did what she repeatedly had said she had no plans of doing. She filed for divorce.

Her divorce complaint against Fairbanks read in part:

> . . . that he has shown a lack of consideration for the plaintiff's feelings and sensibilities, and has constantly and consistently carried on a course of conduct which has caused the plaintiff grievous mental anguish. . . .

> That since, on or about June 1930, against the wishes of the plaintiff and with distant and indifferent attitude toward her wishes and desire . . . he has continuously absented himself from home for months at a time. . . .

That by reason of plaintiff's status and position as an actress, this course of conduct has caused much criticism and unfavorable comment throughout the world . . .

That he has publicly announced that he has no interest in life except traveling. . . . That such conduct rendered the proper discharges of marital life impossible and was such as to destroy the legitimate ends and objects of matrimony. . . .

Certainly Doug was aware of Mary's action and had agreed to it, because just before the divorce suit was filed, a deed of transfer placed Pickfair in Mary's name. The rest of the world, however, was caught unawares. And before the shock could register, Mary was on her way to New York "just to get away from Hollywood for a little while."

She left the day after her suit was filed, December 8, with her secretary, Miss Elizabeth Lewis, as traveling companion. While her private car was being switched from the Sante Fe to the Pennsylvania railway in Chicago, she talked to reporters, but refused to make any comment about the divorce. A day later, she arrived in New York, looking tired, pale and thrown together—she was wearing a tufted wool dress, a mink coat and an antelope hat.

"See here," she said quietly, "I know what's in the minds of you press people . . . don't ask me that."

"About divorcing Mr. Fair . . . ?"

"Don't ask me that question!"

"Why not?"

"Good taste!"

In those days press people were ladies and gentlemen, and they abided by Mary's rules of etiquette. The conversation shifted to why Mary was in New York. She wanted to see the new plays, particularly *As Thousands Cheer*, starring her ex-sister-in-law, Marilyn Miller, and she had also brought her skates along. She hoped to do some skating on Central Park Lake with nineteen-year-old Gwynne who was coming East for the holidays.

And three days later, accompanied by a battery of photographers, she was on the ice, one hand hidden in a Persian lamb muff, gingerly trying to maneuver her way through a figure eight. Her days of trying to play an outdoorswoman worthy of Douglas Fairbanks were over.

⚜ 15 ⚜

Besides ice-skating and seeing the new shows, Mary had one other reason for visiting New York. She was going back to the stage . . . not Broadway, but vaudeville . . . well, not exactly vaudeville, either. She was part of the stage show at the old Paramount movie palace on Times Square.

According to *Variety*, "Pickford rated a guarantee of $10,000 a week and 50/50 split with the house over a gross of $60,000 for her engagement." It was not just a one-week booking—after New York, Mary was set for a two-month tour of Paramount's East-coast theatre circuit. The contract called for her to go on five times a day, seven days a week, in a twenty minute scene from *A Church Mouse,* a Broadway comedy that had starred Ruth Gordon. It was a grueling schedule, but Mary had several good reasons for undertaking it. This gave her the chance, she explained, "to realign myself with the younger motion-picture audience, and also to allow myself to become accustomed to stage routine prior to my return to Broadway." Beyond that, it would keep her busy and prove she wasn't brooding over her troubles with Doug.

There was little time for rehearsals, and Mary was visibly nervous during the first performance, but the audience greeted her warmly. The engagement was a huge success, breaking the house record set by Mae West a year or so earlier, and requiring a squadron of police to keep order on the last day of Mary's appearance. The critics received her performance with carefully-worded good will, a typical comment coming from Howard Barnes of *The Tribune*: "Miss Pickford is restrained and competent."

Perhaps Mary also had reservations about her performance. Earlier, she had commissioned Pulitzer Prize playwright Owen Davis to write a comedy for her Broadway comeback, but she now announced that she was dissatisfied with Davis's script and would not be appearing on Broadway the next season.

She did, however, go ahead with her Paramount tour, playing Philadelphia, Baltimore, Washington and Boston, where two dramatic events occurred. The first started when Mary received a letter from a man who had "valuable papers" which he thought might interest her. Pickford invited him to her hotel suite on the same afternoon she was entertaining Lillian Gish and several other friends. The man arrived with a woman companion and asked to speak to Mary alone; she took him into the bedroom where, after locking the door, he stared at her "with a steely, almost hypnotic look." Mary screamed, her guests pounded on the door, the man opened it and fled with his accomplice.

Mary wasn't sure what her visitors had wanted. "Maybe it was an extortion plot or maybe they had planned to hypnotize me and have me walk out with them so the people in the other room would have thought nothing of it." The extortionists or kidnappers were never caught, and the true purpose of their visit was never clarified, though the press hinted that they were spiritualists. At any rate, Mary was so frightened that she asked for a police escort to Buzzard's Bay where she was met by friends who took her to their home on Cape Cod.

Returning to Boston to finish her Paramount engagement, she received an even nastier surprise. Word reached her that Lord Ashley had filed for a divorce, naming Fairbanks as corespondent. The news caught everyone by surprise. There was a lot of press speculation about why Ashley had waited six years before taking action and why he had cited only Doug as corespondent. It was no secret that Sylvia had kept company with several men since the breakup of her marriage, most notably a rich and handsome speed-car enthusiast, Sir Timothy Birkin. Perhaps, the English papers suggested, Doug had been chosen for his publicity value.

Mary, of course, had known about Doug's affair with Sylvia Ashley for some time. But she had not expected a public scandal; neither had Doug, and he was very concerned about how Mary would react. During a transatlantic phone conversation, she assured him she would do or say nothing that would hurt him. On the whole, she was true to her word. A few days later, she told a group of reporters that there ought to be a "school for wives" that would teach them to be "reasonably selfish. Women ought to learn that kindness is sometimes the most devastating and weakening influence. Wives especially make this mistake. It is the unselfish ones who ruin themselves and everyone depending on them."

Obviously, she was extremely hurt. "Her pride was wounded," remembers Mildred Loew. "She felt Doug had humiliated her in public, and that was something she couldn't forgive." And around this time, she began to drink, not heavily, but enough for people to notice . . . and talk.

Doug made no attempt to talk with Mary in person. In her autobiography, Pickford says Doug "never faced any difficulty he could run away from," and now he had a valid excuse for staying away from Pickfair. He had to remain in England to finish what was to be his last picture, *The Private Life of Don Juan*, for the Hungarian-born, London-based producer, Alexander Korda.

This film had grown out of Fairbanks's enthusiasm for the British cinema. A year before, he had seen a preview of Korda's film biography of Henry VII, and told the press that he thought it was one of the finest movies ever made. In fact, he was certain that someday London would be the film capital of the world, and to help it along, he arranged for United Artists to distribute Korda's productions in America.

He also hoped to encourage the great English actors who had migrated to Hollywood to return to their native land, but most of them were content where they were. So, in 1933, Fairbanks enlisted the aid of Doug, Jr., who agreed to appear in *Catherine the Great,* a historical pastiche starring Elisabeth Bergner. Then a year later, Doug, Sr. decided to return to the screen as the aging Don Juan, an unfortunate choice of role considering his recent escapades with Lady Sylvia.

Doug's championing of British films did not go over well in America. *The New York American* commented bitterly, "Mr. Fairbanks used to be a notable figure in pictures, but he has become somewhat passé, and has gradually descended from feature pictures to program pictures to travelogues and from travelogues to London." Possibly the resentment had something to do with the fiasco of *Don Juan* in the States, but then again, it's not a very good picture. Heavy, static, episodic, it's almost cruel in its exposure of Fairbanks as an aging roué.

Doug did not enjoy making *Don Juan.* Hounded by reporters who hung around the studio or outside his rented Hertfordshsire estate, he was irascible and jumpy, frequently flying off the handle for no apparent reason. Keeping up a front of indifference, he and Lady Sylvia continued to be seen together in public, often double-dating with Doug, Jr., now divorced from Joan Crawford and escorting Gertrude Lawrence (his co-star in a recent West End play). London bachelor life brought father and son closer together, though sometimes Doug, Sr. suspected Doug, Jr. of siding with Mary, and there would be a momentary breach in their friendship.

Dealing with Fairbanks was a touchy business, but by employing tact and patience, several friends were able to broach the subject of a possible reconciliation. Joe Schenck, returning from England in the spring of 1934, said, "There is no question in my mind that Mary and Doug are still very much in love . . . A while ago, Mary told me if Doug would woo her all over again, there was every possibility their difficulties could be patched up . . . And from what Doug said, he gave me the feeling he wanted to try it all over again . . ." A month later, Karl Kitchen started hopping back and forth across the Atlantic, acting as a go-between for Mary and Doug. He predicted that a reconciliation was imminent. German boxer Max Schmeling agreed. Arriving in New York for a championship bout, he reported that during a week-long visit to his training camp, Doug had called Mary almost daily.

Pickford continued to brush aside any questions about her marriage problems. She wanted to talk about only the happy, fulfilling segments of her life: her work and plans for the future. Mary was branching out in all directions. She had her sculpture lessons and her writing, which included a short story ("The Little Liar") and the first of her inspirational books, *Why Not Try God?* (These were followed a year later by another inspirational tract, *My Rendezvous With Life,* and a novel, *The Demi-Widow,* which one reviewer concluded could not have been ghost-written "since it reads so much like the typical Hollywood scenario.") She was still looking for a Broadway script—Frances Marion had been asked to prepare something suitable—and was also thinking of making a new picture.

"Hopefully it will be something with as little talking in it as possible," she said. "I shall weep bitterly if Charlie Chaplin talks in his next picture [*Modern Times*] for then I will know it is the death of silent pictures."

A few weeks later, she announced she was abandoning movies for radio as the hostess-star of a "stock company" that would broadcast abbreviated versions of Broadway plays. The show, which went on the air in the fall of 1934 with *A Church Mouse,* was only a modest success, and was replaced by a second series, "Parties at Pickfair," a disaster. This half-hour weekly program originated from Pickfair, and featured Mary's celebrity friends who were asked to contribute "a song or a few witty sayings." According to one critic, the programs tried to create "the illusion of eavesdropping on one of Mary's dinner parties by way of an unconscionable amount of lip-smacking and talking about mouth-watering food . . . the purpose of the series seems to be to convince the public that Mary sets a good table."

This flitting from one hastily conceived project to the next was not typical of Pickford. She seemed lost, a desperate woman trying to find something to make her forget her unhappiness. She avoided Hollywood as much as possible, and spent more time at the Sherry-Netherland in New York than she did at Pickfair. Her friends were deeply concerned about her welfare. And when she celebrated her forty-first birthday in April, even her dedicated fans had to admit that she looked her age.

Then, in late spring, her depression suddenly lifted. One day, as she returned to the Sherry-Netherland after a Fifth Avenue shopping spree, she was besieged by a group of reporters who noted that she looked "radiant" and "younger than she has in months." And on this occasion, she was willing to answer questions about Doug. Yes, she said, there was a good chance of a reconciliation. Doug was coming to Pickfair as soon as he finished *Don Juan*.

The trip was postponed several times, but finally he sailed on the *Rex* in early August. Arriving in New York, he was in high spirits, but refused to talk about Mary. Instead he entertained the press with tales of his adventures in exotic places, including his experiment with opium, a drug he had taken in Marrakesh without ill effects. For anyone old enough to remember Doug in his prime, when he was lecturing American youth about the dangers of liquor and the sanctity of marriage, this aging café society rake must have been a depressing sight. What a transformation! The champion of clean living had ended as an opium-eating womanizer.

It was not, of course, the first time Doug had tripped over his public image, but before, when he divorced Beth for Mary, his immense popularity had helped him keep his footing. That popularity was gone, replaced by a lingering nostalgia, a very wispy emotion, not enough to sustain Fairbanks through the present crisis. Now all public sentiment was directed toward Mary.

Pickford told reporters she was both apprehensive and optimistic about the reunion. "The future must work out, and it will," she told reporters the day before Doug's arrival in Los Angeles. Then she paused for several seconds. "Excuse me," she finally said. "I can't bring myself to talk about these things so near my heart."

Fairbanks arrived at Pickfair on a Wednesday afternoon; he took Mary for a drive, they dined by candlelight and ended the evening with another drive around the Hollywood Hills. Thursday, they motored to the Santa Monica beach house. Along the route, they were spotted by friends who reported that they were smiling and looked happy. The next day Doug went off alone to Rancho Zorro. He and Mary were going to spend the weekend "thinking it over."

But not until November was there definite word about the status of the Fairbanks marriage. Then Mary came forward and denied "the persistent rumors of a reconciliation." Perhaps she was hoping Fairbanks would contradict her, but six weeks later, when she had not heard from him, she instructed her lawyer to proceed with the divorce suit. On December 28 her attorney announced that he had filed an affidavit showing that divorce papers had been delivered to Fairbanks by mail, and that the trial had already been placed on the court calendar.

Two days later, Doug sailed for Europe. And on January 10, 1935, a pale and visibly shaken Mary left a courtroom after receiving an interlocutory decree of divorce.

Nearly all their friends feel that neither Mary nor Doug really wanted a divorce. But somehow things had gotten out of control. Both felt wronged, both were stubborn, both wanted the other to be the first to give in. Neither was willing to compromise on the all-important question of how and where they would live out their lives.

But there was probably more to it than this. Recalling her

reunion with Fairbanks, Mary later wrote, "Something had gone. It was as though his spirit had fled." And Doug may have had similar feelings about Mary—glamor and vitality were no longer their long suits. An observer of the Fairbanks marriage (who wishes to remain anonymous) said recently, "Mary and Doug were on a mutual ego-trip. Their attraction for each other was based on their fame and success. When their careers floundered, their marriage went to pieces. There was nothing else to sustain it."

It is also possible, as several people have suggested, that Doug never believed Mary would dissolve their marriage. He apparently expected her to patch things up before the interlocutory decree became final. And Mary may well have been waiting for him to stop her. Once again, they were playing a dangerous game of double bluff.

The press, however, accepted the divorce as inevitable. Abandoning all hope for a reconciliation, the papers now began to speculate about the settlement. A spokesman reported that the matter had been worked out amicably, but there was no disclosure of what arrangements had been made. Probably very little property or money changed hands. Mary and Doug's only joint holding was the physical plant of the UA studio, and the land on which it rested. Assessments from the Los Angeles County Assessors for 1932 credited Mary with having stocks worth over $2 million, foreign trusts worth $175,000 and real estate valued at $190,000. Doug's stocks were estimated at $1.3 million, foreign trusts at $75,000 and real estate at $80,000. Pickfair, listed separately and valued at $70,000, had already been deeded to Mary.

Another matter of speculation was when Doug and Mary would remarry. Throughout the next year, Pickford continued to deny rumors of her romantic attachment to Buddy Rogers, and Doug refused to talk about Lady Sylvia. During his absence, Ashley had been seen around London with Irish sportsman, Michael Farmer (one of Gloria Swanson's ex-husbands), but dropped him as soon as Fairbanks returned to Europe.

They caught up with each other in Rome and then went to Naples for a short holiday. Two weeks later, they were house-hunting on Berkeley Square in London. But instead of settling down, Fairbanks took off on a world cruise with Sylvia, Fred Astaire and one of his *Don Juan* co-stars, Benita Hume (later Mrs. Ronald Colman). The party sailed across the Atlantic to the Bahamas and Jamaica; after several weeks in Kingston, they set out on the second leg of their voyage, finally getting as far as Indonesia. In Batavia, Doug learned of an impending stockholders' crisis at UA, and rushed back to the States. But instead of entering at San Francisco, as was expected, he sailed to Vancouver.

There was a lot of curiosity about why Fairbanks had gone so far out of his way, and one explanation was that he was shielding Sylvia, who left Doug in Vancouver and traveled across Canada to Quebec, where she planned to catch a liner for England. *The New York Sun* reported:

> The reason Ashley avoided the United States may have been because of the case of Vera, Countess Cathcart, who was detained at Ellis Island and finally barred from entering America in 1926 on grounds of moral turpitude. The basis for the action was that she had been divorced in England for misconduct. Fairbanks's lawyers apparently feared the same thing, though since the furor over the Cathcart case, the immigration authorities have been careful about the interpretation of the moral turpitude provision. It was then pointed out that it would bar every person divorced on grounds of misconduct, including many distinguished visitors.

Another, more probable explanation is that Doug didn't want Sylvia loitering in the background when he met Pickford at the UA stockholders' meeting.

Doug's reunion with Mary was brief and uneventful. He was able to catch up with Sylvia in Montreal and they sailed together for England. They arrived in London in late July—

less than seven months before the divorce was to become final on January 10, 1936. Weeks went by without any overtures of peace from Mary. By December, Doug was apprehensive and started cabling Pickfair. Still no word from Mary. On January 7, he sailed for New York, on a pretext of business, and started wiring Mary from the Waldorf Astoria. No answer. Giving up, Doug booked passage back to London, and was already aboard ship, when a conciliatory call came from Mary. "It's too late; it's just too late," he told her.

This often-told and very dramatic story may have a core of truth, but some of the details have to be wrong. It's a matter of public record, as reported in at least three New York newspapers, that when the divorce decree became final, Doug was sitting in Connie's Inn, a famous Manhattan night-spot of the period, with Adele Astaire and another couple. The bandleader announced that the next number would be dedicated to Fairbanks and "Lady Ashley"—Adele had been mistaken for Sylvia. Before a note of music was played, Doug was out of his seat and on his way back to his hotel.

On February 26, almost a month after the divorce, Doug finally sailed for London, already decided on marrying Sylvia as soon as possible. Less than two weeks later, he petitioned a Paris court for an exemption from French marriage laws (which required a period of residency); the request was granted, and on March 7, Sylvia Ashley became the third Mrs. Douglas Fairbanks.

Today there is still lively debate about why Fairbanks married Sylvia. Some say love; some say spite—this was Doug's way of getting back at Mary. Anita Loos feels the marriage was motivated by Fairbanks's indiscriminate snobbism. "I met Doug a few months before the marriage and we started talking about Sylvia," Miss Loos recalled recently. "He said, in all seriousness, that he had wronged a lady of the British peerage and felt obligated to do the gentlemanly thing and marry her. It never seemed to dawn on him that the lady was really the daughter of a hostler."

It seems unlikely, however, that Doug was oblivious to

Sylvia's plebeian background—the tabloids were full of accounts of her past history. There is even a story that Fairbanks once turned to a friend and said, "So what if Sylvia's father is a groom? Mary's father was a grocer."

The Ashley-Fairbanks marriage got off to a bad start—their car was robbed while they were honeymooning in Spain—but worked out better than practically anyone had expected. Sylvia was no more a sportswoman than Mary—she always wore floppy hats to protect her ivory skin from the sun—but she was glamorous; she "jazzed" a little; didn't scold or nag; had no ambitions to be the doyenne of Beverly Hills. In many ways, she was a perfect companion for the mature Fairbanks.

And Mary, after five years of fretting over a vagrant husband, must have been flattered by the attentions of such a devoted suitor as Buddy Rogers. He was very serious and very considerate and very young; young enough, at least, to object to his boyish nickname, which suited him perfectly. Curly-haired, with a pleasant, open face, he was as wholesome as the boy next door. When photographed together, he and Mary often looked like an Ivy League collegiate out with his well-preserved stepmother.

Mary kept Buddy waiting for several months. She didn't say no, but she did see other men while he was touring with his band. Buddy was the personification of patience; having bided his time since *My Best Girl*, he was prepared to wait a few more months. Finally, his perseverance paid off. He spent the 1936 Christmas holidays at Pickfair, and a week later, Mary announced they would be married in June.

The ceremony, held at the home of producer Louis Lighton (whose wife, Hope Loring, wrote *My Best Girl*) was "a simple outdoor affair" under a sycamore tree in the garden. Photographers were admitted in groups of four, but no newsreel cameras were allowed on the premises—Mary vetoed them after seeing the footage of the Duke and Duchess of Windsor's marriage. After the service, the wedding party returned to Pickfair for a reception for three hundred, including

Eddie Cantor, Sam Goldwyn, George Burns and Gracie Allen, Norma Talmadge, Mr. and Mrs. Cecil B. De Mille, Dolores Costello, Walt Disney, Mickey Neilan and the Johnny Mack Browns. Doug and Lady Sylvia were staying in Santa Monica, but, of course, they did not attend the reception; neither did they send a wire or letter of congratulations.

Friends explained that the wedding ceremony was not held at Pickfair because Rogers didn't want to be married in a house that once belonged to Fairbanks. He had, in fact, asked Mary to sell Pickfair and she had agreed. He allowed no press photographs taken at the reception. He also made it clear that he didn't like being called Buddy, so the papers referred to him as Charles ("Buddy") Rogers.

The wedding presents included a gold wristwatch from Mrs. William Randolph Hearst—a strangely partisan gift unless the watch was of unisex design—and a group of white figurines on a marble base from Norma Shearer. Mary looked radiant and surprisingly youthful. This was her third marriage, but only her first big social wedding, and though she had been very nervous that morning, she soon settled down and enjoyed herself. The reception was very pointedly an intramural, all-Hollywood affair—none of the diplomats or titled celebrities who had paraded through Pickfair in Doug's time were invited—and yet it was still international news. Mary's "ciel-bleu" dress (a last minute choice) didn't create a color fad as did the Duchess's Windsor—blue gown, but the two marriages got almost equal coverage in the press.

After the wedding, Mary and Buddy left on a honeymoon cruise to Hawaii. Gwynne went along, and on the same ship were Henry and Clare Booth Luce and another set of newlyweds, Jeanette MacDonald and Gene Raymond. A crowd of 5,000 fans jammed the Honolulu waterfront to watch the celebrities' arrival. Buddy was too intimidated to leave the ship, but Mary relished every lei and aloha thrown in her direction. It seemed like old times.

⚜ 16 ⚜

By this time, Mary and Doug had admitted that their performing days were over. Neither was withdrawing from the film business, but from here on they would function only as producers and UA stockholders. Being the more decisive of the two, Mary was the first to put words into action. Early in 1936 she formed a partnership with Jesse Lasky (one of Paramount's original founders), and before the year was out they had produced two films: *The Gay Desperado* starring operatic tenor Nino Martini and Ida Lupino, and *One Rainy Afternoon* with Miss Lupino and Francis Lederer. Released through UA, the Pickford-Lasky pictures were a cut or two above run-of-the-mill; so were their reviews, but business was below par. Lasky and Pickford exchanged cross words, and in 1937 the partnership was dissolved.

Just before her marriage to Rogers, Mary seemed to lose her incentive for work. Her ambitions for a stage career ended with a West Coast tour of *Coquette* in 1934; her flirtation with radio stopped with the failure of "Parties at Pickfair"; she grew tired of writing when *The Demi-Widow* failed to duplicate the success of *Why Not Try God?* After her partnership with Lasky collapsed, she often talked about new film projects—*Alice in Wonderland* was frequently mentioned—but nothing got off the ground. And Mary slowly drifted into unofficial retirement.

Doug's post-Pickfair life followed a similar pattern. In 1937 he told the press that in partnership with Samuel Goldwyn he would produce, but not appear in, a superspectacle based on the travels of Marco Polo, and apparently he did work on the preliminary plans for the picture. Then he abruptly lost interest and sold all rights to Sam Goldwyn (who later filmed it—badly—with Gary Cooper in the title role). A few months later, he had a new idea; he was forming a company, Fairbanks International, to produce a Western epic, *Zorro Rides Again* (later retitled *The Californians*) starring Doug, Jr. But Fairbanks was in no hurry, and the film, the culmination of his boyhood fantasies, was still nowhere close to realization at the end of 1939.

If Doug dawdled over these projects, it may have been because they aroused so little excitement; no one seemed to care about his professional plans. The same was true of his personal life. With Sylvia, he continued to be in all the right spots at the right time: they were in London "for the season," went to Pamplona for the bullfights, to Saint Moritz for the winter sports, to Berlin for the 1936 Olympic games. They were constantly photographed as they boarded ships, "sky clippers" and dirigibles—they returned to New York on the Hindenburg in the summer of 1936. But pretty soon the pictures and the reports of their travels were buried on the inside pages of the tabloids.

They spent a good part of every year in Hollywood, and there was a lot of curiosity about when Doug would introduce Mary to Sylvia. Fairbanks faced this problem in his usual way—he ran away from it. Once Mary and Sylvia nearly bumped into each other at United Artists. "Don't leave yet," Doug whispered to Mary after a board meeting. "Sylvia's waiting in the corridor." But the inevitable finally happened one night at Gloria Swanson's. Throwing caution and Emily Post to the wind, Gloria had invited Sylvia and Doug and Mary to the same party, and when Fairbanks flatly refused to provide an introduction, Gloria happily performed the task.

While Doug cowered in an adjoining room, Mary and Sylvia carried on a polite, self-conscious conversation. Was it true that Pickfair was for sale? It was true. "Too bad," commented Sylvia. "Yes," replied Mary. "But I find I no longer need material possessions." This was Mary's only wicked comment, and it wasn't so terribly wicked. Nor was it particularly accurate. Pickfair was one material possession Mary couldn't do without, and though the house was on the market for a while, it was quietly withdrawn in the winter of 1937. Around that time, Mary bought some polo ponies for Buddy, possibly as a thank-you gift when he agreed to live in the house that would always partly belong to Fairbanks.

When Buddy wasn't touring with his band, he was playing polo, and when Mary wasn't traveling with Buddy, she was opening flower shows or reading in the Pickfair library or sipping a rum cola by the pool. ("One of these drinks," she confided to a reporter, "makes me feel very wicked.") They led expensive lives in an expensive house in expensive Beverly Hills. Though they weren't terribly social, they were society people, Hollywood style. Doug and Sylvia were society people, international style. In California they were part of the English and globetrotting sets—David Niven, the Ronald Colmans, Fred Astaire (who was soon to replace Fairbanks as Hollywood's leading snob).

For the first two years following the divorce, Fairbanks and Pickford rarely saw each other except at UA board meetings where they were waging a bitter campaign against Sam Goldwyn's attempt to gain control of the company. Doug was starting to cut himself off from his old friends, even from Chaplin, who in his autobiography remembers seeing Fairbanks only twice during the late 1930s. Soon his inner circle included only his wife, his son, Chuck Lewis and a few trusted members of his staff.

Fairbanks's world travels ended in September 1939. Two days before Great Britain declared war on Germany, he and Sylvia hastily boarded an American clipper and flew to the States. A day later they were joined by Sylvia's sister, Mrs. Basil Beck, and two sons; then they left for Los Angeles where they planned to sit out the war. They moved into a beach house at Santa Monica, and Doug worked fitfully on his plans for *The Californians* and for renovating Rancho Zorro, two dream projects that were now closely interwoven in his mind.

On Saturday, December 10, 1939, he went to a UCLA–USC football match, and returned home in good spirits—his team had won. The next day, a business associate said he looked "pale and overtired." On Monday, Doug started to complain of pains in his arms and chest; Sylvia called his doctor who immediately recognized the symptoms of a mild heart attack. As had been predicted, Doug's overly strenuous physical fitness program had adversely affected his circulation, a condition that may have been aggravated (as some claim) by too much alcohol. The doctor prescribed total bed rest, a restricted diet and professional nursing care.

Later that day, Doug told his brother Robert that should anything happen to him, Mary should be told "by the clock" —their private catchword since Ella Fairbanks's death twenty-three years before. Fairbanks slept off and on all day, awakening shortly after midnight when he asked his male nurse to open the window so that he could hear the sea.

"How are you?" the attendant asked. "Never felt better," Doug answered with a convincing grin. Then he fell back asleep and the nurse returned to his chair, as Marco Polo, a 150 pound mastiff, curled up at the foot of Doug's bed. The nurse had just settled down when he heard Polo growl. He glanced at the clock—12:45 A.M.—noted it on his chart, and got up to check his patient.

The headlines in the morning papers tell the rest of the story:

DOUGLAS FAIRBANKS DEAD AT 56

The news of Doug's death was known around Hollywood long before it reached the papers. One of the first to hear was Norma Shearer, who lived just down the beach from the Fairbankses. That night she was giving a midnight supper after a film premiere. Doug and Sylvia had been invited, and because of the excitement of the past two days had neglected to send their regrets. Just as her guests were about to sit down to dinner, Miss Shearer was called to the phone. She listened, blanched slightly, then hurriedly spoke to her butler, who quietly removed two place settings from the table. Then she went back to her guests, and only hours later did she tell Hedda Hopper that Douglas Fairbanks had died of a massive coronary.

The next morning Norma Shearer was one of the first to extend condolences to Sylvia. Other visitors included Darryl Zanuck, Kay Francis, Mrs. Fred Astaire and Cecil B. De Mille. The funeral was held in the "Wee Kirk 0' the Heather" at Forest Lawn. Tom Mix wore a black cowboy suit; a string quartet provided music; the pallbearers included Chaplin, Joe Schenck, Tom Geraghty, Chuck Lewis and Sid Grauman (the owner of Grauman's Chinese and the son of the man who dubbed Mary "America's Sweetheart"). Heavily veiled and unsteady on her feet, Sylvia was helped down the aisle by Doug, Jr. and his second wife, Mary Lee Fairbanks.

Good taste kept Mary from attending the service. She was then in Chicago with Buddy and his orchestra. Gwynne phoned her the news, but Mary, who suspected she might have had a sixth sense, already knew. "Don't tell me!" she gasped. "He's gone, isn't he?" Gwynne started to sob. In her autobiography, Mary says she choked back the tears "out of respect for Buddy," but turned to him for consolation: they spent the night "drinking tea and milk" and "talking about everything under the sun but Douglas."

There were many things to talk about. In just a little more than ten years Mary had lost nearly everyone who was dear to her. First Charlotte, then Jack, and finally in December 1936. Lottie had died of a heart attack. The two sisters were never close friends, not even in later years. At the time Mary was broadcasting "Parties at Pickfair," Lottie was selected as the hostess of a "Let's Pretend"–type radio program for children. "One Pickford on the radio is more than enough," Mary shouted, and Lottie quickly turned down the offer. But for all their differences, Mary could not have been unmoved by her sister's death—Lottie was her last remaining tie to a certain Smith family who once lived in Toronto.

Mary had lots of memories to mull over that night, but by morning she had found time to compose a dignified statement about Doug's death: "I am sure it will prove a consolation to us all to recall the joy and the glorious spirit of adventure he gave the world. He has passed from our mortal life quickly and spontaneously as he did everything in life, but it is impossible to believe that vibrant and gay spirit could ever perish."

In the following weeks, the papers and magazines were full of reappraisals of Fairbanks's career, one of the most accurate and heartfelt coming from Frank Nugent in *The New York Times*:

> Doug Fairbanks was make-believe at its best, a game we youngsters never tired of playing, a game . . . our fathers secretly shared. He was complete fantasy, not like Disney's, which has an overlay of whimsy and sophistication, but unabashed and joyous. Balustrades were made to be vaulted, draperies to be a giant slide, chandeliers to swing from, citadels to be scaled. There wasn't a small boy in the neighborhood who did not, in a Fairbanks picture, see himself triumphing over the local bully, winning the soft-eyed adoration of whatever ten-year-old blonde he had been courting, and wreaking vengeance on the teacher who made him stand in the corner that afternoon.

Or, to phrase it another way, Fairbanks's bad years and bad pictures were now forgotten, and Doug emerged in all his old glory—as the brash go-getter of the Anita Loos comedies, as Zorro and D'Artagnan and Robin, as the Thief of Bagdad and the Black Pirate.

Fairbanks had played some small part in ensuring his own immortality. Eight months before his death he donated prints of his key films to the newly formed film archives of The Museum of Modern Art, and through its exhibition and distribution programs the Museum introduced future generations of film buffs to the magic of Douglas Fairbanks. A short time before, Mary had donated negatives of her early one- and two-reelers to the National Archives in Washington, but these films and the later Paramount and UA features were screened only irregularly (and usually illegally) during the next thirty years. Mary had changed her mind about destroying her films, but not about giving modern audiences the chance to ridicule America's Sweetheart.

As a result, Doug's reputation has never diminished, while Mary's place in film history has been misunderstood or misrepresented. Nearly everyone interested in the American cinema knows something about her role in shaping the industry, but about her screen character and what it meant to audiences of the 1910s and 1920s there are still misconceptions. Unable to check myth against fact, people began to think of Mary as a superannuated Shirley Temple, all sugar and no spice. Ironically, she is remembered as the silent screen heroine Fairbanks once described in "A Classified List of Who's Who on the Screen," a series of articles written for *Vanity Fair* in 1918.

> First of all there's the movie heroine. She is invariably one of those excruciatingly sweet young things who once saw Mary Pickford and has never been the same since. She walks with the approved Lillian Gish movement, at a pace which would seem to indicate she is always on her way to a fire. She never sits in the accepted sense of the word—she merely takes a running jump at a chair and lands girlishly on all fours, then draws her knees up on a level with her chin and clasps her hands vivaciously around them. Her hair is always worn in curls—it's the unwritten law of the movies that all heroines, without regard to age, race, color or creed, must wear their hair in curls . . .

Doug's stereotype-heroine was meant as parody—no major silent screen actress was ever that inane, certainly not Pickford. But as time went on, she was remembered only as America's first curlytop Sweetheart, a misrepresentation for which she is partly responsible. Once, in the early 1940s, when she was asked to hand her title to a new starlet, she answered coyly, "It's not mine to give."

By 1970, when Mary sanctioned the first commercial re-release of her films, it was too late. The myth had replaced the reality, and a public that had grown up with Freud, Krafft-Ebing and *Lolita*, took a dim view of a grown woman cavorting about in pinafores or overalls. In New York, the films played to near-empty houses, half of the small audience laughing at the quaint stories and neglecting to notice the skill and toughness Mary brought to her characterizations. Some, of course, recognized the individuality of her talent, but as one buff said, "She's wonderful but, short of a major revolution in taste, there's no way she'll earn the recognition she deserves." Unlike Chaplin's and Fairbanks's screen characters, Pickford's spunky little heroine has not aged well; she can only be fully appreciated as a product of the values and outlook of an America that no longer exists.

Mary's later years lie outside the boundaries of this book, happily so, because the final chapters are not the best part of her story. The nicest thing that happened to Pickford was Buddy Rogers, described alternately (and sincerely) as "an angel" or "a saint." After their marriage, he continually encouraged her to go on with her various careers. And for a while, she did stay active. She wrote a series of newspaper interviews, including one with a "rumple-tied" bandleader named Buddy Rogers; opened an unsuccessful cosmetic line; thought about returning to the screen in *Life With Father;* invested money in a low-budget film company and produced a glossy woman's picture, *Sleep My Love,* starring Claudette Colbert. She and Buddy adopted two children, Roxanne and

Ronnie, but they were a disappointment; Mary has since severed all relations with them.

In the early 1950s, she and Chaplin sold their stock in UA, thereby severing all connection between the company and its founding members. (It had long since lost touch with their original vision; by the mid-1950s, the keepers once again had control of the asylum, and United Artists had really become United Producers.) Chaplin and Mary were often on opposite sides of an issue during their final years at UA, and their friendship suffered accordingly. There were political differences as well—Mary was staunchly conservative while Chaplin drifted farther and farther to the left. Still, in 1954, when Chaplin was branded a Communist sympathizer by right-wing columnist Westbrook Pegler, Mary sprang to Charlie's defense, saying he shouldn't be condemned on hearsay.

Around the same time, Mary decided to make a screen comeback in *The Library* (later retitled *Storm Center*), but withdrew at the last minute, explaining that the film would not be made in color as she had expected. (There was malicious gossip that she had withdrawn because of an unsuccessful facelift.) For the rest of the 1950s she continued to appear at fund-raising functions, but gradually lost her interest in politics, politicians and charities run along political lines. In the 1960s, after a cataract operation, she started spending most of the day in her bedroom; for a while, she came downstairs to see a movie, but the movies of the 60s and 70s were too prurient for her taste, and she called a halt to the screenings.

Today her investments have made her a very wealthy woman—*The New York Times* recently reported she was worth somewhere around $60 million. She sees virtually no one except Buddy, Gwynne (who now lives in Spain), Doug Jr., Lillian Gish and a team of business advisors. For a long time, her old friends kept up with her via the telephone, but in recent years, according to Mildred Loew, "no matter when you'd call, she couldn't come to the phone." Buddy is now her official spokesman. In 1971, when a group of critics assembled at Pickfair to publicize the release of Mary's films, Rogers guided them through the house. Doug's Western Museum . . . Napoleon's china . . . the Japanese salon . . . Mary's bedroom. Outside the latter, Buddy paused and knocked, then opened the door a crack. "What's that, Mary?" he asked. "Give them what? . . . Oh! . . . Mary says to give you her love!"

Allene Talmey recalls meeting Mary at a Beverly Hills dinner party in the mid-1940s. "We were sitting around having cocktails and talking about the war when Mary walked in and suddenly we all shut up. And for the rest of the evening, no one said anything, absolutely nothing, without first casting a glance at Mary. When we got back to the hotel, my husband asked, 'What was that all about? Why was everyone treating that woman like a child?' "

Today people still want to protect Mary. In Hollywood, she is always talked about in whispers: "Of course, you know . . ." "Poor Mary . . . Isn't it a shame?" So, it doesn't seem right to end this account of Mary and Doug on a negative note. But how to avoid it? Only by turning back the clock, rewinding the film, to some happier moment. So—a flashback to 1927. Doug has just bought Rancho Zorro and is rebuilding it as his fantasy hacienda. One of his first improvements is an irrigation dam, and as he and Mary are inspecting the workmanship, they sit down, press their hands and write their names in the wet cement.

Out of this tender moment comes a brainstorm. Their friend, Sid Grauman, is opening a new movie palace and needs a gimmick. How about handprints and signatures in cement? Sid loves the idea, and a new form of immortality is born.

A List of the Feature Films
of
Mary Pickford
⚜ & ⚜
Douglas Fairbanks

Note: The following abbreviations are used in this filmography:
(d) director; (p) photographer; (s) script; (c) cast; (pc)
production or distribution company; (r) release date. An
abbreviation (*) denotes sound.

MARY PICKFORD

Mary Pickford made 143 short films between 1909 and 1912 for
the Biograph, IMP and Majestic companies. (Only a few of the
IMP and Majestic productions survive.) With one exception (*A
Pueblo Legend* in 1912) they were one reel in length. The more
important include the following:

Her First Biscuits: (d) D. W. Griffith; (p) G. W. Bitzer; (c)
Florence Lawrence, Mack Sennett, Owen Moore; (pc) Biograph;
(r) 1909. (Mary's "official" screen debut; earlier she played a
scene in *What Drink Did,* which was deleted from release prints.)

The Violin Maker of Cremona: (d) Griffith; (p) Bitzer; (c)
John Compson, Owen Moore; (pc) Biograph; (r) 1909. (Mary's
first leading role.)

The Lonely Villa: (d) Griffith; (p) Arthur Marvin; (s) Mack
Sennett; (c) Marion Leonard, Owen Moore; (pc) Biograph; (r)
1909.

The Renunciation: (d) Griffith; (p) Bitzer and Marvin; (c)
James Kirkwood, Billy Quirk; (pc) Biograph; (r) 1909.

They Would Elope: (d) Griffith; (p) Bitzer (c) Kate Bruce, James Kirkwood, Billy Quirk; (pc) Biograph; (r) 1909. (Mary gets her first film review. Though her name is not mentioned, she is singled out for praise by *The New York Dramatic Mirror*.)

Getting Even: (d) Griffith; (p) Bitzer; (c) Kirkwood, Quirk, Sennett; (pc) Biograph; (r) 1909. (Quirk and Pickford teamed up in a popular series of comedies, called "the Muggsy pictures" after their leading male character.)

To Save Her Soul: (d) Griffith; (p) Bitzer and Marvin; (s) based on Sir Hall Caine's novel, *The Christian;* (c) Arthur Johnson, Lottie Pickford; (pc) Biograph; (r) 1909.

The Thread of Destiny: (d) Griffith; (p) Bitzer; (s) Griffith; (pc) Biograph; (r) 1910. (The first Pickford film made in California.)

May and December: (d) Frank Powell; (p) Marvin; (s) Mary Pickford; (c) Bruce, Quirk; (pc) Biograph; (r) 1910.

Ramona: (d) Griffith; (p) Bitzer; (s) based on Helen Hunt Jackson's novel; (c) Bruce, Henry Walthall; (pc) Biograph; (r) 1910. (This was promoted as the most expensive picture ever made, partially because Biograph had paid Jackson $100 for the screen rights to her novel.)

Wilful Peggy: (d) Griffith; (p) Bitzer; (c) Bruce, Robert Harron; (pc) Biograph; (r) 1910. (This picture was the result of Mary's campaign to play more spirited heroines than she had in the past.)

In The Sultan's Garden: (d) Thomas Ince; (pc) IMP; (r) 1911.

Science: (d) Ince; (s) based on Mark Twain's *A Dog's Tale;* (c) King Baggott; (pc) IMP; (r) 1911. (This and *In The Sultan's Garden* are the best remembered of Mary's IMP films.)

Little Red Riding Hood: (d) Owen Moore; (pc) Majestic; (r) 1911.

Lena and the Geese: (d) Griffith; (p) Bitzer; (s) Mary Pickford; (c) Claire MacDowell, Mae Marsh; (pc) Biograph; (r) 1912.

Friends: (d) Griffith; (p) Bitzer; (c) Lionel Barrymore, Harry Carey, Robert Harron; (pc) Biograph; (r) 1912. (Mary's first film close-up.)

The New York Hat: (d) Griffith; (p) Bitzer; (s) Anita Loos;

(c) Lionel Barrymore, Harron, Mae Marsh, Lillian and Dorothy Gish; (pc) Biograph; (r) 1912. (Mary's last—and most popular—Biograph/Griffith film.)

Feature Films

In The Bishop's Carriage: (d) Edwin S. Porter; (p) Porter; (s) based on novel by Miriam Nicholson; (c) David Hall, House Peters; (pc) Famous Players; (r) September 1913.

Caprice: (d) J. Searle Dawley; (c) Ernest Truex, Owen Moore, Louise Huff; (pc) Famous Players; (r) November 1913.

Hearts Adrift: (d) Edwin S. Porter; (p) Porter; (s) based on Cyrus Townsend Brady's story, *As the Sparks Fly Upward*; (c) Harold Lockwood; (pc) Famous Players; (r) February 1914.

A Good Little Devil: (d) Porter; (p) Porter; (s) based on the play by Rosamonde Gerard and Maurice Rostand; (c) Edward Connelly, Ernest Truex, William Norris, David Belasco; (pc) Famous Players; (r) March 1914. (Though this was Mary's first feature film, it was withheld from distribution for several months.)

Tess of the Storm Country: (d) Porter; (p) Porter; (s) based on novel by Grace Miller White; (c) Harold Lockwood, Olive Fuller Gordon; (pc) Famous Players; (r) March 1914.

The Eagle's Mate: (d) James Kirkwood; (p) Kirkwood; (s) based on novel by Anna Alice Chapin; (c) Kirkwood, Ida Waterman; (pc) Famous Players; (r) July 1914.

Such a Little Queen: (d) Hugh Ford; (s) based on the play by Channing Pollock; (c) Harold Lockwood, Carlyle Blackwell, Arthur Hoops; (pc) Famous Players; (r) September 1914.

Behind the Scenes: (d) James Kirkwood; (c) Kirkwood, Lowell Sherman; (pc) Famous Players; (r) October 1914.

Cinderella: (d) James Kirkwood; (c) Owen Moore, Georgeia Wilson; (pc) Famous Players; (r) December 1914.

Mistress Nell: (d) James Kirkwood; (s) based on George C. Hazelton's play; (c) Owen Moore, Arthur Hoops; (pc) Famous Players; (r) February 1915.

Fanchon the Cricket: (d) Kirkwood; (s) based on George Sand's novel; (c) Jack Pickford, Lottie Pickford, Jack Standing; (pc) Famous Players; (r) May 1915. (Some historians claim Fred and Adele Astaire played bit roles in this lost film, but Astaire denies it.)

The Dawn of Tomorrow: (d) Kirkwood; (s) based on Frances Hodgson Burnett's novel; (c) David Powell, Robert Cain; (pc) Famous Players; (r) June 1915.

Little Pal: (d) Kirkwood; (c) Russell Barrett, George Anderson; (pc) Famous Players; (r) July 1915.

Rags: (d) Kirkwood; (s) based on a story by Edith Barnard Delano; (c) Marshall Neilan, J. Farrell MacDonald, Joseph Manning; (pc) Famous Players; (r) August 1915.

Esmeralda: (d) Kirkwood; (s) based on a story by Frances Hodgson Burnett; (c) Ida Waterman, Arthur Hoops; (pc) Famous Players; (r) September 1915.

A Girl of Yesterday: (d) Allan Dwan; (s) Mary Pickford, from a story by Wesley C. MacDermott; (c) Marshall Neilan, Jack Pickford, Frances Marion, Donald Crisp, Glenn Martin; (pc) Famous Players; (r) October 1915.

Madame Butterfly: (d) Sidney Olcott; (p) Hal Young; (s) based on John Luther Long's story and Long's and David Belasco's play; (c) Marshall Neilan, Olive West; (pc) Famous Players; (r) December 1915.

The Foundling: (d) John O'Brien; (p) Harold Siddons; (c) Marcia Harris, Edward Marindel, Mildred Morris; (pc) Famous Players; (r) January 1916.

Poor Little Peppina: (d) Sidney Olcott; (p) Emmet Williams; (s) based on a story by Kate Jordan; (c) Eugene O'Brien, Jack Pickford, Cesare Gravina; (pc) Famous Players; (r) March 1916.

The Eternal Grind: (d) John O'Brien; (p) Emmet Williams; (c) John Bowers, Robert Cain; (pc) Famous Players; (r) April 1916.

Hulda from Holland: (d) John O'Brien; (p) Emmet Williams; (s) from a story by Edith Barnard Delano; (c) Frank Losee, John Bowers; (pc) Famous Players; (r) July 1916.

Less Than the Dust: (d) John Emerson; (c) David Powell, Mary

Alden, Cesare Gravina; (pc) Famous Players-Artcraft; (r) November 1916.

The Pride of the Clan: (d) Maurice Tourneur; (p) John van der Broek and Lucien Andriot; (s) Elaine Stern and Charles E. Whittaker; (c) Matt Moore, Kathryn Browne Decker, Warren Cook, Leatrice Joy; (pc) Famous Players-Artcraft; (r) January 1917.

The Poor Little Rich Girl: (d) Maurice Tourneur; (p) John van der Broek and Lucien Andriot; (s) Frances Marion, from Eleanor Gates's novel and play; (c) Madelaine Traverse, Charles Wellesley; (pc) Famous Players–Artcraft; (r) March 1917.

A Romance of the Redwoods: (d) Cecil B. De Mille; (p) Alvin Wyckoff; (s) De Mille and Jeanie Macpherson; (c) Elliott Dexter, Tully Marshall, Raymond Hatton; (pc) Famous Players–Artcraft; (r) May 1917.

The Little American: (d) Cecil B. De Mille; (p) Alvin Wyckoff; (s) De Mille and Jeanie Macpherson; (c) Jack Holt, Hobart Bosworth, Raymond Hatton; (pc) Famous Players–Artcraft; (r) July 1917.

Rebecca of Sunnybrook Farm: (d) Marshall Neilan; (p) Walter Stradling; (s) Frances Marion, from novel by Kate Douglas Wiggin and a play by Wiggin and Charlotte Thompson; (c) Wesley Barry, Eugene O'Brien, Marjorie Daw, ZaSu Pitts, Helen Jerome Eddy; (pc) Famous Players–Artcraft; (r) September 1917.

A Little Princess: (d) Marshall Neilan; (p) Walter Stradling and Charles Rosher; (s) based on a novel by Frances Hodgson Burnett; (c) Norman Kerry, ZaSu Pitts, Theodore Roberts, Gustav von Seyffertitz; (pc) Famous Players–Artcraft; (r) November 1917.

Stella Maris: (d) Marshall Neilan; (p) Walter Stradling; (s) Frances Marion, from a novel by William J. Locke; (c) Conway Tearle, Marcia Manon, Josephine Crowell; (pc) Famous Players–Artcraft; (r) January 1918.

Amarilly of Clothes-Line Alley: (d) Marshall Neilan; (p) Walter Stradling; (s) based on a story by Belle K. Maniates; (c) Norman Kerry, Herbert Standing, Wesley Barry, Kate Price; (pc) Famous Players–Artcraft; (r) March 1918.

M'Liss: (d) Marshall Neilan; (p) Walter Stradling; (s) based on a story by Bret Harte; (c) Theodore Roberts, Tully Marshall, Thomas Meighan, Monte Blue; (pc) Famous Players–Artcraft; (r) May 1918.

How Could You, Jean?: (d) William Desmond Taylor; (p) Charles Rosher; (c) Spottiswoode Aitken, Herbert Standing, Casson Ferguson, ZaSu Pitts; (pc) Famous Players–Artcraft; (r) June 1918.

Johanna Enlists: (d) William Desmond Taylor; (p) Charles Rosher; (c) Anne Schaefer, Monte Blue, Fred Huntley, Douglas MacLean, Wallace Beery; (pc) Famous Players–Artcraft; (r) September 1918.

Captain Kidd, Jr.: (d) William Desmond Taylor; (p) Charles Rosher; (c) Douglas MacLean, Spottiswoode Aitken; (pc) Famous Player–Artcraft; (r) April 1919.

Daddy Long Legs: (d) Marshall Neilan; (p) Charles Rosher and Henry Cronjager; (s) Agnes Christine Johnston, from the novel by Jean Webster; (c) Mahlon Hamilton, Marshall Neilan, Wesley Barry; (pc) First National; (r) May 1919.

The Hoodlum: (d) Sidney Franklin; (p) Rosher; (s) Frances Marion; (c) Max Davidson, Dwight Crittenden, Andrew Arbuckle; (pc) First National; (r) September 1919.

The Heart O' The Hills: (c) Sidney Franklin; (p) Rosher; (s) based on a story by John Fox; (c) John Gilbert, Claire MacDowell, Sam de Grasse; (pc) First National; (r) December 1919.

Pollyanna: (d) Paul Powell; (p) Rosher; (s) Frances Marion, from the novel by Elanor Porter; (c) William Courtleigh, Helen Jerome Eddy; (pc) United Artists; (r) January 1920.

Suds: (d) John Francis Dillon; (p) Rosher; (s) based on 'Op O' Me Thumb,* a play by Frederick Fenn and Richard Pryce; (c) William Austin, Theodore Roberts; (pc) United Artists; (r) June 1920.

The Love Light: (d) Frances Marion; (p) Rosher and Henry Cronjager; (s) Marion; (c) Fred Thompson, Evelyn Dumo; (pc) United Artists; (r) January 1921.

Through the Back Door: (d) Alfred E. Green and Jack Pickford; (p) Rosher; (s) Marion Fairfax; (c) Gertrude Astor, Wilfred Lucas, Adolphe Menjou, Elinor Fair; (pc) United Artists; (r) May 1921.

Little Lord Fauntleroy: (d) Alfred E. Green and Jack Pickford; (p) Rosher; (s) Bernard McConville, from the novel by Frances Hodgson Burnett; (c) Claude Gillingwater, Joseph Dowling, Kate Price, Frances Marion; (pc) United Artists; (r) September 1921.

Tess of the Storm Country: (d) John S. Robertson; (p) Rosher and Paul Eagler; (s) Elmer Harris, from the novel by Grace Miller White; (c) Lloyd Hughes, Gloria Hope, David Torrence, Jean Hersholt; (pc) United Artists; (r) November 1922.

Rosita: (d) Ernst Lubitsch; (p) Rosher; (s) Edward Knoblock, Norbert Falk and Hans Kraly, from the play *Don Cesar de Bazan* by Philippe Dennery and Philippe François Pinel; (c) Holbrook Blinn, Irene Rich, George Walsh; (pc) United Artists; (r) September 1923.

Dorothy Vernon of Haddon Hall: (d) Marshall Neilan; (p) Rosher; (s) Waldemar Young, from Paul Kester's dramatization of Charles Major's novel, *When Knighthood Was in Flower;* (c) Allan Forrest, Marc MacDermott, Wilfred Lucas, Clare Eames, Estelle Taylor, Lottie Pickford; (pc) United Artists; (r) March 1924.

Little Annie Rooney: (d) William Beaudine; (p) Rosher; (s) Hope Loring, Louis Lighton and Tom McNamara, from the song by Michael Nolan; (c) William Haines, Walter James, Gordon Griffith, Carlo Schipa; (pc) United Artists; (r) October 1925.

Sparrows: (d) William Beaudine; (p) Rosher, Karl Struss and Hal Mohr; (s) Winifred Dunn, C. Gardner Sullivan, Tom McNamara, George Marion, Jr. and Carl Harbaugh; (c) Gustav von Seyffertitz, Roy Stewart, Mary Louise Miller; (pc) United Artists; (r) September 1926.

My Best Girl: (d) Sam Taylor; (p) Rosher; (s) Hope Loring, Allen McNeil, Tim Whelan, based on a novel by Kathleen Norris; (c) Charles Rogers, Hobart Bosworth, Lucien Littlefield, Mack Swain; (pc) United Artists; (r) October 1927.

The Gaucho—see Douglas Fairbanks filmography.

*Coquette: (d) Sam Taylor; (p) Karl Struss; (s) Taylor, John Grey and Allen McNeil, from the play by Ann Preston Bridgers and George Abbott; (c) John Mack Brown, Matt Moore, John Sainpolis, Louise Beavers; (pc) United Artists; (r) April 1929.

*The Taming of the Shrew: (d) Sam Taylor; (p) Karl Struss; (s) Taylor, from the play by William Shakespeare; (c) Douglas Fairbanks, Edwin Maxwell, Geoffrey Wardwell, Dorothy Jordan, Clyde Cook; (pc) United Artists; (r) October 1929.

*Kiki: (d) Sam Taylor; (p) Struss; (s) Taylor, from the play by David Belasco and André Picard; (c) Reginald Denny, Margaret Livingston; (pc) United Artists; (r) March 1931.

*Secrets: (d) Frank Borzage; (p) Struss; (s) Frances Marion, Salisbury Field and Leonard Praskins, from a play by Rudolf Besier and May Edington; (c) Leslie Howard, C. Aubrey Smith, Blanche Frederici, Ethel Clayton, Ned Sparks, Bessie Barriscale; (pc) United Artists; (r) March 1933.

DOUGLAS FAIRBANKS

The Lamb: (d) W. Christy Cabanne; (p) William E. Fildew; (s) Cabanne (?), from a story by D. W. Griffith; (c) Seena Owen, Lillian Langdon, Monroe Salisbury; (pc) Triangle; (r) September 1915.

Double Trouble: (d) W. Christy Cabanne; (p) William E. Fildew; (s) Cabanne and D. W. Griffith, from a novel by Herbert Quick; (c) Tom Kennedy, Gladys Brockwell, Monroe Salisbury; (pc) Triangle; (r) December 1915.

His Picture in the Papers: (d) John Emerson; (s) Emerson and Anita Loos; (c) Loretta Blake, Clarence Handyside, Homer Hunt; (pc) Triangle; (r) February 1916.

The Habit of Happiness: (d) Allan Dwan; (s) Dwan, D. W. Griffith and Shannon Fife; (c) Dorothy West, George Fawcett, Mary Harlan; (pc) Triangle; (r) March 1916.

The Good Bad Man: (d) Allan Dwan; (p) Victor Fleming; (s)

Fairbanks; (c) Bessie Love, Sam de Grasse, Mary Alden; (pc) Triangle; (r) April 1916.

Reggie Mixes In: (d) W. Christy Cabanne; (p) William E. Fildew; (s) Roy Somerville; (c) Bessie Love, Frank Bennett, Joseph Singleton; (pc) Triangle; (r) May 1916.

Flirting With Fate: (d) W. Christy Cabanne; (p) William E. Fildew; (s) Cabanne, from a story by Robert M. Baker; (c) Jewel Carmen, Howard Gaye, Lillian Langdon; (pc) Triangle; (r) June 1916.

The Mystery of the Leaping Fish: (d) John Emerson; (s) Tod Browning; (c) Bessie Love, Alma Rubens, A. D. Sears; (pc) Triangle; (r) June 1916.

The Half Breed: (d) Allan Dwan; (s) Anita Loos, from Bret Harte's story, *In the Carquinez Woods;* (c) Alma Rubens, Sam de Grasse, Jewel Carmen; (pc) Triangle; (r) July 1916.

Manhattan Madness: (d) Allan Dwan; (s) Charles T. Dazey, from a story by E. V. Durling; (c) Jewel Carmen, George Beranger; (pc) Triangle; (r) September 1916.

American Aristocracy: (d) Lloyd Ingraham; (s) Anita Loos; (c) Jewel Carmen, Albert Parker; (pc) Triangle; (r) November 1916.

The Matrimaniac: (d) Paul Powell; (s) Anita Loos and John Emerson, from a story by Octavus Roy Cohen and J. V. Glesy; (c) Constance Talmadge, Fred Warren, Winifred Westover; (pc) Triangle; (r) December 1916.

The Americano: (d) John Emerson; (p) Victor Fleming; (s) Anita Loos; (c) Alma Rubens, Spottiswoode Aitken, Tote Du-Crow; (pc) Triangle; (r) December 1916.

In Again, Out Again: (d) John Emerson; (p) Victor Fleming; (s) Anita Loos; (c) Arline Pretty, Bull Montana, Walter Walker, Homer Hunt; (pc) Artcraft–Paramount; (r) April 1917.

Wild and Woolly: (d) John Emerson; (p) Victor Fleming; (s) Anita Loos, from a story by H. B. Carpenter; (c) Eileen Percy, Joseph Singleton, Walter Bytell, Sam de Grasse; (pc) Artcraft–Paramount; (r) July 1917.

Down to Earth: (d) John Emerson; (p) Victor Fleming; (s)

Anita Loos, from a story by Fairbanks; (c) Eileen Percy, Gustav von Seyffertitz, Bull Montana; (pc) Artcraft–Paramount; (r) August 1917.

The Man from Painted Post: (d) Joseph Henabery; (p) Victor Fleming; (s) Fairbanks, from a story by Jackson Gregory; (c) Eileen Percy, Frank Campeau, Herbert Standing, Monte Blue; (pc) Artcraft–Paramount; (r) October 1917.

Reaching for the Moon: (d) John Emerson; (p) Fleming and Sam Landers; (c) Eileen Percy, Richard Cummings, Frank Campeau, Eugene Ormonde; (pc) Artcraft–Paramount; (r) November 1917.

A Modern Musketeer: (d) Allan Dwan; (p) Fleming; (s) Dwan, from *D'Artagnan of Kansas* by F. R. Lyle, Jr. (c) Marjorie Daw, Frank Campeau, Tully Marshall, Eugene Ormonde, ZaSu Pitts; (pc) Artcraft–Paramount; (r) January 1918.

Headin' South: (d) Arthur Rosson; (p) Hugh McClung; (s) Allan Dwan; (c) Katherine MacDonald, Frank Campeau; (pc) Artcraft–Paramount; (r) March 1918.

Mr. Fix-It: (d) Allan Dwan; (p) Hugh McClung; (s) Dwan, from a story by Ernest Butterworth; (c) Wanda Hawley, Marjorie Daw, Katherine MacDonald, Frank Campeau; (pc) Artcraft–Paramount; (r) April 1918.

Say! Young Fellow: (d) Joseph Henabery; (p) Hugh McClung; (c) Marjorie Daw, Frank Campeau, Edythe Chapman; (pc) Artcraft–Paramount; (r) June 1918.

Bound in Morocco: (d) Dwan; (p) Hugh McClung; (s) Dwan; (c) Pauline Curley, Edythe Chapman, Frank Campeau, Tully Marshall; (pc) Artcraft–Paramount; (r) July 1918.

He Comes Up Smiling: (d) Dwan; (p) Hugh McClung; (s) Frances Marion, from Byron Ongley and Emil Mytray's dramatization of Charles Sherman's novel; (c) Marjorie Daw, Herbert Standing, Bull Montana, Frank Campeau; (pc) Artcraft–Paramount; (r) September 1918.

Arizona: (d) Fairbanks; (p) McClung; (s) Fairbanks, from a play by Augustus Thomas; (c) Marjorie Daw, Marguerite de la Motte, Theodore Roberts, Kate Price, Frank Campeau; (pc) Artcraft–

Paramount; (r) December 1918. (Whether Fairbanks really wrote and directed this film has been questioned; some sources cite Albert Parker as director, Dwan as writer.)

Knickerbocker Buckaroo: (d) Albert Parker; (p) McClung; (s) Fairbanks; (c) Marjorie Daw, William Wellman, Edythe Chapman, Frank Campeau; (pc) Artcraft–Paramount; (r) May 1919.

His Majesty, The American: (d) Joseph Henabery; (p) Victor Fleming; (s) Elton Banks (Fairbanks); (c) Marjorie Daw, Lillian Langdon, Frank Campeau; (pc) United Artists; (r) September 1919. (This was the initial United Artists release.)

When the Clouds Roll By: (d) Victor Fleming; (s) Tom Geraghty and Lewis Weadon, from a story by Fairbanks; (c) Kathleen Clifford, Frank Campeau, Albert MacQuarrie; (pc) United Artists; (r) December 1919.

The Mollycoddle: (d) Victor Fleming; (p) William McCann and Harry Thorpe; (s) Tom Geraghty, from a story by Harold McGrath; (c) Ruth Renick, Betty Boulton, Wallace Beery; (pc) United Artists; (r) June 1920.

The Mark of Zorro: (d) Fred Niblo; (p) William McCann and Harry Thorpe; (s) Elton Thomas, from Johnson McCulley's story, *The Curse of Capistrano*; (c) Noah Beery, Claire McDowell, Marguerite de la Motte, Tote DuCrow; (pc) United Artists; (r) November 1920.

The Nut: (d) Theodore Reed; (p) McCann and Thorpe; (s) William Parker and Lotta Wood, from a story by Kenneth Davenport; (c) Marguerite de la Motte, Barbara LaMarr; (pc) United Artists; (r) March 1921. (Charles Chaplin and Mary Pickford were "extras" in this film.)

The Three Musketeers: (d) Fred Niblo: (p) Arthur Edeson; (s) Edward Knoblock from Alexandre Dumas's novel; (c) Adolphe Menjou, Marguerite de la Motte, Barbara LaMarr, Leon Barry, George Siegmann, Eugene Pallette; (pc) United Artists; (r) August 1921.

Douglas Fairbanks in Robin Hood: (d) Allan Dwan; (p) Arthur Edeson; (s) Elton Thomas; (c) Wallace Beery, Sam de Grasse, Enid Bennett, Alan Hale; (pc) United Artists; (r) October 1922.

The Thief of Bagdad: (d) Raoul Walsh; (p) Arthur Edeson; (s) Elton Thomas; (c) Julanne Johnson, Anna May Wong, So-Jin, Snitz Edwards, Charles Becher, Brandon Hurst, Winter Blossom, Tote DuCrow; (pc) United Artists; (r) March 1924.

Don Q, Son of Zorro: (d) Donald Crisp; (p) Henry Sharp; (s) Jack Cunningham, based on Hesketh and Kate Prichard's *Don Q's Love Story;* (pc) United Artists; (r) July 1925.

The Black Pirate: (d) Albert Parker; (p) Henry Sharp; (s) Jack Cunningham, from a story by Elton Thomas; (c) Billie Dove, Donald Crisp, Anders Randolf, Sam de Grasse; (pc) United Artists; (r) March 1926.

The Gaucho: (d) F. Richard Jones; (p) Tony Gaudio; (s) Elton Thomas and Lotta Woods; (c) Lupe Velez, Eve Southern, Gustav von Seyffertitz, Albert MacQuarrie, Mary Pickford; (pc) United Artists; (r) November 1927.

*The Iron Mask: (d) Allan Dwan; (p) Henry Sharpe; (s) Elton Thomas, from Alexandre Dumas's *The Three Musketeers* and *The Man in the Iron Mask;* (c) Marguerite de la Motte, Stanley Stanford, Leon Barry, Gino Carrado, Dorothy Revier; (pc) United Artists; (r) February 1929. (This film has two or three dialogue scenes in which Fairbanks addresses the camera and speaks in verse. A silent version was released to theatres which had not yet been equipped for sound.)

*The Taming of the Shrew—see Mary Pickford filmography.

*Reaching for the Moon: (d) Edmund Goulding; (p) Ray June and Robert Planck; (s) Goulding, from a story by Irving Berlin; (c) Bebe Daniels, Edward Everett Horton, June MacCloy, Bing Crosby, Jack Mulhall, Helen Jerome Eddy, Claude Allister; (pc) United Artists; (r) February 1931.

*Around the World in 80 Minutes with Douglas Fairbanks: (d) Victor Fleming; (p) Henry Sharp and Chuck Lewis; (s) Fairbanks and Robert E. Sherwood; (pc) United Artists; (r) December 1931.

*Mr. Robinson Crusoe: (d) Edward Sutherland; (p) Max Dupont; (s) Tom Geraghty, from a story by Elton Thomas; (c) Maria Alba, William Farnum, Earle Browne; (pc) United Artists; (r) August 1932.

The Private Life of Don Juan: (d) Alexander Korda; (p) Georges Perinal; (s) Frederick Lonsdale and Lajos Biro, from Henri Bataille's play, *L'Homme à la rose*; (c) Merle Oberon, Benita Hume, Binnie Barnes, Heather Thatcher, Melville Cooper, Gibson Gowland, Natalie Paley, Athene Seyler; (pc) United Artists–London Films; (r) November 1934.

Index